brings to light new philosophical insights and ideas.

Because human beings continue to evolve, informing our everyday understanding of the world, Langan shows how vital it is for us to think through the sense of human being and how great a challenge that is in today's society. His work offers insight into human being that invites readers to think and live more deeply in their humanity—and to face the challenges of a rapidly changing world by reawakening perennial quests for love and the divine, and the very search for meaning itself.

About the Author

Thomas Langan is Professor Emeritus of Philosophy at the University of Toronto. He is the author of numerous books, including *Surviving the Age of Virtual Reality, The Catholic Tradition,* and *Tradition and Authenticity in the Search for Ecumenic Wisdom* (all available from the University of Missouri Press).

About the Editor

Antonio Calcagno is Assistant Professor of Philosophy at King's University College at the University of Western Ontario and author of *The Philosophy of Edith Stein* and *Badiou and Derrida: Politics, Events, and Their Time.*

HUMAN BEING

HUMAN BEING

By Thomas D. Langan
Edited by Antonio Calcagno

UNIVERSITY OF MISSOURI PRESS
Columbia and London

Library of Congress Cataloging-in-Publication Data

Langan, Thomas.
 Human being / by Thomas D. Langan ; edited by Antonio Calcagno.
   p. cm.
 Includes index.
 Summary: "Langan draws on a lifetime of study to offer a new understanding of
the central question of our existence, turning to phenomenology and philosophical
anthropology to help us better understand who we are as individuals and communities and what makes us act the way we do"—Provided by publisher.
 ISBN 978–0–8262–1843–8 (alk. paper)
 1. Philosophical anthropology. I. Calcagno, Antonio, 1969– II. Title.
 BD450.L286 2009
  128—dc22
 2008049348

♾™ This paper meets the requirements of the
American National Standard for Permanence of Paper
for Printed Library Materials, Z39.48, 1984.

Designer/Typesetter: FoleyDesign
Printer and Binder: Integrated Book Technology, Inc.
Typefaces: Charlemagne and Palatino

To Antonio Calcagno, without whose insight and patient support this book would not exist—and to the students, past and future, who catch from him the passion for wisdom.

CONTENTS

EDITOR'S PREFACE

On the Task of Becoming Human

I came to know Professor Thomas Langan as an undergraduate student at the University of Toronto in 1988. Over the years I have come to know his philosophy and have worked with him to help develop and articulate his thought. His five volumes published by the University of Missouri Press represent a lifetime of mature thinking and living. It is a pleasure for me to be able to say a few words here about this philosophical anthropology.

Anyone who knows Professor Langan would undoubtedly say that he takes seriously the challenge and responsibility of becoming human. Though one is born with many natural givens, the task of making sense, appropriating, and deepening what is given to us as human beings living in a world with others is a profoundly engaging undertaking. Modern philosophy, for better or for worse, has presented Western philosophy with a rich legacy of the individual ego or subject. This subject is a center of free decision making and understands what is proper to him- or herself, in large part, due to modern conceptions of property. Though this egocentric notion of subjectivity was vital in overcoming many forms of social and political oppression, and there are still more to be overcome, one of its oversights is that it never developed a full conceptual framework to understand the very history and having-been of human being in general. This is to say, although there is something rich and exciting about individual human beings that possess a concrete identity in the world and in time, there is also a large and overarching legacy or *positum* of human being that continues to develop and grow as long as human beings continue to exist, develop, and philosophically think about their existence. Human being, understood in its broadest sense, is constituted by histories, religions, cultures, sciences, worlds, politics, and so on, all unfolding and colliding in time. Globalization has allowed us to see and grasp more vividly the meaning of human being, offering us a global perspective of who we are and how we came to be through the ages. Given the vast changes of our world in the past twenty years or so, we can view human beings as singular and general. In this volume, Professor Langan argues that we must see and understand the relation between ourselves as individual human beings and the being of humans as it has unfolded in time. Human being, therefore, must be viewed from two perspectives. First, there are individual human beings; second, there is a larger sense of human being that continues to shape and inform our individual beings in the world.

These two perspectives inhere in and mutually inform one another. The goal of this work is to show how these two perspectives interrelate, ultimately uncovering the basic constitutive layers of what it is to be human. Over the ages human beings have worked hard at uncovering and developing the meaning of their beings, contributing to the larger sense of human being in general. As readers will see, Professor Langan points to certain key constitutive elements, including rationality, freedom, developing sense of worlds, space-time, and so forth. Here, I would just like to point to two central insights, namely, transcendence and responsibility.

Every individual ego-subject is limited by his or her own self-knowledge. One can never know oneself absolutely. Knowledge gathered by others, of course, helps fill in the gap of our own self-knowledge and knowledge about the world. It is this very dwelling with others that allows us to build ourselves and the world around us. To understand ourselves and others more fully, in order to become more fully as human beings, we need to reach out of or step out of ourselves. This very stepping out of ourselves and reaching to others to make sense of ourselves is what Professor Langan calls transcendence. It is also what permits us to recognize not only our individuality but also a collective legacy that can be studied through human appropriation and interpretation, namely, human being. Transcendence not only allows us to know and build our becoming but also allows us to make the philosophical leap to understand human becoming in general, through time and cultures and worlds. It is this transcendence that allows us to see the larger human and divine realities that help make us who we were, are, and will become.

But transcendence is not simply an act of human will or fiat. We do indeed have the ability to engage in such an undertaking through our own free decisions. The material and spiritual realities that we find or create are not merely subjective projections and creations. They have an objective thickness to them, an objective reality and force that shape and influence, even sustain, us, making our very existence possible. These objects that stand over and against our own individual ego-subjectivity penetrate and make demands on us; they call us to respond in some way or form. For example, the physical laws of gravity do exist, and they act upon us constantly. If we are to live in a world shaped by gravity, then we have to understand and take gravity into account in most things we do; we respond to gravity. Likewise, if the desire to know more about ourselves and understand humans in general is to be fulfilled, we have to respond to others. This response to the other or to all that is other than me is the fundamental sense of responsibility developed by Professor Langan in this work.

Transcendence and responsibility are key structures that unfold themselves as human beings begin to try to make sense of who they are and what they have been and will become. They make possible any comprehension of human being, understood from the two perspectives outlined above. The world and the legacy of the being of humans make certain demands on us; to understand and deal with such demands fully and responsibly is not only a practical task but a deeply philosophical one as well. The work that you are about to read is an exploration of what it means to be human, but it is also an invitation to all readers and all humans to take seriously the task and responsibility of human being.

AUTHOR'S PREFACE

Human Being has been deeply informed by the work of my previous volumes but also seeks to bring to light new philosophical insights and ideas. The earlier volumes focused on larger structures, including tradition, authenticity, being, High-Tech X (HTX) in the age of virtual reality, and the Catholic tradition.[1] This volume shows how these larger structures come to bear specifically on being human. Human being is to be understood in two primary senses. First, it is a specific way of being, and it refers to a specific kind of being, an individual human being who lives and dwells in the world. I proceed to describe phenomenologically his or her basic ontological constituents: the worlds in which he or she dwells, the importance of various grades of relations, and the human urge to make sense of all that one encounters in existence through adequate appropriation. Here, in this first sense of human being, one can say: a human being exists, it is a specific *x*. One can also say that this being exists in a specific way: it feels, wills, thinks, and relates to others; it loves and hates; and so forth. Yet this specific human being conditions and is conditioned by a larger sense of human being. Second, and more important, human being is a phenomenon that unfolds in time and has its own history; it is a fluid *positum* or thesaurus, understood in

1. HTX refers to the High-Tech X. The reason I have chosen this initialism is because I am trying to designate a phenomenon that has come about through the rapid changes in technology. Technology has created a virtual reality and altered our own personal sense and experiences of time and space. Not only do we live in a radically changed world, but technology is advancing at such a rate that new worlds are constantly being created and new relations fostered. The X refers to the implicit possibility of new worlds and relations that are present in technology but have not been named yet. Readers will see references to HTX throughout the text. See Thomas Langan, *Surviving the Age of Virtual Reality* (Columbia: University of Missouri Press, 2000).

the literal sense of a treasure house, continuing to unfold and develop through various cultures, histories, and contexts. Philosophically, it is a kind or species of being that comes to be known through philosophy and philosophical anthropology, albeit not exclusively. Human being has a collective significance. Martin Heidegger claimed that *Dasein,* or the human existent, had a specific being and was related to Being. The meaning of Heidegger's Being has been the source of much contention, as Heidegger never finished the second part of *Being and Time,* which was supposed to clarify the meaning of Being. Human Being is the collective result of the experiences of humans throughout time, stemming from various cultures and creeds. Human being has a history, a past, composed of various traditions and significant events. This past continues to inform our present and our future. We continue to forge human being by our living here and now as human and in a human way. It is the goal of this book to explain how human being, understood in this second sense, is a specific kind of being that has a history, which continues to inform the present. But present and future anticipations can bend back to change meanings or our understandings of how human being existed in the past. Human being continues to evolve, informing our everyday horizons of understanding of and acting in the world. I show how vital it is for human beings to think through the sense of human being, and how great a challenge that is in today's society. In a world structured by highly pervasive and complicated technologies, the need to make sense of who we are and the legacy that has informed us as individual human beings, out of a fragmented digitalized existence, is paramount. Without a more developed philosophical understanding of human being, both in its general and in its specific structures, we humans will not be able to cope with the fast-developing worlds that surround us. Our task is twofold: to understand the world and our being in the world so that we can better manage it and ourselves. There is a direct connection between how we understand what is at stake in being human and how we live our lives. In order for human beings to understand themselves, they require an understanding not only of themselves but also of human being in general. A discussion of human being will facilitate these two tasks.

My method in this book is two-pronged. It investigates deeper structures of human being while also demonstrating how, through philosophical questioning, such structures can be appropriated and made meaningful by individual human beings. *In nuce* this leads to the following conclusion: human beings can face the challenge of a rapidly changing technological world by reactivating perennial human existential structures put on the back burner, including love, the divine, and the very search for meaning itself.

I first attempt to show how fundamental a "philosophical anthropology" is to this project: larger societal, global, and cosmological awareness must coincide with a developing awareness of what it is to be human. I then proceed to discuss how we find ourselves situated in various worlds and how time structures the way in which we relate to these worlds. Imagination, analogical thinking, will, and the category of the weird are introduced to describe often-forgotten dimensions of what it is to be human. In discussing these realities, I show how philosophy can help to understand them. It is the unique capacity of humans to appropriate the meanings of worlds, relations, selves, and others, including the divine Other. The category of the weird, a peculiar intervention on my part, is meant to account holistically for that which is strange, destructive, and contradictory about human nature. Philosophy has traditionally emphasized the rational, the conscious, and the deliberate as distinctively human categories. The weird has tended to find a place—usually in terms of psychopathology and sin—in psychology and religion. Yet any serious philosophical anthropology must take the weird into account. I offer the notion here in the hope that readers may find it original and take it seriously when they ponder what it is to be human. Ultimately, I argue that, in order to manage the radical global challenges we are experiencing, we will have to reexamine the fact of the human capacity for transcendence, both toward others and toward the divine. A balanced and serious philosophical appropriation can lead us to rediscover love and religion. Not all that original a philosophical or human proposition? I believe that by engaging philosophically the being of these specifically human realities in lived experience and in traditions—the Christian tradition, for example—we can bring love and religion to bear more meaningfully on present-day human existence.

What is novel about this book? It demonstrates how our "worlds"—the larger structures discussed earlier in my work—must be rooted in the deeply personal and communitarian life of the individual human being and human being in general. It also demonstrates how serious thinking about the question of "being human" uncovers and consciously engages structures of basic existence that are often taken for granted because, as Heidegger says, they are too ready-at-hand. Furthermore, it is an effort to recover important dimensions of the "subject" bequeathed to us by modernity. The subject has been seriously challenged and compromised by the huge political, social, and technological changes we are currently experiencing. Yet the appeal to reason, self-consciousness, science, and common sense certainly has its place within any given philosophical anthropology. How could it become relevant for us here and now, in our individuality? This book proposes a way to raise once again the central question of what it is to be a human person, offering a possible contemporary approach. Rather than strictly focusing on the individual human being, this work seeks to situate the human being in relation to its larger ontological context, namely, human being in general.

This book can be read separately, but it assumes some knowledge of the four previous volumes. I did not wish to repeat what was already discussed in the previous texts, but I certainly do draw on earlier insights. This, however, should not discourage any reader from picking up this text. Exploring the nature of human being is a long-standing tradition, and my work can be read as part of this tradition. As such, readers interested in our "nature" as human beings and its implications for human relationships, love, religion, thinking, willing, and meaning will find this work useful.

ACKNOWLEDGMENTS

This book grew out of lifelong interaction with people whose passionate love for truth drew me into active philosophy. It attempts to weave together insights generated within this intense dialogue. It hopes to persuade new generations to join in the age-old struggle for wisdom, by casting light on the dynamic structures, at once consistent and ever expanding, within which this struggle must be waged.

I therefore wish to mention here how deeply indebted I am to the Jesuits of St. Louis University, especially to Father Maurice B. McNamee, who launched me into thinking; to Etienne Gilson, coauthoring with whom showed me what it means to love Being; to Jacques Vidal, who introduced me in his Parisian salon to the leading actors in post-Heideggerian Continental philosophy; to Hans Urs von Balthasar and Karol Wojtiwa, whose Communio community was such a tremendous support for many Catholic thinkers of my generation; and to Jude Dougherty, who kept me in constant touch with international philosophical encounters.

I would like to thank here all those who cooperated directly with my work in progress, helping me see reality with the eyes of contemporary science (Michel Vaillant), of politics (Iain Benson), of contemporary psychiatry (Ed Hersch), of contemporary information technology (Bruce Stewart), and of eternal theology (Brother Bernard Audigier).

Finally, I would like to express my gratitude to the students whose friendship and thirst for truth kept me on my toes, and who, to my great joy, have become philosophers themselves—Frank Cunningham, Michael Gorman, Ingrid Stefanovich, Nick Zunic, Giuseppe Butera, and, above all, Antonio Calcagno, the midwife of this book.

HUMAN BEING

INTRODUCTION

The Love of Wisdom

STRANGER: The differences of human personality, the variety of men's activities, and the inevitable unsettlement attending all human experience make it impossible for any art whatsoever to issue unqualified rules holding good on all questions at all times.
—Plato, *Statesman*

Have things changed all that much since Plato's brilliant observation? Today we do know more about the most complex entity in the universe, the human being. (In an average body there are 1.45 trillion cells, each cell containing more bytes of information than one hundred sets of *The Encyclopedia Britannica*.)

I propose a very modern set of dynamic structures that will help us understand ourselves better: whether a healthy human adult is aware of it or not, he needs to reckon with *various genera of worlds,* which, in our search for wisdom, must be explicitly related. One of these worlds consists of several billions of presently living humans, "the world's population." A second kind of world includes hundreds of millions of intersubjective worlds, from a solitary friendship of two persons to populations as huge as China's. As though that is not enough of a challenge, modern "historicity" has made matters still more complicated: human being looks quite different to followers of distinctive traditions, each with its own founding faith, many of which reach back millennia.

If you want irrefutable evidence of our confusion about ourselves, and the contradictions between traditions and worlds, consider the present-day tensions and conflicts between and within certain Middle Eastern nations, including Iran, Iraq, Israel, and Lebanon. People and groups are divided along and between religious, class, ethnic, language, and political lines, and here I am just listing general and obvious lines that allow varying worlds to converge and diverge. *Whatever worlds we mostly live in, we need help to deal wisely—philosophically—with the variegated approaches to reality proposed to us in various worlds, and to keep order* between the various worlds within which we operate.

Any intelligent philosophy needs to confront the fact that anthropology is a historical science of overwhelming complexity. I do not mean that our anthropological understanding changes over time, but more strikingly, I want the reader to consider that human being itself evolves physically and spiritually as mankind projects its future.

Given the staggering variety of pluralistic views of man in our present world and every human's reaching out into the future, we need more than ever what Plato was explicitly seeking: some plain WISDOM, a wisdom that can make some sense out of history, the worlds within which human beings find themselves, and human being in general.

WHAT IS WISDOM?

One does not hear "wisdom" mentioned very often. Today's philosophical challenge is to build wisdom on clear worlds connected understandingly. Historical relativism without clear principles is shifting and murky.

In this present work, I invite the reader to build on reliable foundations revealed more clearly in contemporary times than ever before. The foundations will be clear, although the content of many worlds and how they relate to one another remain challenging because of the complex dynamics. You shall see that much can be done to clarify relations between different kinds of worlds, indeed different kinds of truth, in "the weaving of a wisdom."

The first book I published with the University of Missouri Press is titled *Tradition and Authenticity in the Search for Ecumenic Wisdom* (1992). There my project is summed up in one rather cumbersome title: I seek to develop a method for achieving "authentic" personal existence through "wise" interaction with the multiplicity of traditions available to us, treated ecumenically (that is, on a world scale), embracing every aspect of truth. By linking "tradition" and "authenticity" I sent a signal in the first volume that I was going to be preoccupied with traditions insofar as they "hand on" *(tradere)* in their respective worlds something positive and true that can be part of what one can build on. Of course, all traditions can also hand on "fixed ideas," "old wives' tales," deep-rooted errors, and more.

The first four books, now published, explore this critical operation of wise appropriation and judgment and the specific methods it calls for. As I worked to appropriate a great tradition important to me (see volume 3, *The Catholic Tradition*) and later to sketch the present world situation (volume 4, *Surviving the Age of Virtual Reality*), I was developing an "ontology" and "epistemology" that became the basic propositions of volume 2, *Being and Truth* (1996). (Volumes 2 and 3 evolved simultaneously over a half decade of my teaching and rewriting.) In volume 5 you are now encountering my attempt to develop further my understanding of the notion of "authenticity," seen as the lucid and developed attitude toward reality that ought to be most fundamental to being human (and is surely limiting the portrait of the human being!).

Authenticity is experienced as a "drive": "love of wisdom," "philosophia." Striving for wisdom entails a continuing struggle (mostly with oneself!) to grasp and correctly relate *ever wider horizons* within which to embrace reality, and find reliable meaning in it, with *ever deeper foundations* critically related to our struggle to be fully who we ought to be (the sense of "authenticity").

In present times, we can easily see the sense of our opening up wider fields of meaning. Looking inward to the complexities of a single cell, while casting our view of the universe to include myriad of galaxies, within all this dynamic structure of cell and galaxy relating, there is radically new knowledge to contemplate.

The development of methods for clarifying the complex interactions of kinds of worlds of meaning will continue as long as there are human beings. In Chapter 2 of *Human Being* I shall begin to explain more thoroughly what I mean by this dynamics of worlds. Later, I will also show how these worlds are extensions of human being but also how they dynamically and reciprocally bend back on human beings, challenging, limiting, and even expanding what we understand and appropriate as human being.

If wisdom is a drive that can grant us access to a deeper appropriation and understanding of ourselves as human beings, either human beings thrive by fulfilling a vision (and it had better be genuine, and we had better get it right!) OR we *just happened*, and it is then up to us, collectively and individually, to create a direction for ourselves out of the structures at hand. Whatever we make of ourselves had better allow us to grow.

This "either-or"—either there is ultimate meaning or there is none—animates the radical *"Gigantomachia"* dividing modern, in fact all, human self-understanding. Such is the warning of political philosopher Eric Voegelin. If "authenticity," as I intend the term in its "large sense," demands we see reality within the widest and most fundamental horizons we can currently open, and that our sense of reality be founded in the deepest levels of being, then utmost attention should be given to the clash between the two seminal positions at the heart of this *Gigantomachia*. I shall call them respectively "the mythological" and "the revelational."

In both families of tradition, the role of myth in envisioning our ultimate situation is respected. But in what I am calling "the mythological" or "humanistic" traditions, all leaps beyond previous horizons of interpretation, all new transcending "enlightenment," are treated as purely human accomplishments, the wondrous work of the human imagination, even "mysterious," so long as neurophysiology has not advanced sufficiently, but nothing more.

Modern science itself acknowledges the importance of the struggles of the human imagination for "sense." Mythical imaginings—models—play such a role; it is indeed proper to call the "humanistic" tradition a tradition of myths: works of art, flights of scientific fancy (ultimately criticized by rigorous methods), the myths that preoccupy psychoanalysts, civilization-forming religious myths, language as symbolic, and so on.

In the "theistic-revelational" traditions, the mythological is, of course, attended to by scholars, but the theistic anthropological scientist believes as well in "breakthroughs of proffered insight" illuminated from *beyond the horizontal transcendental field of meaning of mere human interpretation,* letting shine forth a new light. These breakthroughs are believed to emerge in the horizons of human history, founding and shaping religious traditions of great breadth and long endurance that go beyond the merely human. These alleged *"breakthroughs from above and beyond"* have not only affected human self-understanding at the base of the civilizations, but some continue to claim for themselves *merit as evidence for intention in the unfolding of the universe by the ultimate transcending Source.* In short, the theists believe in revelation beyond the merely mythical, and consider such revelation essential for the full human grasp of reality and human being. Revelation, they are convinced, furnishes light for criticizing the limits of the merely mythical. I shall show later that such a split here between two approaches is less fatal than it seems.

As readers of my earlier volumes know, I adhere to a revelational tradition. Nonbelievers need to know something of those "vertically transcendent" traditions if they are to deal authentically with human being. In the present work, wisdom demands that I seek insights from phenomenologists from the other side, for whom "revelation" is a fantastic yet significant human construction, even if there is no "God"; I must learn from physicists who remain hostile to notions of "design"; I must learn what I can from resolutely atheistic neurophysiologists and psychoanalysts, however difficult.

Of course, in the midst of all this we should be attentive as well to the traditions of all "worlds": the East, to Islam, to the Hindus, and other traditions of revelation. Rejection of the "supernatural" elements of a revelational faith does not, in any case, render its human insights meaningless.

Further, to see human being in the vast and demanding way modern knowledge makes possible calls for a synthesis of overwhelming dimensions. Undertaking such folly may be tolerated in the work of an old philosopher. Rather than breaking new experimental ground, I hope to offer balanced contributions to the synthetic vision of what it entails to be human. It is my hope this will encourage the reader to expand his or her own thinking about humanity, and help in his or her own quest for authentic horizons with new perspectives.

Thus far, I have maintained two important principles. First, in order to understand human being we must maintain that the drive pushing us to seek this very understanding is wisdom. Second, to know and understand oneself as human being and to understand oneself as part of human being that has a history, legacy, and meaning include giving an account of oneself and the nature of human being in general. We do this by understanding that we are immersed in worlds that converge and diverge. In order to understand "authenticity," we must begin by seeing how human beings come to understand themselves as human. This happens primarily in and through temporality.

Human beings and human being are temporal; the understanding of this occurs in and through time. Human existence is a stretching process. As existentialists point out, conscious human *ek-sistenz* "stands out" toward the partially "not yet" of a future, the subject "doing truth" and struggling to live up to that vision. This process we might call *the ongoing personal quest for wisdom*. The individual's thought always imaginatively stretches forward, until the day one's bodily foundation is damaged or worn out, no longer supporting this élan, the fullness of grasping what stretches forth in a "field."

Attending to any object brings past, present, and future together, to give the object at least a temporary place in the subject's world of meaning, that is, of "sense," of direction beyond the immediate present. *This may sound too immanent—too idealist/subjectivist—as though we give sense. We shall see in due course the givenness at the core of what is to be interpreted.*

Awareness of transcendence permits us to open new horizons of meaning in a temporal context; it literally refers to the stepping beyond ourselves, beyond our "present" here and now. "Horizontal transcendence" is a basic fact of what it is to be human: in the midst of the attractions and collisions of objective forces in the universe, we have no choice but to struggle to make our way—or die. In this process, the human subject "goes beyond" the focal center of his awareness—the present bit of cosmic time and space already accessed through his body—to envelop this new "bit" in a field of meaning. Sensing, handling, classifying any object, the subject "goes beyond" the givens to "shed light on them," giving them meaning from the subject's own standpoint:

— from the present: sensory receptors gather the data presently being processed in the brain
— from the past: memories permit recognition and provide vocabulary for interpreting the givens
— toward a future within the subject's world of meaning, a future already provided by attending to the object for even three seconds, but can also be extended to others and in time

It is one of the strangest things about human being—that what I am here describing most people find obscure. How can this be, when such horizon-deploying interpretation is happening in our conscious life at every instant, all day long? Every act of whatever kind of knowing and everything we do consciously are made possible by horizontal transcendence.

This fundamental fact of horizontal transcendent space and time is underplayed in many philosophies. Yet there is no way to deal with "human being" adequately today without coming to terms with transcendence. In this book, I shall not be "playful" at all about it, alas; I will even attempt in the following chapters to make a case that one should take "vertical transcendence" *seriously.*

Because of the temporality of human being, and the "horizontal transcendence" it entails, the method of exposition of the present study is not linear. It is, rather, *a series of conscious expansions of horizons of meaning.* I will attempt to show how response to new givens keeps stretching our context of meaning both timewise (historically) and spacewise (cosmically), affecting how we live. My efforts to fix on paper descriptions of the dynamics of reflective human being, I fear and hope, will demonstrate why it is that common sense has so much trouble thinking dynamically and in terms of interacting horizons of meaning. The way we interact with and respond to these ever expanding and complicated horizons or worlds of meanings is by no means a smooth trajectory. There is struggle. CONCEIVED AT A PLACE AND A TIME, THE HUMAN BEING PASSES THROUGH AN ENDURANCE WITH "OBJECTIVE" PAST, "INTERIOR" PRESENT, AND "MYSTERIOUS" FUTURE, the stage of a *polemos* (Greek for "struggle") for transcendence.

THE FIGHTING, STRUGGLING HUMAN BEING

This study will deal with our struggles *to manage* (contemporary verb intended!) the increasingly demanding variety of worlds, in our effort to become an authentic "self" in the large sense that I shall explain. At the very core of human reflective being is a dimension of *opposition* (suggested in the *ob* of *object*), struggle. *Homo sapiens* (the struggle for knowledge), *Homo faber* (the struggle to create), *Homo ludens* (the struggle to play and enjoy), and *Homo militans* (the struggle to dominate, extinguish) are examples of this struggle and opposition. *Polemos*, struggle, is inextricable from human existence, at least in the cosmos. Voegelin dramatizes it on a global scale, calling it *Gigantomachia*. The power of the human cosmos is at issue. This struggle is a characteristic that may emerge from the playful *(Homo ludens)*, but it is not peaceful. "Competition" can be civil, but it too is about clash of power. The canny Greeks saw *polemos* as an essential aspect of nature, in which we participate. Nietzsche's phrase "Menschlich, alzu menschlich" (Human, all too human) reminds us that the German thinker considered *polemos* a central human reality. History has revealed the terrifying proportions of *polemos* in the cultural realm (lithium hydride bombs are objects of practical art, and extermination camps are a purely human invention—neither is in any sense playful). All cultural achievement risks erosion from its cosmic base up. *Polemos* dramatizes this weakness.

I see easily at least three kinds of human *polemoi* requiring the development of strategy and tactics:

1. The physical world. Without it the other kinds of struggle could not arise or take the forms they do. Lifelong we need to learn to take care of and train the body, to develop motor skills, to fight off attacks, from microorganisms to hunger. Physical illnesses affect all our abilities to "struggle." The gravely ill responding to grace may succumb gracefully to their destiny.
2. The external participation in the "intersubjective world," where we meet other human beings, who bring us to strife of all kinds, including clashes with the desires of other human beings who can hurt me not only with physical weapons but "spiritually." (Later we shall see that this spirituality goes beyond the merely psychological.) We share our world with different kinds of creatures, from the neighbors' cats to CEOs running the institution from which we gain our livelihood. We must learn to survive in such a complex intersubjective world.
3. Time and space: the personal site of the "interior struggle" between aspects of our individual being that are not harmonized. We must learn "to get it all together"—bodily struggle, internal personal tension, intersubjective strife—as the psychiatrists say, in order "to feel human."

A CALL TO CRITICAL EDUCATION

How to manage all this? I see the present tome as a *"how-to manual"*: how to achieve authenticity, ultimately how to deal with both our horizontal and vertical transcendence, becoming a full self *(autos)*. This is achieved by responding to the breadth of horizons of interpretation, depth of the foundations on which openings of transcendence reside, and receptivity to the breaking into our worlds of that mysterious vertical transcendence that brings new vision. In short, an appropriation of human being can assist us in this quest for authenticity. Education should be aimed at securing peace. "From *polemos* to good management to peace" would make an appropriate motto.

How do we achieve "authenticity," expanding our selfhood horizontally and vertically, with sufficient criticism of our own way of projecting the future? It should be remarked that deep penetration of the center also gives meaning; meaning does not only happen horizontally and vertically. Without the struggle for authenticity, management becomes superficialities, "rearranging deck chairs of the HMS *You-know-what*." Existence, of course, is more than management: "authentic existence"— the free existence of a human being—implies testing one's loves: clarifying what I wish to make mine. *"Authentic," after all, means "truly proper to the self (autos)."*

Our present planetary-scale cultural context has us caught up in *an unprecedentedly powerful set of social processes, unbelievable in number, in force, in rapidity of development, and in sweep.* This has spawned new mindsets, new symbols, new kinds of institutions, breakthroughs in "information processing." It has created instruments that were before unthinkable. In this swirl of complex activity, how best to respond to those vast intersubjective processes demanding attention in our own increasingly hectic personal worlds?

To be "authentic," maximally conscious and free, such personal management presupposes *education of new width and depth.* We must learn to open up ever wider world contexts of meaning as we interpret the givens of our existence; we must also learn the "virtues" that free up response to the givens entailed, however breathtaking they may turn out to be. Generations are being molded to computer-game scenarios, often twisting and forming reflexes in ways few examine critically. This may not in the final analysis be the most desirable form of education!

In the present study there will be many indications how to educate, how to mobilize the wise to their proper end. Let me offer here a few examples of what needs consideration in any foundational educational process.

The call to "authenticity" is based on human being's innate "freedom," the inborn "transcendence" mentioned at the beginning of this study. We constantly open new horizons for ourselves, projecting toward the future, attempting to direct the processes in which we are involved toward the ends we are seeking. In German, *Die Freie* is open space, as in "He broke out into the free." Human freedom implies the opening of a time and space within which things are allowed by us to appear and thus to have a meaning so that we can deal with them. This "space" can be personal, or it can be intersubjective. But it is always in human time and space that objects are allowed to appear.

Such freedom to create meaning from the given data implies a responsibility, the capability precisely to "respond" genuinely to reality as it offers itself to us. The nature of "responsibility" will be carefully examined in this study. *Spondere* is a Latin root recognizable in the word *spouse*. It means "to commit." *Re-sponse* implies commitment. Commitment . . . to what? To the "data"—whatever my horizon-deploying interpretation allows to stand there objectively, that is, *ob,* "over against" me, for at least a moment. Even the most intrusive object surging up in my world usually allows me some leeway to refuse "commitment," to refuse to respond to it: at the stage of crawling the infant may flee the other person physically, or blank out an image mentally. For a positive example, imagine the subject escaping into timeless abstractions, treating as "eternal" things that are in fact growing and declining and so require planning. In a positive response there will always be a finite fund of remembrances, hence limits to wanting to open the future. The young infant is hampered by lack of experience. Is there any general way to judge in a given instance reasonable parameters of "openness" to the "data"? How much are we able to digest into meaning? How does the ability to judge in response to "data" develop within a human life? We shall see later what the issues are when we examine interpretation within different kinds of worlds, with distinctive presencing.

I shall take this moment to call attention to the foundational relationship between two persons, essential to every kind of relationship between human worlds. Consider the reciprocal "gift of self" dimension involved in encounter between subjects. The first contact between a child and *ex utero* reality is taken from the person assisting to put the infant in the arms of its mother. The mother cannot presence to the child until the gift of birth, a result of cooperation between cosmic reality and the mother's acceptance of the new life. The infant must have some (minimal) ability to notice the mother, although having no name for her. Eventually, the newborn will re-spond to the other human being by a look, later also by a smile (one of nature's great inventions). Conscious, free commitment on the infant's part to communication is a somewhat later development. Eventually, the child will become able to give something back to his parents and casual admirers. The smile eventually will come to mean "You please me. I want to please you." For many years the child may take the family for granted. With maturity he may begin to appreciate all that the family members have given him, and to resent aspects of their interactions that he judges negative, sometimes even disastrous. There may come a phase when the child judges sweepingly, "This little family world is oppressive. . . . I'm out of here." Much of what may have been tendered by the family with positive intent, as gift, may now be taken by the adolescent as power play, *polemos*. The responding "gift of self" may be deferred, or refused.

THE PERSON

If authentic selfhood develops through increasingly generous reflective response to "the gift of the givens," then development of education calls for "a phenomenology of gift." An exploration of "the conditions of the possibility of enhancing the student's openness to receiving gifts, and in turn learning to give back generously, is what education" is all about. (I am assuming here that "moral virtues" can be taught. It will be a task later on in this anthropology to make credible the age-old tradition of acquiring moral virtue.)

In the present study the term *person* will be reserved for the most authentic aspect of the temperament-inheriting self: its loving, generous, and "freest" opening. Given the history of the word *person*, this is not an arbitrary attribution: the early Fathers of the Church distinguished the three *"personae"* of the Triune life of the Absolute. The human "person" is mainly led out of the limits of the primitive "self" by the gifts of other "persons" who work lovingly *and methodically*, striving to educate a person authentically. Nothing is more central to self-development than the generous and enlightened persons in our lives who offer this "drawing out."

I will show how the capacity of a self to manifest personhood by the giving of self renders creative being perceptible and contagious. This is evident not only individually but also socially—for instance, in codes of law, artistic breakthroughs, in heroic or holy lives. These "luminous" encounters with "human being" breaking through continue influencing the still struggling selves living in later time.

"Dasein soll seinen Helden waehlen: The human existent should choose his heroes." Martin Heidegger declared this, rather abruptly, in a famous paragraph toward the end of one of the most influential philosophical works of the twentieth century, *Being and Time*. Nowhere in his work does he elucidate this principle directly. In the context of our reflection on "person" I shall offer a hint of how I understand this.

Human being should blossom into personal being. Part of our struggle toward authenticity is wise response to personal influences, allowing the best of ourselves to respond to the gift of the other. It is vital to reflect on how one achieves responsible imitation of genuine heroes and avoids fanatic following of pseudoheroes. *Polemos* is not the way, but the contagion of genuine love can be.

THE AUTHENTIC AND THE WEIRD

I have somewhat confused the issue of whether many human beings seem little conscious of their call to authentic existence. With some it seems as though they were never touched by "a luminous event" of any depth and breadth. *Authenticity is far from automatic.* Realizing human freedom is indeed a struggle between our inborn transcendence and our inborn limits. I shall explain.

Each of us is situated concretely in time and space, within definite and, one hopes, expanding horizons. We have also suffered damage, often self-inflicted, that will hinder our recuperating the implicit: intersubjectivity brings not just gift but also polemical power plays. Trauma can bring about a catastrophic narrowing of one's horizons. Indeed, weird things can happen.

Weirdness is a very real and most regrettable dimension of human being. I introduce this word in all seriousness. It contrasts with the straightforwardness of the *genuine (Echt),* which often presents as calm and banal but can also be very exciting. A *straightforward* rational person has trouble coping with the weird. The very word itself is troubling: the root is *wayward.* The German word "Un-*heim*-lich" means the same thing: "without a home." Human weirdness is an *unheimlich* phenomenon, one in which the person cannot settle down, a mystery so much with us that it is worthy of serious thought, as the rabbis of old saw when they painted the amazing canvas of "the Fall." *Ho de poioon ten aletheian* (He who does the truth comes to the light), says St. John in his gospel: "The light has come into the world, and men loved darkness rather than light, because their deeds were evil. For every one who does evil hates the light, and does not come to the light, lest his deeds should be exposed. But he who does the truth comes to the light that it may be clearly seen that his deeds have been wrought in God" (John 3:21).

In our search for authenticity, we will have to deal with the weirdness of "hating the light." The Greek word for truth, *aletheia,* means "unveiling," literally, taking away the veil of forgetfulness (remember the river Lethe, the challenge at the beginning of Dante's *Inferno*). What is this "veil"? *It is the unintelligibility of brute force.*

Science keeps penetrating below the attractive and routine surface of things, unveiling heretofore unsuspected levels of being. But truth is often veiled in ways more sinister than merely the material limits of the finite: veils of pathological DENIAL, the obscurity of wanting to dominate, of raw power, as though I were the center of the universe, misuse of situations and things to entice or force the other to serve me in fear. We can keep fooling ourselves when many who know us "see right through" the subterfuge. Perverse human obscurings of reality may be healed thus: "doings of un-truth being un-done by the friend or the psychoanalyst"; something more "personal" and empathetic than empirical research is required, as psychiatrist Karl Stern pointed out so forcefully. It is a central role of the educator to attempt to bring light where before there was darkness or sheer power.

HOW ARE WE THROWN MORE DEEPLY INTO MURK AND WEIRDNESS?

Given the complexity of our interacting worlds (in subsequent chapters I shall clarify considerably the relations between the different kinds of worlds), how do most of us, so long as we are mentally healthy, manage to feel so familiar with our own immediate settings? Are we guilty of ignoring *polemoi*, paying little critical attention to how the worlds work, locking ourselves in familiar surface structures so as to avoid the *angst* of the unfamiliar as much as possible? Are we terrified of the intense anxiety that goes with recognizing ourselves trapped in the little internal world we make our prison through lack of self-criticism? Does this anxiety hinder our own appropriation of who we are as human beings and human being in general?

When suddenly thrown more deeply into ourselves by unexpected "catastrophe," we find many aspects of our "interior" murky. We do not understand the hold of certain impulses on us; we find ourselves being uncharacteristically selfish and unloving. The weirdness of the foreign surging up from the domesticated calls for exploration. For instance, this nagging feeling that I am throwing myself into my work more to lose myself than because my job has great significance in the ultimate order of things: Is there any ultimate order of things? If so, what roles do the different kinds of worlds play in forming the dynamics of our lives?

I believe most of us tend to take the inner confusions of human being far too much for granted—*as though they are inevitable*. Should someone close to us be caught up in frightening mental pathology, we do begin, however, to get concerned. Why should there ever be serious confusion within? Why endless wars without? Why perpetual *polemos*, interior and exterior? Is painful collision the inevitable consequence of finite freedom? Are internal peace and external community inevitably so difficult to attain? *Is insane destruction inevitable in human affairs?*

We should never take evil for granted—"It just is; learn to cope as best you can." Whatever the reader's notion of being, I believe it makes sense to ask: Is there something basically wrong with human beings? Is there something, however, in each of us that could be basically right? What can we do to find the right path?

A quick question for theists: If all human beings are the creatures of a good God, why would he ever have made us so prone to confusion and suffering? Humanists: Are these conditions, which we often experience as intense sufferings, simply inevitable pains of a blind evolution? Is there a ground to keep searching for "wisdom," that is, a meaningful reliable way to live?

UNTANGLING THE STRANDS:
DISTRACTION VERSUS OVERSPECIALIZATION

Is a meaningful search for maximum vision and "authentic human being" really possible in a world as complex and seemingly confused as ours? Would it not be prudent to blank out as irrelevant much of the landscape over which we are now soaring: "too much to handle"? Like pilots concentrating on a flight path, most of us choose to focus attention on a few *cosmiota* of greater attraction, absorbed by a few main traditions. The dynamic structure of our life will then be—let's face it—a personal, partly quirky way of being in the cosmos: inevitably a weird "lifestyle."

I suggest we can do better: being human, we cannot in any way blank out the need for an all-embracing vision of human being, although it may be mixed up, poor in scope, superficial, often more than a little crazy; still, it is "my world," and I personally must confess that I aspire to expand my world to embrace all of reality. It should be remarked right from the start that an embracing vision of humanity must not be understood as some immovable Platonic idea. Human being is constantly evolving and is incarnating itself through time in various cultures and worlds, operated upon and conserved by individual human persons. They do this through their institutions, languages, religious beliefs, art, culture, science, histories, and so forth. In short, human being is the collective *positum* or thesaurus of all human thinking and doing. It conditions who we are and who we will become, but it is not absolutely determining, as it always works through human freedom. For example, the notion of modern Western science has evolved from Descartes and Galileo forward, but its history is enfolded and has helped bring about our present-day attitudes toward science, ultimately creating a scientific world. Given the multiplicity of kinds of worlds in which we are involved, we find imposed an entire *hierarchy of related ongoing balancing acts.* Stay mindful of the reality that all these different kinds of worlds are dynamic, expanding, and contracting (for example, the once vast world of steam railroading has shrunk to a few operating museum locomotives).

Maintaining equilibrium within and between worlds demands certain disciplines. First, we need disciplines to avoid vaporizing our focus into mindless distractions. We need to keep reassessing the relative impor-tance of our roles in the several main worlds in which we live. We ought consciously to make time for *contemplation* illumining all the important worlds. Further, we need disciplines to help us *keep our world as wide open as possible.* There is some "built-in" protection in our lives from ideologi-cal oversimplification: things and people aggressively keep invading "our world," involving us in every manner of process, distractions, and treasured "breakthroughs." Aerial combat to keep them out of our "air-space" is itself a form of such involvement. But there is also built-in sup-port for such blind spots: ideological commitment and pathological fear of the uncontrollable tend to blank out such invasions as "irrelevancies," with the greatest of skill being exercised through "denial" and "suppres-sion." These must be vigilantly criticized.

How to develop a strategy to follow a via media between distractedly going off in all directions rather than stubbornly pursuing a preeminent goal, closing oneself off from challenging "data" in other traditions? I am seeking to convince the reader that in our virtual times, not only can we keep trying to move toward a balanced overall world, but if wisdom is aspired to, we must try. The need for explicit strategic thinking with a wise balance between many sources of demand is now better understood and more vital than ever. Being finite, we do indeed need to specialize, but at the same time we must act in keeping with who we truly are: not only be "authentic in the small sense" ("be yourself") but more fundamentally be "authentic in the large sense" ("be human")—face all the important realities and learn how they relate dynamically. The two logically require one another: priorities and balance, form and dynamics.

FREEDOM AND TIME: "STOPPING TO THINK"

Time, of course, is of the essence. The infamous "lack of time" in our lives is not only a pressing practical problem but also a clue to the dilemmas of "finite freedom" at the foundation of the articulation of our "horizontal" time-space worlds. *We seek everlasting meaning in the midst of fleeting realities.* Our life is a constant struggle to "make time" for what we consider most meaningful.

In villages, there is always time to smoke a pipe and exchange stories: "In the village, one can feel the presence of spirits, and think of the Great Spirit." But you and I do not live in a village, and pace McLuhan, a great friend of mine, there is no "global village." The quiet necessity of feeling the presence of transcending spirit is ground up in the frantic hurly-burly of our high-tech life, in which Marshall the guru was too immersed.

Even today, however, daily life follows "commonsense" rhythms of a postindustrial kind. We can rely on changing things not to change in the aspect we need to count on for now. That, as we shall see, is perfectly rational. But "taking for granted" certain "permanences" can also distract us from noticing signs of coming obsolescence for which we should account in our strategic planning (they can prove fatal). Where necessary and possible, prepare for the foreseen still remote but eventually big change. Planet Earth and everything coming and going on it will disappear, however badly we depend on it. Our strange human freedom makes us responsible for the space we live in but also for our time.

THE SOCIAL NATURE OF THE SEARCH FOR TRUTH

Paradoxically, we cannot achieve "authenticity" alone. It is obvious that the individual left to himself or herself cannot get an adequate hold on his or her present situation, not now, and never in the past. Many fail to recognize how radically they depend on collective resources provided by traditions of various kinds. In these *cosmiota*, one works symphonically with others, not just for immediate practical purposes but to discover deeper reality, because they love truth and want to pass it on.

Awaiting us is a vast communal wisdom, both explicit wisdom (religious, scientific, technological, and so forth) and implicit (social class, profession, ethnicity), *both kinds of wisdom launching individuals on the path to authenticity.* We are all formed by the institutions in which we participate. If the world open to us is confusingly complex, it also provides us with unprecedented support in the struggle for clarity. We are in need of enduring processes of "sorting out."

When human beings saw the world more simply, aristocrats in the brief but splendid periods of high culture secured for themselves the leisure to sit around and employ this "freedom" to invent what some Hellenic sages came to call "philo-sophia." Not just the notion of "sophia" but methods for "erotically" pursuing her. This was achieved at a cost: enslaving others to do the menial work.

Today the small bands of high-tech moguls in government and information and corporate management are not so blessed with time hanging heavy upon them. As I said, to "manage" our lives authentically, today more than ever, we need to invest in the many interconnected worlds we share ever more tightly with all other humans. This suggests how radical the truth of the old ethical principle is: Proper management of my life implies participating in "the common good of all." Every one of my free decisions contributes to the direction in which humanity will invest. This may seem to rock the most hallowed principle of contemporary popular ethics: My feelings are my ultimate beacon, the key to who I really am! No one has the right to tell me what to do. My responsibility to others beyond should be restricted to sensible political compromise. Absolutist convictions have no place in the "public square"! Religion, if you have to suffer it, should be utterly private. Yet it is worth pondering.

PRACTICAL METHOD: RATIONAL SIGHT AND INSIGHT

Sorry, I cannot disguise it: the main goal of the present book is to show that being fully human implies *philosophical insight.* To make the philosophical-insight statement credible, there is simply no alternative method to the one I will follow: patient description of what I believe I see, with "seeing" ranging from turning my eyes on the apple tree to verify my wife's claim that the first blossoms are showing to mathematical insight and musings on the propositions regarding cosmos, the universe, the reasons for wondering about a multiple of universes.

WHAT DOES IT MEAN "TO SEE"?

Seeing: a primordial word! Pierre Teilhard de Chardin began his most famous work, *The Phenomenon of Man,* with this statement of the purpose of his study: "Voir et faire voir!" (To see and to make others see!). The Greek philosophers distinguished the "theoretical" and the "practical." *Theory* comes from a word that meant being attentive to what the gods *(theoi)* have to tell you. They were the first we know of (because of a colossal invention—writing) to grasp what is at stake in the human act of "seeing," a startling phenomenon. They made seeing an explicit theme for reflection, for the first time in history. This was a vast leap in "insight": human beings became conscious of their "re-flection," *bending back anew to be able to see that they see!*

An animal can see, but human seeing seems to require something more: the creation of a conscious distance between a self-conscious knower and the known (which much of the time is unaware of being observed). This reflected-upon distance, this ob-position (*ob* as in *object*), this intelligent space, makes possible the higher meaning of which humans are capable, including the very idea of "ob-jectivity!"—of being consciously "thrown over against" and being capable "of being dependent upon"!

What did the Greek thinkers make of this human "seeing"? *The highest goal of man.* So they considered "practical activity" (*praxis*), while necessary, to be inferior, "ancillary," one might say. They pressed slaves (*ancillae*) or draft animals into doing much of the work necessary for mere survival, ensuring the minimum cosmic foundation required for pursuing the noble seeing.

"Seeing" is understood differently in the Hebraic tradition, because at its core it is believed to be a revelation, a loving encounter and re-sponse between God and man as persons, not gods as alien, difficult masters, but the unique God as Father. Father and child see differently: the Father takes the initiative of a new kind of presencing, one that brings about a new kind of divine-human relationship.

Both the Greek and the Hebraic traditions emphasize that you become what you see, and that seeing is a special call of the human being. As the term *eros* suggests, as the Gospel of John affirms and as I pointed out, truth is an activity. "Doing truth" is an essential part of the life of the maturing human being, passionately so, indeed (given our sin, "polemically" so).

Human beings *learn to see*. (Even the highest animals seem to see in the limits of inherited neurophysiologic possibilities.) In each human life, seeing changes almost endlessly as the individual matures. Over the span of human history, what it means to see develops as humans' observations increase in complexity. I hope this book will be a help in seeing in depths and breadths more worthy of a human being—both to me and to you.

THE HEART OF THE MATTER:
LOVE AS LIBERATION FROM OURSELVES

I am not going back on what I promised at the beginning of this introduction: I am not attempting to draw my reader into Buddhist contemplation any more than preparing Bible-thumping invocation of the most magic of words, *loving*. I shall try, however, to give *reasons* for proposing love, this most awesome of all mysteries, as the key "method" to wisdom, the most liberating *hodos*—"way" of life. Liberating from what? From slavery to our selves.

For that ringing declaration to make any sense at all, we shall have to try to come to know better our selves. What is it about the human "self" that makes it possible for us so to relate to ourselves to the point that we can "tie ourselves in knots," as common language so well puts it? What particular kind of seeing can point the way to untying such knots?

Any psychiatrist will tell you how difficult it is to help a patient see himself more truthfully. The early philosophers—and today Teilhard de Chardin—were right about that: without love you will not see properly. *To love well and to know are intrinsically linked*, as Hebraic language intuited.

To be freeing, love has to be directed knowingly—it cannot be pure *eros*, in the sense of a blind desire; then it will lead to *polemos*, unless it is intrinsically linked to wisdom.

This forces us to face an operational paradox: clearly, "love" can be blind, mere groundless fantasy. I cannot know my self *(autos)* if I loathe what I have made of myself; it is equally impossible if I make an idol of my present state.

Love can open us into the most daunting reality to which we can accede, the interior world of another person. But the extent to which I enter the depths of another depends on my access to my own depths. Through their love, others lead me more deeply into myself. *The Love that drives us into full existence is thus at once a form of tradition, handed down to us by others, at the very root of ourselves and human being.*

I do not assume the reader's agreement to any of the challenges I have just proposed. The massive reality of meaningless and destructive acts, the pain and anger in the world, the cruel power plays acted out in the name of love tend to make soft cynics of us all. The wider our world, the more suffering we encounter, the more difficult it may seem to love, the more irrelevant wisdom may seem. The most daunting challenge for anthropology is mustering credible evidence for a wise response to such evil—a response credible because it does not attempt to evaporate the mystery.

In our hedonist society suffering is acknowledged, but contemplating it is generally not "in." We prefer proposing solutions to eliminate it: "Let us make our HTX means of production and distribution more effective, more equitable." "Let us clamp the power of the state more securely over the 'multinational' behemoths, and thus force improvement of lifestyles in the fourth world."

If we can make no sense out of suffering, we can make no sense out of life; we cannot respond to the challenge of being human. After Auschwitz, life must still make sense. Before Auschwitz, the symbol of the supreme reality of suffering was the Cross. The *polemos* over the crosses erected in memoriam at Auschwitz was not a superficial *"mal entendu."*

Loving wisdom, the attempt to accept the painful *polemos* necessary to achieve the best integrated vision of the world in which I stand—an insight into what "human being" is—and to discipline myself to respond generously to the reality I am offered, is not merely still possible. It is ever more *necessary*, the essential need of human being, as it has always been.

In sum, using a phenomenological approach I have developed, I shall be concerned with the following trajectory:

1. There exists a human drive to know oneself as a human being and as part of larger, more encompassing human being.
2. The drive to be authentically human compels us to understand and appropriate for ourselves the different worlds in which we dwell.
3. This implies a discussion of freedom, responsibility, and an overcoming of the weird and murky *polemos* or struggle inherent in existence (note there is necessary and good *polemos*, too). This can be achieved by moving toward love.
4. An effective move toward love can be made through an understanding of the givens of worlds, traditions, others, and self through insight and vision.
5. To engage love is one of the principal ways we exist as human beings but also is one of the principal ways to understand and live human being in general.

2

TIME AND WORLDS

Shades of Marburg, Freiburg, and the "Left Bank"

Authenticity was a "buzzword" in the passionate days of "existentialism" just after the Second World War. In the writings of Jean-Paul Sartre, it seemed to support an extremely individualistic notion of the self. (Remember the climactic line of *Huis clos* [No Exit]? "L'enfer c'est les autres" [Hell is other people].) As we saw in my opening chapter, it is the "small" individualistic sense of "authenticity" that persists in some psychiatrists' use of the word. It can easily take on a rather negative, isolating sense.

Heidegger was interpreted by some in that way, but that was a flat misinterpretation of his notion of *Eigentlichkeit*. To be sure, the root, *eigen*, does mean "one's own"; *property* in German is *Eigenschaft*. But in Heidegger's *Sein und Zeit* (Being and Time) (1927), the "being-there" of the human existent—the *Da* of *Dasein*—essentially involved "being in the world with others" *(Mitsein),* which constituted part of the very being of who one is . . . of the *da*. Moreover, in *Being and Time, Eigentlichkeit*—authenticity as "ownness"—has to do essentially with a consistently unfolding life. The horizons, in enfolding one's own "throwness into the world" (past) and "anticipation of death" (future), call for the effort to embrace ever more explicitly *the widest possible context of human existence, namely, human being.*

Caution! I am transforming the sense of that possible: "possible" so far as the wisest human beings now know it, from initial "throwness in the world" to the finality of death, not only of the individual, not only of mankind, but of the cosmos itself, to the extent we can speculate about its final state. Furthermore, if Heidegger is correct, the phenomenon of human being must be understood in two fundamental senses. There is, first, the individual sense (my own or *eigentlich*) sense of being, and, second, there is the larger context of human being in general that spans worlds and time. Human being is the work of individuals and communities through time, creating a plethora of worlds. Reciprocally and dynamically, this larger sense of human being conditions individual human beings through time.

All realities in the cosmos can have relevance for our building the wisest course for ourselves personally and for all mankind. All the while the foundation remains cosmic, rooted in the real depths of matter and organism. "Authenticity," a fundamental attitude that can exist, of course, only by being incarnate in knowledge of reality, is an *attitude* that forms and reinforces itself as the person re-sponds generously to the gifts of things presencing in everyday experience and from "e-ducation," a methodic engagement with reality. The climb from "individual" through "self" to "person" leaves none of the lower levels of growth behind, for the higher are rooted in the lower, and the lower further illumined by progress toward larger horizons in the higher consciousness. So right from the start I am sketching a crosslike figure of the human being. *Horizontal:* the opening of a time and space of interpretation. *Vertical:* the levels of the human being's climb from the infant preself "individual" through "self" to "person." Having prepared the way, now we need to understand better how these come to articulate themselves.

This vertical progression and rotation from below to highest and from highest illuminating further our cosmic foundation entails necessarily a horizontal progression as well: you cannot make progress becoming a "self" or from "self" a "person" without deploying ever wider and deeper horizons in your present opening into THE world and into different "little worlds." This will become clearer through the examples I shall offer. One accesses the larger reality of human being by exploring and navigating this structure of multiple and converging and diverging worlds.

The techniques of inquiry that the high-tech world of our time has progressively discovered now need to be *extended to the widest, most primordial, and most anticipatable unfolding of cosmically based time and space.* Essential to this progression is the leading up of "disciples" from the cosmic depths of human being to higher levels, by those with the developed consciousness capable of advancing. That higher level, paradoxically, may best be termed "a more profound existence." It is from the heights of today's knowledge that we illumine more deeply the cosmic and the neurophysiological foundation of even our most exalted leaps of insight into the distant and long ago.

The self is "auto-nomous"—"a law *(nomos)* unto its self"—but only to a degree. The self, while remaining responsible for itself, is essentially called to be communitarian. This is the ideal human scene: *many partially autonomous, self-responsible "lawgivers" willingly harmonizing their desires and actions, making and upholding together the law of a rationally ordered, loving society, respectful of the cosmic, given so far as we know it, building, from nursery on, mutually responsible selves.* Such an ideal of a rational communitarian "intersubjective" dimension of human being collides with the reality of *"polemos," collision and struggle, both of contending selves and of tensions within a solitary self.*

The sense that cooperative structures can be made to bring more tranquil existence to human being enjoys greater respectability today than in nineteenth-century "positivist" times or in the glare of a Nietzschean "Will to Power." Our highly technological world has emerged from two planetary-scale wars and inhuman ideological regimes into a time when more persons than ever seek consciously for structures of fairness to allow fruitful competition between caring selves.

There are several reasons for this improving atmosphere: the kind of phenomenology I am calling on has made an impact in bringing thinkers back from extreme "positivism" to the more fluid and more complex realities of intersubjectivity. This leads to reflection on a larger gamut of kinds of "objects" worthy of serious "methodical" response. These are objects understood in the weave of relations in which they get their sense. Then consider what has happened in physics itself: relativity theory and quantum mechanics dissolved overly simple classical mechanical notions of fixedness. And finally the implications of the temporal dimensions of "fields" and the sense of the past continuing to mold the future as historical studies became more "existential," and physics itself became "historical." The revelation of time now stretches from the "cosmic singularity" to the "end of the world," expanding our imaginations.

Now consider the role the project of "authenticity" in the large sense plays in this recent awakening of interweaving dynamic structures and levels of meaning. First, commitment: authenticity helps deepen an ontological sense of the contrast between "greater" authenticity and the "lesser" and much used psychoanalytic sense of the term. In psychology "authentic" has something like the sense of the self as it really is concretely here and now in these individuals—confusions, denials, and all. Authenticity in this lesser sense is wrapped up in the obscurity and masks emotionally obstructing the person's consciousness of honest confrontation with himself. They ought to be taken with the seriousness they deserve as "negative realities," if I may so dub them. Psychological authenticity is close to the sense of "genuineness," in Heidegger's sense of *echt*. Second, the self, being essentially relational, consciously (and "spiritually") connects directly or indirectly (and potentially) to all of being, in all the complex ways we are discovering. This connectivity includes one's authentically being aware of knowing he is related objectively, through that part of the cosmos that is his body, to the entire objective cosmos, whether or not, and to what degree, he is aware of this truth. All these connections within him, many structuring his outreach to the objective of all various kinds, are contributing to full selfhood. Every kind of known relation reveals itself to be part of the intelligibility of any object.

In our high-tech times we should struggle continually to make as evident as we can the foundationally real, even in the perhaps shadowy reaches of the widest, deepest, oldest continual context, both cosmic and historical. We ought not to be afraid to confront the weird in all its terror, for this vast context surrounds and penetrates the self, calling to us to respond to this full intelligibility, parts of which the subject may be shutting out pathologically. In this anthropology *the person in "authentic situation" is motivated by an attitude of bringing in the whole of being as explicitly as we are able to know it, and struggles to respond to all of it.* This is an ideal the human being, alone or collectively, cannot reach. But we are called by the realities revealed in our time to struggle to break down barriers to whatever form of truth an individual may be ignoring or denying. The psychiatrist may be uninterested in criticizing the patient's religious beliefs, save those that affect his ability to function as a balanced self. But the philosopher by vocation, as Dr. Hersch has suggested, must take seriously all science and all the kinds of theological claims that have molded whole civilizations.[1]

While "Being" illumines through that social being who is human, what it illumines genuinely is reality. Much of reality does not have its origins in the human-social or depend on it in large part. Earthlings affect a tiny part of the universe; it is all so slightly messed up by us: one planet considerably, one moon ever so slightly, probes to a couple of other planets, and now . . . serious talk of "swallowing up the Van Allen

---

1. Edwin L. Hersch, *From Philosophy to Psychotherapy: A Phenomenological Model for Psychology, Psychiatry, and Psychoanalysis* (Toronto: University of Toronto Press, 2003).

belts." (That will not disturb even our closest neighbor, Mars!) The colossal remainder is unperturbed.

PRESENCING WORLDS AND THEIR TEMPORALITY

Philosophy draws on things that are given and that come to take on meanings as we interact with them. How we interact with and understand what is given form worlds. When human beings began to examine the structures of life, they saw (recently) that the simplest cell is a rigid operation already enormously complicated for our understanding! (I shall continue to recall the fact that there are more data in one cell than in one hundred sets of *The Encyclopedia Britannica*.) In more advanced life forms we can imagine something of their "interior life." But our experience of genuine interiority and freedom to expand capability we human beings alone enjoy occurs only in our own "interiors." (The cell has no self-consciousness.) The key is a kind of fresh input from beyond what was available genetically at the start of the path, which grows as awareness broadens and deepens.

Most human "selves" do not achieve "authenticity in the largest sense"—the self explicitly committed to seeking out the widest and deepest horizons of meaning. What enables the thrusts forward by the individual are new future-opening cosmic elements acquired by him along the way. In every act of interpretation both the previous acquired capabilities and the new future-opening creative element meet *now*, at the center of one's consciousness. The whole developing horizon unfolds "horizontally" along the time-space surface of the path of life. However, in every interpretative act the vertical levels are having their present influence. Whether the present act is one of searching for a pen or a moment of exalted vision into the meaning of a mathematically expressed formula in quantum mechanics, it happens now. In the present moment the human being achieves the holding open of horizontal time and space, which allows the object to be intelligible at its scale of grandeur. The scope of vision a self can achieve in a particular act of horizon-opening interpretation at the level of his maximum capability depends in large measure on that vertical level of possibility for knowing that she or he has accomplished and stored in memory.

In the chapters to come, kinds of presencing will loom as increasingly important. Without our presencing, nothing very human is going to happen. Hence, the need of developing methodically our understanding of ways of presencing and of methodically ("virtuously") increasing control of the positive aspects of our own willingness to presence in response to every sort of being. We must work against unhealthy incapacity in the form of the vice and pathology of denial. We must not hide from reality.

Retained results of my past, including all the formative influences of many intersubjective worlds, are deposited experiences that pass through me (selectively) at the present center of decision. Past results are called into action selectively in function of my present particular capabilities and visions and desires, as I react to the sensibly given. These visions and desires, interweaving at a bodily level only partly under conscious control, affect the ways I now open myself, directing my world projectively toward the future. What then comes out of the future as I go into it is deposited in the ever growing past.

The singularly important factor of what in all this interpreting is true here confronts us with yet another ambiguity: the tension between what "really did happen to the self over the years" (the "objective" history—aspects of which may be testified to by others but is "known fully only to God") and his present subjective history (what he presently allows "to be the case," selective and somewhat inaccurate, perhaps even madly distorted as he irresponsibly DENIES vitally important versions of "reality," projecting pure fantasy instead).

There are two different truths at work here: It is true, but perhaps forgotten by all, that I at age ten sobbed inconsolably when my model train set was destroyed in a fire. It is also true that now I do not remember having so reacted. This interplay between what has really impacted one and what he now believes forms right now his forward pro-jecting vision. From the ex-tension, the leap into the new element in the future, new light falls on past and present. The event right now of a credible witness testifying that I was distraught may convince me to change my view of the past event (unless I am for some reason adamantly opposed to such a testimony).

Experienced past and anticipated future meet in ongoing process in the critical moment, the present: only *now* is decision being made. The "thickness" of the "moment" of presence varies; one instant my regard is fleeting, another I can ascend and look widely around, and then with intense sustained concentration, future vision grows out of past experience brought to the center of attention in large and rich sets of past-established relationships. *The more authentic the person, the wider and richer the*

horizons of interpretation he or she opens up, the more critically examined the
truths illumined, the thicker and brighter and truer his or her wisdom.

The intellectual virtues required to sustain a thick, rich, true presence enhance one's capabilities of amassing much that is good. The moral virtues (to be examined later) that are strengthened by a vast, rich, and genuine wisdom advance a great goodness, as reciprocally the exercise of moral virtues strengthens the vision. Goodness can be found without authenticity in the sense of a vision of the widest and deepest horizons presently available. But authenticity requires the moral support of goodness.

An all-englobing challenge of harmonizing two different kinds of fundamental time, and within them many different kinds of truths, is inescapable for a contemporary authentic search for wisdom: first, the "lived time" of the human spirit interior to which presences to each of us in the world and, second, the real processes of the objective things themselves unfolding for our inspection at different rhythms. These objective processes appear within the horizons of our worlds but reveal themselves to be not merely human constructions.

Again, caution! These two kinds of time do not correlate with the horizontal and the vertically transcendent, but belong respectively to the "interior" of subjectivity and the "exterior" of the cosmic (including that most intimate object, the body of each of us). It will help once again to elaborate both:

1. The internal time of the human spirit is essentially bound up with the remembering pro-jective interpretation carried out by human subjects. This "lived, reflective time" varies in emotional intensity: the proverbial minute while the dentist drills is longer than the quarter hour lingering over a Starbucks. In interior time there are then subsets of different "interior time experiences." The choice in all cases has to do with the person's actual personal interior life, a strong role being played by current desires, and behind it all *cura* (*Sorge*, "*care*"). The sense that time goes faster for the old than for the young has a physiological realty.

2. Human consciousness when interpreting observes many objects caught up in natural processes. They reveal their own different kinds of endurance (including rapidity of change) in one of a given variety of real time and space. The new oak tree's "slow" pace of growth (by our standards) has nothing to do with what any of us think about

it, unfolding at its own rhythms in a cosmic setting where rains and storms come and go, seasons flow, nature provides nutrients, and humans inject fertilizer from time to time.

None of this givenness of the objective time of the various processes and endurances has anything to do with what we may think about them, except the acts of fertilizing that have their origins in certain humans' notions about fortifying plants. Even in that case, the act of injecting the chemicals is a fact, an objective process that has been unleashed, say, five times in the life of my young oak. The truth (interior) of our knowledge about these matters does, however, depend on the correctness of the interior life's judgment regarding what is grasped through the senses of the reality of (exterior) objective processes and forms. This includes our consciousness's ability to grasp different kinds of "objective time." What I aim to achieve in looking over my healthy oak is one thing, the accuracy of my observation—the objective truth—another. I must be on guard not to let the desire of the first twist what I am willing to admit is happening in the second.

THE DIFFERENT GENERA OF WORLDS MAY ENFOLD ONE ANOTHER, AND EACH REVEALS DISTINCTIVE KINDS OF PRESENCING AND OF TIME

I have promised to explore the fact that, within the known ultimate (the "authentic," objective) context, the very different kinds of worlds—personal, social, the highly technological world, and the cosmos—enfold one another. Each genus "enfolds" in different ways, with distinctive kinds of "presencing," forming a complex structure of interaction. In fact, each of these genera of worlds reveals many different varieties of presencing of its own. Yet the dynamic, complete interaction between the genera of worlds happens so familiarly—"automatically" (or so at first it appears)—my personal world being rooted cosmically in my body and my interpretative horizon openings being fed by remembered experience and many habits. We deploy these shifting foci all the day long, taking largely for granted their contribution to the life of our spirits.

Each genus of world has its indispensable role in making possible human being as we now know it. For instance, I earlier pointed out that individual human beings are the only creatures that can openly "reflect upon critical worlds." With increasing, educated critical awareness, we learn to invent more powerful forms of learning and research.

The "mind-set" of each self will then be at once the same, in that all healthy human beings participate in all four genera, and are different—within the same kinds of horizons with different personal histories, outlooks, and developed talents: an airline pilot's outlook on life and his capabilities are different from those of a bush pilot or an opera singer.

The set of relationships between different genera of worlds is complicated by the fact that *each genus is ontologically different.* By "cosmos," for instance, is generally meant today, as we have seen, an objective reality, the universe as a partially known set of real objective relationships among particles, atoms, molecules, radiations, and every kind of real thing—the falling snow, the tree bending in the wind—in an unfolding universe that founds and enfolds the individual human being. The objective universe "enfolds" all these relations and things really in an all-inclusive field of energies. By the cosmos's "enfolding" is meant, then, not so much a set of interpretative horizons by which we come to know something of the universe as it is, but, rather, in this case, it is more an acknowledgment that all other kinds of worlds (including the most imaginary) have as a condition for their possibility their *being constituted and related to one another in a real space-time of a universe.*

DEEPER INTO FOUR GENERA OF WORLDS

Personal World

Every manner of world I know about meets me at the center of my personal world. So we might start our reflection here. There are also certain essential features about how things and other human beings presence to me and I to them, which we recognize are also indispensably foundational. In normal daily life I awake to find myself in a familiar setting, so customary I am scarcely aware of the fact that I am responding to what I see and feel by "automatically" recognizing, within the immediate sensory receptions I have no trouble interpreting correctly, a familiar, reliable setting in the intersubjective world. "Oh, here I am, not at home in my Toronto house but in a room of the Regina Delta hotel." It took me two seconds to jolt awake. Now I know that if I pull back the curtains I shall see, nineteen stories below, the old Union Station—now a huge gambling

casino, but coming as a relief there will also be the freight trains roll-
ing along the Canadian Pacific steel backbone of the country. Instantly,
I know from past trips to the Regina Delta what my routine is going to
be—shower, shave, dress, descend to breakfast—and I know the preor-
dained schedule, built around my commitment to be on time for a nine
o'clock meeting four blocks from the Regina Delta. I know where I am,
why I am here, how I got there, and where I am to go next . . . and that I
must pack my bag and take it along, as I must rush from the lunch after
the meeting directly to the airport. Nothing problematic interrupts this
flash review of today's schedule until . . . I actually open the blinds: Gads!
A blinding blizzard dumping on my plans! After a moment of shock I
acknowledge that "Mother Nature," a familiar cosmic presence, is not
to be taken for granted. Despite this nasty surprise, nothing spins out of
control in my personal world: I know about these blizzards, I know that
the meeting will take place, as all the principals are already in town, and
I know that my departure in the afternoon is now a question mark. Past-
present-future have been further illumined.

In "my" personal world the reality of an external reality presences
insofar as it is related to me personally. I am the ultimate and immediate
reference point. Time and relations with others are organized and revolve
around my own schedule and timely needs. I appropriate and respond
to that which is given in a manner in which I see fit. Truth is very much
my own; it is my experience of what is real and present within my context and my world. Notice that there has to be a fundamental receptivity
to that which is given in the outside world; I do not create the world,
but I react and respond to it. By being affected by this external reality, I
become conscious of my self as a self and begin to appropriate for myself
that which is given to me. The emphasis in this world is on the self, but
it implies neither a selfish way of being in the world nor a philosophical
solipsism. Here, there is a shift of emphasis. I am in the world, and reality is given to me; I do not create it, and it is not merely a projection of
my own fantasy and will. I respond to that which is given, and I begin to
respond to that reality in a very primordial way, that is, in and through
my own personal world. This personal world necessarily is connected to
a larger world, namely, the intersubjective world. I access this world by
shifting my attention away from the self and toward a larger reality.

Intersubjective Worlds

Every interpersonal world—every family and every intimate friend-ship as well as casual acquaintances, and from there on up the scale, remoter and larger intersubjective worlds—is constituted by cooperat-ing individuals working into that world from their personal perspectives (however little they may know!). The personal programs of each moti-vated by their personal cares put a different urgency on particular pro-cesses for each individual in a given intersubjective world.

Within every world except that of intimate friendship there will be individuals very present and others remote to the point that they affect me only through their contribution to the dynamic structures of the *cos-mion*, like accidentally bumping someone in a crowd. "Oh, sorry!" suf-fices. All sorts of *cosmiota* introduce special kinds of presencing and endurance that participants must learn to handle (for instance, there are many really weird families, Mafia gangs may manifest peculiarities you do not care to hear about, and there are "way out" kinds of employment, such as in the Cirque du Soleil). Intersubjective realities do not dissolve the participating individuals from their share of responsibility for the rel-evant "institutions."

Personal worlds are also, then, "foundational," but in this sense they are different from the way the cosmos founds: only because individual human beings, themselves founded in a cosmic hold on the universe, can open sensorially and cognitively on the vast cosmos is it possible for them to enfold the universe psychologically. Universally, then, the subject can hold various insights in memory, and on that basis build up a knowledge not only of the universe but also of intersubjective *Mitsein* worlds shared with others. Through his presencing in a given *cosmion*, he brings effects of his interior life, externalizing them in language and action.

Introducing Mitsein

Mitsein ("being with") worlds provide structures of human work-ing together. When a single individual interprets a thing or an objective world without another human being answering or participating in the interpretation, *Sein* is present but not *Mitsein*. There is no "with" because there is no response. The subject expresses something, the object, even if one is talking about some person as an object who cannot in this set-ting respond; there is no intersubjective communication. Together just two persons might exchange ideas or sentiments, perhaps building a firm friendship. In an exchange of sentiments among many, a large *Mitsein* will occur. A person may enter into a long-lasting complex set of relations between other human beings. In another way, *Mitsein* worlds may be quite different. Consider these modes:

1. In a concrete intersubjective setting: two or more of us are physically (or telephonically) present, each reading in the expressions and actions of the other, or interpreting voices over a telephone, and through interpretation of what he says divining what is going on inside him. (A variant: I may read a letter or a document, imagining in the process of interpretation what were the intended horizons of interpretation projected by the author or authors.) Note also as I explain my intentions to the other and reflect on my own actions, I discover more of my own interior life. This is close to

2. —the other mode, which is self-centered and imaginary. Intersubjective *Mitsein* worlds of both modes—"the cosmic-direct" and "the imaginary" (which, by the way, does not necessarily imply either "unreal" or "false")—usually today receive some of their meaning from the largest of the *Mitsein* worlds, "THE world," that vast web of traditions, institutions, symbol systems, and characteristic processes that constitute our high-tech world. Considerations generated on a vast technological scale can affect both the high-tech world itself and many millions of *Mitsein* worlds, having an ongoing molding influence on how each self interprets himself and the worlds and THE world.

Normally, one person's influence on THE world is infinitesimal, adding up only "statistically," but a James Madison–Thomas Jefferson duo palpably changed the world. Technology now makes possible the destruction of mankind in a matter of hours, requiring the action of a rather small number of nuclear launchers. A modest *Mitsein* might destroy humanity! With *Mitsein* and larger human realities, including the worlds of technology and the cosmos, time and presence become more expansive and more complicated. They are expansive in the sense that they are more comprehensive in that they affect and include more people and more complicated relationships between them and the worlds in which they dwell. Time and presencing become more internally complicated as well in that relationships between persons and their worlds intensify and become more complicated. A larger array of people become intertwined in the lives and worlds of others.

With this "enfolding structure of kinds of worlds," the reader will see that it is not only when one reaches the ultimate level of the authentic person resolutely struggling to open to all of being that humans need to start becoming savvy about this complex plenitude of worlds of so many kinds. More pragmatically, every manager worthy of her salt, on whatever scale she is responding to reality by strategizing, needs *to ponder the dynamic world structures relevant to her plans.* If she does not, her enterprise will be overtaken by deadly surprises. Educationally, we build up (and are built up) gradually to the level of cognitive capability where authenticity, we hope, becomes a central issue where we may begin to care about "the ultimate context of our responsibility."

Becoming explicitly aware of the context in which we daily dwell and operate is further complicated by the fact that there are within the near-cosmic setting, constantly impinging on one's personal world, so many intersubjective worlds forming social structures. Some are as small as families (which can be intense) and others as huge as China, Sunni Islam, the Catholic Church, and (surviving even the Justice Department's attack) Microsoft. The largest can also deliver a big charge in our personal lives, whereas others are a feeble presence. "Pressures" can change. Consider how recently Islam has become less remote and more important in the lives of many Occidentals. We can easily recognize categories of intersubjective worlds that affect in some instances just about everyone.

All thoughtful people experience, in and through their own participation in these social structures, *Sein* and *Mitsein,* the incomprehensible weight of just some of the 6.2 billion individual human worlds, each with, at its center, its own cares, its will, its foibles, and many its own craziness. All, individuals and institutions alike, confront us with truth claims, all demand their place in the sun, all are capable of wielding power, not the least the screaming infant at Sunday mass.

Truth claims of many different kinds reverberate on the meaning of other truths, requiring an ongoing widening and deepening of our natural faith. It is to show this that, later in the present chapter, I shall offer the present study's initial exploration of the highest-scale genera of intersubjective *Mitsein* worlds. They have molded almost all of us: family, religion, social class, *polis, ethnos.* As already explained in my earlier volumes, each of these make present their own complex truths. Each of us can be related to or affected by these larger social or intersubjective truths.

Technology

As a next step I propose to turn once again to our highly technological virtual world and to the myriad of little intersubjective worlds out of which it is woven. Most educated people living in our technological world are aware just how new this planetary-scale world is, especially in light of globalization. They experience the novelty of what it is imposing on us, every year new shocks. Common sense expresses the unprecedented rapidity of social change. High-tech and fast-paced technology has changed the way we do business and the way we interact and socialize with one another. With the high-tech comes virtual reality, and this world exists and continues to shape us, from entertainment to banking. In one sense, this virtual world created by technology requires less face-to-face and less personal interaction between individuals. But it also facilitates meetings and encounters of another kind. Unless a natural or man-made catastrophe of planetary-scale intervenes, whatever evolves from the present technology will continue to be planetary in scale, and unique, ever THE world, affecting the myriad of personal and intersubjective worlds. It will remain in continuity with the line of development that has brought mankind from Christian Western civilization through the Industrial Revolution to the high-tech virtual world. In that sense, as Fukuyama said, we have indeed witnessed "the end of history": the outlines of the world order into which mankind is being ever more intensely enfolded have been largely achieved.

Meanwhile, nations, or "folk," do not entirely disappear, not thus far anyway, and vast masses of people still chafe against the bit, but both phenomena are rapidly being "marginalized." Consider the extent to which technology and virtual reality affect just about everything, yet control of any of its almost limitless aspects is always extremely selective and usually of limited geographical distribution. Does the UN exercise a greater molding influence on the virtual world of technology than Microsoft?

Technology and virtual reality indeed reveal themselves to be unprecedented, overwhelming developments. Only the initial explosion onto the scene of the great river valley civilizations two millennia before Christ is in any way comparable in its suddenness and many-faceted social reality. Viewed against the background of the emergence onto the planetary scene of European maritime power in the sixteenth century, colonization, the Industrial Revolution, and then technology's exponential expansion in power and influence on every aspect of human being, including religion, the technological reveals that it is extremely powerful compared to the tribal organizations that were absorbed into the resulting "cosmological empires," as Eric Voegelin called Egypt, Sumer, then Babylon, and China.

The Cosmos

Think back over the narrative of the three genera of world already presented (my personal *cosmion*, the intersubjective *cosmiota* (for example, the hotel, Air Canada), the technological and virtual), and you will see clearly the objective reality of the cosmos—the physical universe as such and that little speck of it that is the most complex of all cosmic complexities, my body and the bodies of the other players. Throughout the pages to follow the cosmic foundations will be frequently underscored. The cosmos refers to that structured whole that results when all the genera of worlds relate and interact with one another. It refers to that ever complex reality of relations and worlds that encompasses all that is, including human being and individual human beings.

At the cosmic end of the hierarchy, as the "natural world" is not in its depths first and foremost an interpreted humanized world but a system of real things, and real relations between them in no way presently depend on human interpretation for their "objective" being, there are among those things many kinds of objective reality remaining unknown to us. Only parts of those that we presently interpret fall within the present grasp of our minds. And only a yet smaller part of that "interpreted nature" of the cosmos as a whole does mankind understand very well. But we know from past experience of discoveries of nature that the remaining vast reality continues to work away on us from without and from within without our being aware. The more profoundly a world is rooted in nature, the weirder it can seem to us at times, just as, at the other extreme, worlds perched at the top of a hierarchy of human inventions produce their own brands of weird effects in the realms of the imagination.

A group of astrophysicists' imaginings of the cosmos is not so much a cosmic reality in itself as forms of "spiritual being," aimed at helping scientists manage better what they have been able to discover and to leap imaginatively toward the real they are trying to glimpse. In the intersubjective conscious world of science, a vast planetary-scale world in which most try to keep communications of data open and expression of theories as clear as possible, all this enormous spiritual activity affects the objective cosmos only to the extent that some few work to alter real things in light of the theories. Most visible are the domes of great telescopes on remote mountaintops while particle accelerators are hidden in the ground and probes are sent to distant planets. The Astrophysics Society of Harvard University can meet and talk all night about a hot star that is erupting gases from both ends; the only reality they will have added to the physical cosmos is a negligible amount of carbon dioxide from their lungs! However, if a group of engineers meets on an austere island to blast an asteroid by launching a nuclear-tipped missile, the cosmos is really affected rather more than it was by the emission of CO_2 in the Harvard discussion, yet, in the context of the whole cosmos, the pulverizing of the asteroid, or even our obliterating mankind through nuclear winter, changes not all that much materially.

The formed imagination and the familiar language one brings to every pro-jection of the future give that future a built-in and more or less wide (although often superficial) cultural orientation. Foundational to that "familiarity" are cultural habits, those into which we have been, as it is said, "acculturated," symbol systems into which we have been immersed, laws and "rules of the game" we have come to learn through practice.

MANAGING WORLDS

Beyond the highly technological, the most complex and confusing of the genera of enfolding worlds are the myriad of little social worlds, *cosmiota* interweaving with other little worlds to form yet larger *cosmiota* of a seemingly endless variety. In contrast, the structures of the cosmos, including the living cell, are orderly. The physical cosmos, founding all material things, is primordial. But human social worlds are charged with imagination and rapid creativity, a spiritual creativity built on the base of cosmic materiality. Every day of our lives, from infancy on, we struggle practically and very often theoretically with their embrace, and with their interconnections, in (to put it mildly) a challenging variety of ways, both in a time-space extent and in a hierarchy of significance. The world of IBM enfolds the worlds of their suppliers, but each of the supplier companies is an institution at the service of a distinctive tradition, and is linked to other institutions—other customers, other parts suppliers, the financial institutions that finance them and handle their cash, and so forth—to all of which IBM itself has only indirect relations.

It is obvious that much management time and attention is spent harmonizing the demands made by the relevant little worlds. But among the "managers," do not forget to include yourself: each individual and the societies in which you play roles, from manager to customer, from voter to goalie, from bank, to office, to church, to hockey club, all call on your limited time, attention, and energy. A moment's reflection on this daunting complexity should bring home this truth: WE NEED A STRATEGY!

We cannot avoid being swept up in some of these social worlds. Even a psychopath locked in a cell must accept intravenous injections if he refuses to eat—"a hard-wired high-tech connection." Others, which theoretically we could choose to ignore, may yet be of extreme importance to us, and for a variety of reasons. One could invent a scale for cosmic "importance": at one end of the scale, some social worlds offer rich possibilities for re-sponse-ability, while, at the other, many offer mischievous distraction, excellent for running away from the seriousness of life.

In the incredible variety of tangled relationships, all these worlds, however different, have something in common: the dynamic framework of each is constituted by their institutions and the cultures, expressed in appropriate symbol systems and transmittable skills, that they hand down, by imitation and education. *Your interpretative opening onto* THE *world and various social worlds will be heavily influenced by the institutionalized experiences to which you have been privileged, a good part of it, increasingly, through elaborate, costly formal education.*

The highly technological world has no one overarching institutional incarnation, and so one's "take" on virtual reality and technology is heavily influenced by the traditions and their institutions in which he has been living in a most committed way. Do not forget that behind your TV lies a nest of institutions responsible for what is disgorged from your plasma screen. Most of us know little about these institutions. One's sense of Royal Dutch–Shell, a vague awareness of a vast petroleum empire, may be reduced concretely to his regular purchase of Shell gas because he receives "air miles," a singularly minimal contact with the petroleum giant!

Recall that three kinds of enfolding worlds are not institutionalized at all: the cosmos, in all its naturalness; my individual world (I personally am not an institution, nor do the habits of my character constitute a kind of institution); and the intimate *Mitsein* world of a friendship, for all the little arrangements two or three friends may agree upon to facilitate meeting, truly a minimal "institutionalization." The family, on the other hand, is an institution, stretching over generations and legalized by the state, a structure with definite roles to play. (If two friends hammer out a set of arrangements for their friendship, they may have wandered into the land of [minimal] institution.)

Consider for a moment why normally my personal world ought not to be thought of as an "institution." Although I participate in many institutions, at the base stands me as central source *of* "ME." The network of motor skills and the treasure house of memories and cognitive tools, especially symbols, are organized within my body by my mind. This rich operational structure shows almost nothing like explicit, reflective "institutionalized" protocols and perks. Its operating system allows a flexibility and creativity that any institution would envy. (Mediation of even first-class minds through institutionalized structures is necessary and constricting, both *helping* intersubjective creativity and *dampening* it. I alone decide finally what among the vast resources of my mind and soul I am going to exploit, ranging from a flash of a moment to a lifelong consistency.) Finally, give one more thought to that very important (most important?) *Mitsein*, a friendship: we may meet regularly within an institution, say, at the university, and we may even set a regular timetable that fits with the college's, and we may always go to the same little restaurant because we can count on their fidelity to their tradition, providing good food. But what makes the intimate world of the friendship exist is not these ancillary arrangements but our essentially noninstitutionalized free gift to one another of some glimpses of our interiority.

As I pondered this last question—how a friendship may be endowed with a (minimum) of institutional organization, that is in no way of the essence—it not only occurred to me that a family is, in contrast, an institution and even legalized. But also I have no intimate friendships that call for any regular meetings at all. In fact, the more I survey my concrete reality, I realize that the only intimate relationships in my life are with members of our immediate family, and Dr. Antonio Calcagno who works faithfully with me on my books, and a medical doctor and his wife whom we see quite regularly and share some of the goings-on of our families. This causes me to wonder if perhaps intimate friendships are rare, at least in our high-tech society.

Switching to the opposite end of the scale, note that the most powerful planetary-scale institutions are having little success to date in controlling the environment, and beyond what is accomplished on this planet, only the tiniest effect on even the nearby planetary solar cosmos. Yet the structure of my individual world, founded on my body's objective place and time in the cosmos, provides the resources that deploy at the moment my whole being, "body and soul," according to what I consider appropriate and whatever the themes involved. In all this, my "interior life," especially and most foundationally my "natural faith" and my character, plays the central role.

Both my natural faith and my character are more surely and immediately affected by the exercise of my liberty than are the institutions on which my external acts may have an impact. In institutions my acts of freedom are mediated through my sense of my role and in function of the role-playing reactions of others who themselves act according to their assigned functions. It is in this way that this acting-together has its institutionalized impact. And it is for this reason that my institutionally constrained acts are less free than my strictly personal ones, yet the possibilities offered me by the institutions are vital sources of my life.

In an intimate friendship, cosmic and personal realities—the organic and the historical about each of the individuals—present challenges to the relationship and place constraints on it. Sometimes the institutional role of one or both forms a personal characteristic that is a constraint or a challenge. A simple example: A man and a woman who, having worked together for some time in the same firm, gradually forge a strong friendship. Suppose they experience as a constraint how they can behave toward each other, not only the cosmic fact that they are of the opposite sex but also the sociohistorical fact that both are married. Each may recognize in his or her own heart this cosmic reality—a sexual attraction—but both, being committed to their marriages, find it inappropriate ever to mention what both know to be a fact. Because of the genuine being of the institutions that are the respective families, the cosmic and the social realities, the two coworkers are morally quite right to keep this truth unexpressed, and to avoid circumstances that might place them "in temptation." Would it not be appropriate also for each of them alone to spend some time in serious contemplation of the grounds for their priorities as part of an exercise of strengthening their commitment?

The moral challenges posed by the cosmic reality in and through which we function are quite different from the moral dynamics of a friendship. The dynamic structure of the cosmos as a whole is unfolding objectively according to whatever laws govern its development since the "initial conditions" of the Big Bang, with a hierarchy of organic principles later emerging and becoming effective in and through animal and human bodies. These given practical principles function in themselves, whatever may be the little bit we have managed to learn about them, and the even smaller treasury of knowledge for exploiting them. But in social worlds the situation is fundamentally different: *Our advances in understanding the institutional structures of social-historical worlds actually alter the very sense of those structures.*

One could say about objective, organic structures what appears at first to be the same thing: once human beings come to understand aspects of their working, the potential for dealing with those structures changes. But with social structures, with their immediate implications for human freedom, that new illumination about them changes their very status: from "real but unreflected upon human artifacts affecting human actions" to "human artifacts *now more manipulable by those who see them for what they are—humanly generated and humanly alterable rules changeable simply by altering attitudes.*" Because institutionalization demands the creation and the encoding of rules and structures of command, institutions can be quite well grasped through the history of their protocols and collective historical accomplishments. That knowledge affects the way the institution will be further incarnated through our conscious role-playing.

The example offered above of the unexpressed mutual sexual attraction can serve to strengthen the point I have just been raising, that the very sense of institutional structures can be changed by the participants' coming to regard them in a different way. Suppose one of the two colleagues weakens one evening on a business trip, and while enjoying a dinner together, he or she suddenly expresses the previously mutely shared truth. Depending on the intention and to some extent on how the other responds to the announcement, the sense of their respective marriages may be altered by this very exchange. Suppose the man "breaks the mold": "You and I both know that we have a powerful 'thing' for one another. We both know that our relations with our spouses have become routine, indeed stale. In fact, to be frank about it, we know that you and I have grown up while they are stuck in boring routine. I have come to adore you, and I know you have a great affection for me. I see no harm in our just naturally expressing what is already a commitment in the heart." Not (yet) altered in socially recognized institutional reality, the two marriages are in fact already changed in their profound interior sense, having ipso facto become "marriages under siege." Note, too, that the strictly business relationship the two enjoyed until now is altered into a clearly ambiguous mess, if I may so put it. What until then were two marriages going their normal way may be transformed through the exchange of a few sentences into two marriages entering a new phase of siege "from outside" and from within.

This brings us to a fundamental ontological principle: each institution is illumined by the overarching *being* of its own demanding, intersubjective world. The being of the institution resides mostly in the minds of those making it function. Things like buildings and machines and even written rules are secondary, and in any event are disposed in certain ways because of the notions of the human beings responsible now or earlier on in the institution's evolution. The officers of an institution complex enough to require offices, enjoying the overall view and controlling the greatest power to inflect the direction of its development, pass on, through symbols, "action plans" in keeping with their interpretations of the institution's visions developed through its traditions. Those faithful to the institution respect, usually, its internal laws, and external law imposed by the wider social institutions.

In the family we do not consider the parents to be "officers," because the roles of father and mother have such a large natural component and the institutional structure is traditional and relatively simple—and their plans will not always be very explicit. But the institution does have a hierarchy—parents at the top, their authority becoming ever more challenged as the children "sow their wild oats" of adolescence, with a shifting, implicit "pecking order" among the children.

In our little example of the blossoming office romance, the children, indeed the other spouses, do not yet know that a growing danger has just become more explicit and by that very fact entered a still more dangerous phase. This is a real (but "subjective") ontological change: the intersubjective being of the two families has changed without most of those affected knowing it. Note too that a serious mutual decision can make everything right again: "This is folly. We shall stop seeing each other outside of strictly office circumstances, and never speak of our mutual fascination again." If that declaration truly expresses a genuine change of attitude—from drift into sexual love, to "going public" by mutual declaration, to expression of a new attitude of "coming to our senses," both making a genuine, lasting commitment not to go down the romance road—the being of their relationship could now be described as "a sensible commitment each to hold back any romantic passionate inclinations."

It is important to point out this kind of hierarchy of ever larger, more encompassing worlds moving through cosmic time as a key to understanding how the strategic planning of our lives occurs. Here I have expressed it with perhaps a bit too much of a technological, managerial consciousness. As later on we explore more seriously the challenge of thinking through the horizons of "the analogy of being," this thrust of "the analogy" as I already expressed it will become clearer: not only an attitude (moral when genuine) of constantly seeking to discover and clarify the largest and deepest horizons but also *a determination to put our most serious principles into the amplest context.*

THE IRREDUCIBILITY OF THE PERSONAL WORLD AND OF INTERPERSONAL WORLDS

As we step back and allow our regard to roam over all of being, we are aware that at the personal end of the scale there are truths about us individually that are not meaningfully universalizable: they express each person's creative uniqueness, his own style. Aspects of this uniqueness can indeed be forever foreign to another person's life, a combination of factors, some of which are shared with all human beings, others with particular groups but other features unique to the individual. The uniqueness of each person is a central point, along with the reality of commonalities. (We shall see later how both figure in the analogy of being.) Nor should we forget our potential for egoism, which is related to our uniqueness. Do not forget that every aspect of every person also points beyond him to the larger picture.

For each world in which we participate we discover ourselves artfully tailoring for ourselves a slightly different persona, suited to distinctive kinds of roles in scenarios that can be quite world-distinctive but will also be "person-distinct": you act differently with the kind supervisor; you do not want to let her down. At sixteen I became more a railroad "tower man–telegrapher" than a tenth grade student. Although in a classroom milieu I had to put that scholastic persona up front, the two roles were daily time separated.

THE COMMON ELEMENTS IN ALL PERSONS

But before the cynic cries, "Voilà! Everything is relative!" go back again to the other side of the human "equation": all personae and roles and symbols and particular works and concrete acts and "defining moments" that concern me meet in and radiate from the one real individual self that I am, anchored somewhere at a given moment in the one cosmos. There is displayed a unity even when the person who has been drawn out (educated) by loving gifts offered by other persons has come to suffer from an extreme case of multiple personality disorder. The qualified recognize the disorder and proceed meaningfully with therapy. For the individual, enjoying sound mental health is the critical, integrating judgment of the self.

As one sorts through the various roles the objective cosmic individual plays, one searches for signs of not the individual (no need, for that is objectively clear) but the person forged by his responses to generous gifts of others. We have resources for dealing with the negative dimension in the *polemoi* with which we must contend. As we respond we commit *(spondeo)* ourselves in ways that thread through not just many moments of action and expression but also the many personae and roles that take on a certain dynamic consistency. Within his life, a consistency in which constructive and destructive elements collide, the person must find his way. Some of these aspects of the active person may show enduring signs of distortion as the result of traumas or of mysterious origins of psycho-pathological disorder. In less disastrous cases the individual may confront honestly his problems and seek help to deal with them.

What gives generically the same point of reference—human nature's common kind of opening a world of the self, onto THE world and into the myriad of little interpersonal worlds—is the great similarity in persons of the rich cosmic-bodily foundation of our human individuality. Those familiar intersubjective worlds are there for the infant from the first instant of her opening onto her surroundings. The resulting reactions are spread out from her center of awareness to embrace the multiple centers of activity. (These can be several persons cooing and admiring, plus a stuffed animal being agitated in her face, which multiple-centered world of activity the baby now makes of what she can from her still very limited perspective.)

The Others—objects and individual human beings—are massively at once and at all times in the self's awake consciousness, insistently present as co-operators in various worlds. The personae of the other human beings and their "natures" play and clash with the baby in shared settings. The personhood of the other selves compassionately seeks to draw the baby out as a person, or another can do the opposite: push the baby into confusion and tyrannical limits.

To sum up the "sameness" side of the dialectic: Despite all the complexities, the little worlds, with their multitude of distinctive roles and often bizarre and unique situations, reveal common human and cosmic traits. All these are replete with objects showing some familiar facets, so we rarely feel completely disoriented. Confused, yes: most people recognize that a diesel locomotive is not really a "choo-choo"; all of us non-physicists will, however, admit we have never encountered a familiar quark, not even an electron (a stream of electrons, yes, when I changed a lightbulb with wet hands), and that most of the "theology of the particle physicists" is simply weird to us. We are indeed "lost" in those unfamiliar worlds, but at the same time we are cuddled in the familiarity of common situations and well-known objects.

FROM THE OBJECTIVE SOURCE OF THE DIFFERENT KINDS OF TRUTH TO THE SUBJECTIVE SOURCE: HUMAN INTERIORITY

We shall gain further help in relating different kinds of truth to one another by considering how they are generated in the first place. Objectively, the foundation of all truth lies in whatever accounts for the natural unfolding of the cosmos, from its origins (still wrapped in mystery) through all its evolving complexifications, about which we are beginning to know, especially our bodies as necessary (but not sufficient?) conditions for the human spirit.

Subjectively and reflectively, all worlds, including the cosmos as interpreted, have their sense thanks to discovery from deep within the most "interior" of all worlds: the human self's little cognitive-caring world of its own. It is there that all sense arises as a self builds its capability of seeing interconnections between every manner of thing and idea: the individual soul has the potentiality of a profound interior life, the depths of which are reached in critical meditation on what has been and is being learned. This learning comes both from the exterior and from the interior of the serious thinker:

—The EXTERIOR: the cosmos, both that little bit of it that is my body, which can sense itself, and that part of the cosmos exterior to me, that segment onto which my senses open.
—The INTERIOR: consciousness, including memory, imagination, and reason, into which all that the body discovers can be, little by little, integrated. From the various depths of reflection surge the intelligibilities and symbols that glow in all the horizons of interpretation the subject caringly deploys in all worlds as it projectively ek-sists.

The only locus of "interiority" I experience directly is my own individual soul. It is where all the sense of THE world is preserved for me, and it is from those remembered depths enjoyed by all healthy persons that the horizon openings surge up. This includes the horizons of myriads of social worlds, much of the content of which is mediated through the ex-pressions of the participating "other" subjects, but always for me as interpreted by me, as I embrace them in my horizons. I shall explain.

Worlds exist intersubjectively primarily in the shared wisdom of many souls. *Wisdom* here is used in the "local" sense. Local wisdoms are integrated into wisdom in the ultimate sense as aspects of being as a whole. This happens as various subjects are glimpsing in the elaborate conceptualization "the analogy of being," of which few are aware. For an intersubjective world to exist, each soul contributing to that particular world has to ex-press itself directly (I say something now in the hearing of another, sometimes written in a letter) or indirectly (as in a past contribution to a cultural object the sense of which others can decipher later—a written text, for instance, or a machine I have built).

In the interior depths of souls, in communion through all means of expression, is formed the sense of the cosmos itself. Again, I emphasize this is not the cosmos's dynamic, unfolding, objective causal structure but the *meaning* of those real structures as it unfolds for me in consciousness. So far as we currently know, the human soul is the only means the cosmos has evolved to think itself. (Whether before the beginning of the universe the Source consciously planned the cosmos's development is one of the questions fought over in the *Gigantomachia*. To this we can add the belief in some great traditions in the existence of finite pure spirits—angels and devils, a widespread belief, even some quite sophisticated scientists remaining open to that belief.) Starting from the depths of man's reflection, this human indicating and, "higher" yet, conceptualizing of the cosmos and of THE world have succeeded eventually in reaching out to the distant galaxies of the impersonal cosmos.

But concurrent with the beginnings of methodic astronomical observation recorded by the first civilizations, something else that remains most significant happened: beyond all social worlds and the cosmos itself, man reached toward "the vertical transcendent," producing magnificent mythological imaginings, eventually, according to the founding claims of the Abrahamic tradition, the Transcendent Source; the way has been prepared by its inspiration within certain imaginative souls, crossing an infinite gap to come among men in prophetic ways. Or, if the "postmodernist" skeptics are right, the mythical imagination of man invented the whole immense story of the prophetic incursions in history. Invented or revealed (or a mixture of both), stories of "the vertically transcendent" demonstrably changed the course of human history more fundamentally than anything prior to our present-day high technology. (This hint about the technology implies that within the vast world of the virtual and the technological are found many lights still flowing from earlier beliefs in revelation.)

THE PERSONAL WORLD AS FOUNDATION OF HUMAN BEING: SUFFICIENT CONDITIONS—COSMIC AND PERSONAL—FOR BEING HUMAN

In light of these preliminary musings about the cosmic foundations of our worlds, one should ask whether the humanly most important and absorbing world is then the foundational cosmic reality itself, that is, is it a necessary, sufficient condition for human being? But the objective cosmic is not sufficient condition for the full blossoming of humanity. So should we acknowledge that the humanly most important foundation is, rather, the individual personal world?

In arguing for the personal world as the full foundation, I shall put the following point at the center: *The foundations of the human being lie in those aspects of cosmic reality that have been taken up into consciousness; processed following the normal, healthy biophysiological and psychic structures of the knower as motivated by his cares and desires (Sorge); and further formed through his responses to his encounters with Others.*

Response to this psychic "in-form-ation," including the information about, and processed through, the dynamic bodily substructure, is then *the foundation for my actual individual personal world and for my participation in all the social worlds in which I am involved.* It is there, interior to my personal world, that meaning is basically to be found for me and heeded by me so long as that degree of human being that I enjoy can last. The human without explicit conscious meaning is not up to that point fully human, and the person who has through disease lost much awareness no longer functions fully humanly.

Yet the individual human being is to be respected as precious from conception because of its potential to develop to the point of being e-ducated to personhood. Even the development of selfhood is for the sake of the potential to personhood. A loving person can (and should) love a severely handicapped individual incapable of re-sponding to that love, in the same spirit in which a person respects the unborn baby in the womb that likely will develop postpartum into a self capable of loving re-sponse. On the grounds that the most respectable thing is the human being, it is argued by many that extraordinary supports and not destruction should be the symbols of respect for human dignity even in this most painful case. The most severely mentally handicapped child who has attained the age where it is certain he will never return any attention is to be taken care of, out of respect for the most treasured thing in this world, humanity, however deficient the level of functioning of this individual who nevertheless lives if fed and kept at an appropriate temperature. (A human being in a coma with no reasonable chance of recovery may have life support withdrawn.)

A caveat to help keep the balance here: it is not just "those aspects of cosmic reality that have been taken up into consciousness" that are critical to our human being. Underscore the *necessary* in "necessary but not sufficient conditions," and then understand it to mean: treasure all objectivity, not forgetting the reality of hidden objectivities below the obvious surfaces of all appearance, mine and the surfaces of every manner of objective thing. Until now we may be oblivious to many of these objective foundational elements, but we gradually come to recognize their essentiality. It may be learned in due course that the person in a coma for ten years can awaken from it and reveal that he was conscious of much that was going on. Regardless of the kind of presencing, we should stay sensitive to the hints of the "always more to the cosmic than meets the eye."

Much cosmic reality, operative in my body, surrounding and bombarding me in every setting, formative since the creation of everything, is present in the most spiritual of human achievements. My spirit as well as my body have been and are in fact being molded, through and through, by the cosmic reality. More cosmic reality is presented with every presencing of whatever kind. Much about that reality we suspect, but we grasp little of what lies beyond even our most creative leaps of imagination. At the same time, reciprocally, our spiritual initiatives—our presencings included—are affecting and molding the cosmic body, mine and those of others, and through us all together the cosmos itself.

As I have insisted, the intersubjective worlds are not to be understood merely as real things "out there," visible as they may be through their formative influence on cultural objects (for example, the directors of the surety company sitting gravely in the boardroom as distant prospects are bantered about). Rather, intersubjective worlds are most significantly spiritual because they are shared visions: each intersubjective world is founded in a set of images in every participant's imagination, only partially, imperfectly coinciding.

If the participants in any intersubjective world collectively decide not to sustain that world, it can cease to exist altogether, even when the worlds are as enormous as the Third Reich and the Soviet Empire. But so long as such a world is sustained, then, if those cooperating in it for whatever reason choose to ignore realities that objectively constitute an aspect of the things that interpreting world embraces, the cooperating interpreters may collectively be setting the stage for unpleasant surprises when the neglected reality at last imposes itself. In the end all of these overlooked (or energetically denied) realities are likely to have consequences, perhaps worse than Asian or U.S. economic meltdowns.

The following commonality founds our hope that all objects of whatever kind and scale and all persons, however the different sorts of presencing produce meaning, are eventually integrable in one wisdom: *All worlds have in common the interpretative horizons held open by human beings in whatever sort of time and space. As we ponder ever more complex interweaving of connections between things of literally millions of sorts, we are encouraged by the light that enables us to keep revealing connections, enabling us to make "sense" of many but related kinds, always more sense so long as we work to find it. The fact that all the while we see ever more complexities, more potential connections needing development, questions requiring elaborate research for answers, all this is encouraging to wisdom, and we need not despair of ever knowing such a gigantic complex universe.*

Most mysteriously hidden away in all this are not the constituents of distant galaxies but the interiors of human "spirits." *Skill on the part of the respondent in "seeing the other's point of view" plays an essential role in the quality and truth of the intersubjective communication.* Matters coming into consciousness, presenting themselves with evidence of their arriving from beyond the subject's interpretative world, can often insistently demand to be respected. Recall William Blake's evocation in "Auguries of Innocence" of this sense that the very otherness of what insists ties us to the whole of reality:

> To see a world in a grain of sand
> And heaven in a wildflower.
> Hold infinity in the palm of your hand
> And eternity in an hour.

To be sure, the cosmic foundation of such otherness can at times seem somewhat remote, mediated, like the "stock-trading option," through levels of image and conceptual construction and the symbols—preponderantly words—in which we represent them. It can all become very "virtual" indeed. But if we so desire, we can find our ways back through these layers of interpretation—the words, the concepts, the images—to that core of otherness, ultimately cosmic otherness, in what has been interpreted. Even the falsest interpretation has some sense; it throws its own light on the object.

This chapter tried to show how human beings live in, understand, and form worlds. As human beings change, evolve, and become more complex, new worlds emerge, including virtual and technological ones, and old worlds like the cosmos take on new and more complicated meanings. These worlds are dynamic and unfold in time, understood both horizontally and vertically; they live and condition human being and are part of the larger sense of human being. These worlds are objective, concrete, and accessible to human understanding. As complex wholes unto themselves and as relating wholes, they shape one another but also shape and condition individual human beings and the way they live their lives. These worlds, through space and time, are the ground in which human being in general plays itself out, developing, emerging, and even receding.

3

DYNAMIC FREEDOM AND THE FINITE STRUCTURE OF HUMAN EXISTENCE AS CHARACTER

Finite freedom is always situationally conditioned: the human being, possessing a definite set of capabilities in the face of a definite set of concrete challenges and possibilities that always present themselves in a setting, may at times seem more "put upon" than free. Depending on the aspect of human being at issue, persons can seem more or less determined. That is a potentially misleading illusion due to the fact that no one can describe any dynamic situation all at once. In perfect balance of the determinations and possibilities that are at work, there remains an effort to relate the various forces.

Commonsense man is so preoccupied with intense activity he is obliged to take for granted many aspects of experience. Some of these taken-for-granted objects may later on prove to have been more important than the concern we earlier gave them. For instance, the owner takes for granted that the house he lives in will be there on the familiar street when he comes home from work. He relies on the ground underlying the building as it has always been there. Normally, he gives no thought to its longevity. But the scientist steeped in modern research will be aware that the most solid, seemingly unchanging things in the world change, and this at different speeds, often hard to predict. With a wider view, the very sense of futures has new meaning. As much of our experience is in the commonsense realm, our pursuit of the reality of human being is rooted in ordinary experience. But the critical thinking philosopher in the pursuit of authenticity must envelop commonsense worlds within the vast horizons of authentic knowledge. Allow me to explain.

Authenticity in the large sense invokes historicity. The pursuit of genuine wisdom demands that we attend to the widest and most profoundly

rooted dimensions of being that we as of now can attain. In our techno-
logically advanced world most individuals enjoy more freedom to exercise a wider range of powers than could have been dreamed possible
before the Industrial Revolution. Powers of analysis, of communicating
instantly with all parts of the globe, of flying, powers of organization of
kinds unknown before, are all now at the disposition of the well educated,
hence the challenge for the evolved forms of education to exercise those
various kinds of power responsibly, establishing a scale of importance
directive of maximally fruitful aspects of our limited time and energy.

Every person's and every kind of thing's "boundary conditions" (as
scientists call them) consist of both characteristic capabilities, indicative
of the type of being it is, and capabilities peculiar to the individual in a
concrete situation—the universal and the concrete working together to
reveal being. The challenge of achieving wisdom lies in the formation
and consistent pursuit of the ultimate goal; central to the pursuit are its
loves. The wise searcher has to find a foundation and a motivation in a
vision that, seeking to make sense out of the entire sweep of life, leaves
out nothing real and valuable that one encounters. Part of love requires
that we educate ourselves, that is, build our character or souls such that
we are more capable of carrying out the demands of love.

What is meant here by "soul" is not only the core of the person's interiority *(le quatre intérieur)*, where one ruminates and decides, but also
the constitutive principle that accounts for the whole being *(ens)* of this
subject, his or her being human rather than feline ("feline human" is an
easily recognizable type of human soul, and it comes in different sizes!).
The soul accounts for one's being this irreplaceable instance, this act of
existence that is the given human being and not another. The material
reality—the organic molecules—is animated (in Latin *soul* is *anima*) in
such a way that both the exterior appearance of the body and the style
with which it moves "in things" are basically governed by the soul, and
meet "within the depths of the soul" the person's profoundest reflective
thoughts and feelings.

FREEDOM

Freedom is a given and can be seen to operate within both human
and nonhuman worlds. It is understood to be that capacity to act as one
chooses or desires. Physicist Alan Guth, writing an account of his contri-

bution to the development of the theory of "the inflationary universe," invokes at the particle level "degrees of freedom," meaning the ability to move around characteristic of each elementary type of motion.[1] As I understand it, that is not at all an exaggerated "downward extension" of the term *freedom*. Those particle and atomic movements are manifestations of the basic, limited power of the particle or the full-fledged atom in its very restricted but nevertheless real capability of radiating or of combining with certain other kinds of atoms or particles to form new atoms or to provide more or less long-lasting forces, and of various kinds: what water continues to do is very different from what free hydrogen gas does; how hydrogen and helium atoms endure ("what they are free to do"), their resisting many kinds of assault, is very different from what happens during the long half-life of uranium 235, with its exceptional radioactivity. But not even by extension can one meaningfully call this freedom, that of a kind of "life" (the term *half-life* of a given kind of atom is something of a misnomer). Neither free hydrogen nor water can, by any stretch of language, decide which of its inherent possibilities it is going to take advantage of. But if we observe the opposite extreme of molecular construction in man, as human attention moves up the chain of increasing complexity, we observe not just statistical averages of results of different elementary motion but also the emergence of ever more complex, regular interactions and dependencies, weaving and manifesting ever richer dynamic forms, as one finds, for example, in complex ongoing chemical processes. At some point, when those much more complex protolife forms appear, because at last we encounter in them information governing much more complex processes, enabling them to direct themselves toward host organisms that nurture and play a role in their reproduction, we can justifiably introduce a new category: "protolife."

I agree with physicist Murray Gell-Mann that life begins with the very complex organization of what he dubs "information searching and computing units," a complexity with capabilities of reproducing itself at least by division.[2] Just as the atom in one of the more solid molecular structures gets its full meaning from the role it plays in the molecule, while retaining the (very limited) possibility of flying off erratically but freely

1. Alan Guth, *The Inflationary Universe: The Quest for a New Theory of Cosmic Origin* (New York: Basic Books, 1998).
2. Murray Gell-Mann, *The Quark and the Jaguar: Adventures in the Simple and Complex* (New York: Holt Paperbacks, 1995).

from the molecular structure, so now, at all higher levels, individual cells and animals of all forms, while usually tightly bound together in a social structure, can still behave erratically, in ways even damaging to the integrity of the herd or family. Erratic exercises of freedom are most often damaging to the higher forms, molecular, cellular, or animal, but they can also constitute one of those random mutations that become the start of a breakthrough innovation in evolution. When consciousness (information plus reflectivity) is introduced at the higher levels of information, while the social dependency remains great, the reflective or the pathological behavior of a single role-player can be critical, more so than in a wolf pack, affecting as it can the interiority—the consciousness—and hence the being of each member of a close-knit society.

Freedom becomes most dramatic when, from somewhere within the soul of the higher animal, the ability to transcend the givenness of present experience appears. It is fruitful to reflect on evidence of this in the animals, and to see the different levels of their capability. But I shall pass that by here.

Given that there is nothing like absolute freedom, that is, a freedom that is free from the conditioning forces of one's being situated in the world along with one's own individual being and the legacy of human being in general, all freedom is incarnated and housed within individual persons. Also, it is housed in our collective consciousness and institutions. Freedom has a history and is part of the larger legacy of human being, understood in a more encompassing sense. One primary way of grasping and accessing the larger reality of human being is through a freely chosen decision to study and think about its legacy throughout various histories and contexts. Human being is present in collective memories, institutions, art, culture, science, and so on. All human decisions to think and act, whether individually or collectively through time and place as concretized in the reality of human being, can begin, and significantly so, in human freedom, always through a decision to turn one's attention to a specific object or question, or to decide to do or think something through. To speak of freedom is to speak of it in specific contexts, in reference to specific individuals and to human being in general. The primary locus of human freedom resides in what philosophy has traditionally called soul, that principle of animation and mind that has been identified with the metaphysical aspects of human being; it has also been identified theologically as the source where humans meet the divine. I would like to argue that depending on the quality of the soul, that is, the character of the individual, freedom comes to express itself in various ways. I make appeal to the traditional philosophical categories of small-souledness (pusillanimity), great-souledness (magnanimity), and mean-spiritedness.

An interplay of wider, richer horizons, giving scope to virtue, sharpening intelligence, inspiring others, and healthy bodily development can, altogether, stretch the soul. A weave of mutually reinforcing capabilities strengthens and deepens the physiological base beyond the initially, genetically given and *in utero* nourished powers. It can even "lift off," soaring spiritually in the midst of a declining physical capability. In brief, one can become a bigger person with a still more generous, powerful soul even in the face of sapping physical strength (up to a physiological limit, of course). Keep in mind that these gifts that strengthen the spirit are generous acts of freedom from the attentions of other people and from the divine through prophets, whether real prophets or would-be gurus.

CHARACTER OR QUALITIES OF SOUL: "SMALL-MINDED," "MEAN-SPIRITED," AND "SMALL-SOULED" ARE DISTINCT CHARACTERISTICS

The "small-minded" person is ungenerous, his self-centeredness and mediocre intelligence combine to limit his vision, and he does not give up easily control or possession of the little resources he has. Small-mindedness is worse than small-souledness, for it is small-souledness sans a liberating, vision-lifting education. A small-souled person may be slowly coaxed out of his cave, opening himself unto the sun; the capabilities of his little soul being generously aided by loving others to grow, step by step the person may be drawn out, opened onto larger vistas, eventually impressing others by his growth. "Mean-spiritedness," the worst of all, comes from a combination of a petty streak—including narrow vision—and strong evil inclinations, a propensity to nasty behavior when control is threatened, or purely gratuitous aggression. Trauma can produce aggression, but I wonder whether there are not also some souls born with a mean streak mysteriously built in. Mean-spiritedness has to do primarily with the moral dimension, less than with the inheritance of a "noble" or "an ordinary" (smaller) soul. I am holding out the possibility that genetic dispositions to attack the world in most unpleasant ways seem to manifest themselves in some cases. Studies of certain kinds of psychopathic personalities have highlighted a startling missing sense of hurting the other in some stage of development, often at adolescence; seemingly quite independently of traumas to themselves, they begin to display a lack of a sense of what they are doing to hurt others. In his classic study of this phenomenon, *The Mask of Sanity*, psychiatrist Hervey Cleckley concluded tentatively after a quarter century of observation that a neurophysiologic abnormality was the likely root cause.[3]

I have just suggested that small souls are tempted to small-mindedness but do not necessarily give in thanks to the graces of enrapturing love and genuine education. Conversely, big souls ought to be expected not to develop mean-spiritedness, but they can, perhaps as the result of a series of poor decisions in difficult circumstances, and great temptations. But when big souls turn nasty, then watch out! The result is a big nastiness, perhaps more in one department of life than in another. The same "big soul" can be a generous and wonderful leader with business associates and miserable in his relations with his wife.

Small souls may succumb to little bitter meannesses, but very often they can be sweet, with as good a possibility of eventually achieving holiness as the big-souled. Whatever holiness the small soul achieves will be characterized by a relatively limited version of what is inherited from a tradition in the form of a grand vision. This simpler version of the grand vision may be put into practice in gentle, quiet ways, with only a moderate physical "push." The holy small soul will have cooperated to achieve integrity. It is important to remember that souls can grow beyond earlier limits of vision. And one can gain strength of determination through enticements and through very positive disciplining.

The effects of "mean-spiritedness" on others can be multiplied by the effects of persons' stations in life (social class and office). If the society is fairly mobile, the "big souled" tend to gravitate to higher positions by virtue of their capabilities. Mean-spiritedness can have further-ranging catastrophic effects in a nasty CEO than in a tyrannical shopkeeper limited to persecuting his own family and cheating a few customers.

In all three modes—big-souledness, small-souledness, and mean-spiritedness—moral conditions, matters of character, are of course always present, molding courses of action, in the process further developing character, both of the agent and of those affected by his action, influencing the attitudes of those following together a given course: all

3. Cleckley, *The Mask of Sanity* (St. Louis: C. V. Mosby, 1964).

such "following of courses" have in turn a global effect on the being of all the worlds in which the persons concerned are active.

The small-souled but generous-spirited may have a strong influence on a little circle. I assume he will be operating in a "small circle" because his smallness of soul, by definition, entails a vision that is not inspired to vast scope, and I am presuming him to possess a somewhat modest approach to things, probably quite circumscribed by local traditions, limiting him to small circles.

The person of small soul who also happens to be mean-spirited can cause abominable suffering in the few who cannot escape him. The big soul, which for whatever reason becomes racked with resentment, developing through bad decisions mean-spiritedness or perhaps even an exceptional cruelty, may become an immense force of destruction— another Timur Lan, for instance, one of the giants of horror in the midst of constructing a far-flung but short-lived empire, who changed the course of world history. Timur Lan was a great soul who displayed a legendary gruesomeness by unleashing unimaginable suffering comparable to Stalin's starving of the Ukrainian peasants and Hitler's Holocaust. Hitler and Stalin are both examples of little men with unlimited ambition and cunning who managed to keep control of a vast structure of state while they contributed to deforming entire populations.

Saint Thomas Aquinas's notion that the soul can be stretched, I must admit, appeals to me. Rising to one challenge after another, it would not just be that one's virtue strengthens, that one's store of symbols grows (hence, imagination becomes more potent), and intelligence, with its many creative kinds of operations, develops through use. On top of all that, one allegedly could, so to speak, intensify "spiritual energy" by accepting the gifts of infused energy that from others reach into the depths of the soul as it is then "drawn out" and motivated—"charged up"—by others. Obviously, one could, through discipline and a good strategy for physical health, increase his physical energy, which helps feed the spiritual energy.

THE HUMAN FORM:
A DOUBLE TRANSCENDING OF PRESENT EXPERIENCE

In human being's transcending, the givenness of present experience happens in two dimensions of imaginativeness: through imaginative reconstruction of what might have happened in the past and by antic-ipation-imagining, in function of an interpretation of the present situa-tion, what is going to happen. The most startling form the latter may take is genuinely creative imagination: heretofore unimaginable possibilities become projected for the first time and may prove of lasting truth.

Breakthrough to new vision, which can refer back to previously uncon-sidered possible primitive beginnings or forward toward new futures and even imaginings of final ends, can happen through acceptance of a gift: an intervention of what seems pure inspiration can shatter old limits and allow the person to be pulled beyond himself, if he will seize the opportunity. Suddenly, he sees that some of his past limits are not fatal— free acceptance of "fate" equals death! His imagination transcends the past limits, and he receives the strength to believe solidly in new dimen-sions of his future calling to be realized.

Because we freely accumulate, both personally and socially, a history of reflected-upon experiences, the reach of the anticipation these allow can be built by the mature person back to birth. One has no memory of the experience of birth but vicariously and anecdotally he builds up the image and out to death and even beyond, by a similar process of imagi-native and vicarious experience. The accumulation of wisdom in our tra-ditions now enables us to form hypotheses even about "the singularity," the beginning of the cosmos, and the end of the universe's familiar struc-tures. It allows us to project "eschatologically," from "prophesy," as, for example, in Christian belief in the Creation and in the return of a Savior at the end of time.

So, for the human being with his finite freedom, there is something even beyond anticipation: this lies in those amazing possibilities of sheer creative imagination just mentioned, some of whose new images may never be intended for realization; they may be pure fantasies enjoyed for their own sakes, while others are produced by an artist, not just for enjoyment but for their own sake in a stronger sense because they are a new being of a lofty kind. Beethoven's *Eroica* symphony is a statement that is about more than itself, but it is also in itself a unique example of a new kind of being, crashing into the world from the moment of the two opening chords, like blows of an Olympian fist on the counting table of destiny. In that creative moment the history of music was forever changed, as Napoléon, to whom the *Eroica* was originally dedicated, also forever altered the soul of Europe.

The mystery of the vast difference in scope of vision achieved in particular souls, a mystery that grows especially impressive when we contemplate the greatest of prophetic, scientific, and artistic breakthroughs, adding to what becomes the commonly passed on visions of high culture through its advanced education, this aspect of the mystery of human being can scarcely fail to astonish the seeker after wisdom. The in-breaking of such inspirations, transcending previous interpretative horizons, keeps open the question of that "vertical transcendence" I have suggested is beyond the usual limits of interpreting horizontal transcendence.

DEPTH AND SCOPE OF VISION

"Depth" (ever deeper into the fundament) and "scope" (ever wider horizontally), back to the beginnings of the universe and out to its present fringes and anticipatorily toward the cosmos's end, space and time, come first of all out of the richness and intensity of remembered experience. The most sweeping forms of this experience are built up in, and handed down by, great explicit traditions through elaborate systems of symbols into which generations are educated by its institutions. Human being is a highly institutionalized being. Human freedom operates within the institutions giving structure to various kinds of little worlds. As we have seen, the giving of new structure comes out of past and future. Let us now consider each dimension in greater detail, and hope to improve the sense of our capabilities.

The quality of one's receptivity to experience is central to the exercise of freedom: the intensity and the openness, indeed the generosity of interest and the related clarity of our vision of what is offered to us to see, all these aspects are conditioned by the freely chosen and cultivated attitude of seriousness (*gravitas*) driving our wanting to see, and that attitude of seriousness is based in our true loves. The quality of our receptivity is basically dependent on the store of relevant information we have received and treasured, needed to interpret appropriately (the right application of the relevant information) and adequately: there has to be enough to be relevantly serious for the occasion. And finally, that receptivity depends on "intelligence," which sums up "clarity and depth of insight."

All of these factors involved in clarity and depth of vision are aspects of "size of soul." And they are all subject to improvement through gifted education. Temperamental or acquired intensity coupled with a gift of creative imagination can project individuals of low and limited culture into the stratospheres of human accomplishment. Recall, for instance, Thomas Edison, of humble social origins and without much formal education, who was issued 1,295 patents in his life. This great soul was not only creative but politically clever: Edison knew how to get other people to advance his causes. And think too of Abraham Lincoln, whose total time in formal education, including reading for the law, was less than a year! The greatness of his soul reverberates in every line of the Gettysburg and second inaugural addresses, indeed in most of what has been recorded of his life. A great soul is not necessarily an always light-filled soul. The shining light was sometimes also blackened by deep bouts of depression.

Traditions molded by souls of this magnitude animate generations, sometimes for centuries. The greatness of nations can be viewed in reflection off the immense souls who have shaped their collective vision. In the case of Honest Abe, along with a vast and rich continent, the gift of a number of immense souls is what marks in a special way the traditions of the United States of America, traditions strongly marked by the independence bred by Protestant Christianity.

The handing down of forms through tradition is possible only because of (1) the character necessary for nondefensive reception, linked to (2) the free and continued deployment of creativity, arising from the mysterious "depths of the soul" of those responsible for the handing down (it is necessary to keep "recharging" the underlying insights); (3) talent for imagining new forms, required for adapting the old to apply practically to new circumstances and discoveries; and (4) finding adequate ways to express them anew, while respecting the sense incarnate in the time-honored expressions of the tradition. It does no good to imagine a new form of organization, say, for management of a corporation, if one cannot find the effective words through which to transmit the new vision and to motivate those who have to put it into practice.

The richness of remembered experiences is not just quantitative—one expects a sixty year old to have a richer experience than a five year old, but most of it could be banal. Richness is an effect of both the objective greatness of particular experiences (to have been exposed to Rembrandt's *Night Watch* is in terms of the object potentially a greater experience than contemplating a rare hockey player's card) and the knower's subjective greatness: intensity of attention, doggedly determined reflection upon it (a sign of gravitas), brilliance of insight, and finally that most mysterious of factors, linked to capacity for imagination, not just the brilliance but the "depth" of insight, the mysterious ability to penetrate the surface of what presences to see into (*intelligere*, literally "to read into . . . to gather in") the phenomenon right to its fundament. The most prodigious of such "breakthroughs" always strike us as grand leaps of imagination. Think of the modern paradigm: Einstein's papers of 1905 and 1917.

Teilhard de Chardin pointed our attention to the fact that a degree of interiority is found already in the simplest cell, and that the different degrees of interiority are related to intensification and complexity of "centeredness." He described the progressive intensification of centeredness as large molecules become the simplest living entities. The cell, with its nucleus, is many orders of magnitude more complex than any inorganic or organic compound, and dramatically "centralized." Its sense of "self"—"self" being here an analogous term—is limited to no more than a self-centered set of tendencies that move it to defend itself from predators as best it can, although cells also manifest tendencies to cooperation. Moving up through degrees of animal "self-awareness," centeredness becomes most intense, and true selfhood, that is, personhood, appears in full human self-consciousness, which, paradoxically, at the summit of its development through love is not "self-centered."

CONSISTENCY THROUGH CHARACTER, GOOD AND BAD

The way many related, reinforcing personal acts build up habits, which again freely interact with one another in the ongoing strengthening (or weakening) of "character," is similar to the way any dynamic balancing act continuing between a series of ongoing centers of causation englobes and, when we come to understand it, adds to the "intelligibility" of the local process phenomenon. Without character, "the backbone of the person," there would be no consistency lasting long enough to render recognizable a fundamental "process"—the "building up" and maintaining of the personality. (A madly inconsistent person flying off in spurts unpredictably might still be called a kind of personality, that of the mixed-up kind or the deranged fellow.) Were it not for projects one holds on to and the building up of capabilities that make possible carrying through those projects, one would develop no lasting strengths. Nor would the sad sack be able to undermine so effectively some of his virtues were he not repeatedly and fairly consistently assaulting them with the effects of bad acts. One or two evil acts rarely destroys character, although they may be striking symptoms manifesting with sudden clarity a long, subtle process of weakening that has heretofore gone on unspectacularly. His consistent conviction that he is seeking to maintain a set of good habits may be compromised by his inability to control a certain passion, say, the impulse to drink alcohol when he is likely to lose control of some subprocess, becoming, for instance, temporarily irritable and "touchy." This menace can begin to undermine his carrying out consistently the demands of the larger vision of his natural faith.

Significant onetime events also happen in our lives in the form of accidents, sometimes life-shattering, just as there occur also sudden, unexpected gratuitous opportunities, "gifts." One "accident" can require reordering of priorities, launching new processes. A single gift of love can reorient a life.

Habits can protect to a considerable extent against unwanted foreseeable onetime life-changing events. For instance, it is good to develop the habit of always being careful crossing the street, or, just having been introduced to a person, avoid making shocking remarks to be amusing. In both cases one will have abstracted the general sense of a typical kind of situation: "crossing streets" and "being introduced" will have developed general prudential rules for each type of situation. Once a sudden opportunity has been recognized, quick adjustment of ongoing processes will probably be required, just as with the accident, in order to take advantage of the felicitous happening.

The vast majority of my actions involve many processes I am freely working in my life to control, requiring ordering relations between them, some steady, some readily shifting. In other words, what is required is "management." The intersection of processes within me and goings-on "out there" in nature and in the many social worlds in which I am caught up provide—to put it calmly—multidimensional challenges! It is becoming arguable whether the world of high technology and virtual reality has grown so dynamic and multidimensional as to exceed our personal organizing abilities. Part of a good dimension, character is at work providing its particular moral consistency to all this in the midst of dynamism, through the cardinal virtues.

My free decisions to alter the course of some aspect of my life, ranging from minor shifts in certain habitual ways of dealing with particular kinds of issues all the way to undertaking radical conversion, demand deliberate altering of processes, however aware I may in fact be of the full range of implications. When other events impact from the outside without my invitation, they become integrated into certain courses of action. Sometimes, again, this happens without my being terribly aware of the impact they have actually had, or of my (perhaps very passive) freedom at work allowing them to have this influence. Ignorance, thoughtlessness, denial all have their effects and feed on one another.

As I sum up the factors involved in ensuring healthy (and ultimately authentic) consistency in one's life, bear in mind the dialectical reciprocity existing between each level in this hierarchy, that weave of intellectual and moral habits of wider or narrower scope, essentially (but almost never exclusively) good or bad. Again, I am referring to character not in the abstract but as built upon and at the same time further molding underlying attitudes. Those attitudes are at the same time aspects of one's natural faith that influences all motivations to act.

ATTITUDE AS ESSENTIALLY SPIRITUAL

I invoked at the start of the spectrum of capabilities most obviously accumulated in the body the formation of habits providing quite focused skills, because it is the easiest way to observe habit being built up. What is less obvious is the "spiritual" dimension at the base of this "building" of skill in even the most "earthly" activity. I shall avoid using naively the much abused terms *matter* and *spirit*. Attitude is essentially "spiritual" in this sense: it is in the order of human cognition and persistent willing intertwined. It is reflective, and it is essentially about meaning. An attitude can embrace mentally many kinds of things and ways of "holding oneself." Recall Heidegger's *Verhaltung*, how one holds oneself; "steady on the course," the pilot puts the plane not only on the right course but into the right "attitude," referring to tipping the aircraft down or up or leaving the flight level. Some moral attitudes send us climbing into spiritual heights; others point us to the doldrums.

Certain fundamental attitudes can have as their subject all of being itself. Consider, for instance, the person who holds "heads up" toward the widest horizons and deepest foundations. That is what I meant when in *Being and Truth* I rather poetically characterized "spirit" as "soaring." Another may adopt an attitude of firm closedness to any such "frivolous" thinking as the kind of philosophizing that brings one to issue pronouncements on all of being, accompanied by temptation to think of "soaring" without a glider. Not a rare attitude, I would think. Negativity and skepticism are common "nose-down" attitudes headed for a crash with the earth!

An attitude can be a "stance" gained in one fairly narrow activity that may come to translate to yet more "spiritual ones"—for instance, becoming determined and courageous in champion swimming can translate into a fearlessness about staying stuck to a desk long hours while solving mathematical problems. I am not thinking of a body tone only but of knowing that if I really want to accomplish something that involves a physical discipline, I can do it. We should think of "will" less exclusively in terms of particular acts and more in terms of complex sets of acquired capabilities that underlie whole courses of action.

Psychiatrists have much to say about "bad attitude," "antisocial attitudes," "neurotic attitudes." Once again, slang captures the sense: "Man, has he got attitude!" meaning someone is looking for a fight. Vicious twists in the tendrils of the psyche may have roots in organic brain pathology, but the "bad attitude," I would suggest, is still essentially spiritual because its central effect is in the order of meaning and the exercise of freedom. In every manifestation of attitude, an image *(Bild)* is at work. "Image" is spiritual because it is "noetic," another way of saying that it is about meaning (Greek: *nous, noein*).

The physical component in building even the most "spiritual" intellectual and moral virtues must not be overlooked. Never forget the cosmic base. We see this more easily in the negative: physical breakdown can impede the exercise of virtues solidly built up over a lifetime; a clinical depression can alter a saint's way of living out his faith. But let us close this subject on a positive note: without the discipline of respecting with exceptional self-control a daily schedule of silent reflection, no one can develop a way of profound contemplation.

No appropriate world makes its contribution only in anticipatory image. Required too is actual physical experience, once one participates in pro-jectively opening the appropriate world: Until I let myself be indentured into the world of domestic cooking, entering it largely through actually doing culinary physical acts, accompanied by a bit of science required for the art, I never realized apples were so difficult to pare, slice in four, pit, then cut up in slices. I discovered too how important is the appropriate knife. A symphony of new little skills needed to be developed together so various processes could be dominated and coordinated, this in the midst of constant revelations about the being of vegetables, the capabilities of spices, the quality of instruments—cognitive content and actual skills of fingers, taste buds and nostrils all being worked up together into a great art! Now a whole new world of capabilities opens: a new vocabulary, all sorts of heretofore hidden processes, strange but necessary instruments, new art forms—not just delicious dishes but balanced menus (suggested in terms of the little world of the planned dinner)—and inevitable roles to play, each of these elements presenting previously unknown challenges, each requiring the acquisition of further new habits, including many refined motor skills, processes begetting processes, images and more images, all interweaving to form the fabric of this little culinary corner of life. Such a weaving of skills, images (forms, textures, colors, decorations), and symbols (measures and words and recipes), requiring moral virtues of responsiveness, persistence, and fairness to all cooperating in the enterprise, awaits every human being who allows himself to be led into all the worlds, each having its own similar dynamic structures.

CHARACTER TO CARRY OUT AMBITIONS: PASSION, PRIDE, AND LOVE

In any project that is being carried out, not just dreamed about, attitude is at work in the form of passion: the person projects himself forward from the present out toward the imagined goal with the decision to devote a part of himself to achieving that goal because he wants what he imagines it represents. I have chosen the word *passion*, here meant in the colloquial contemporary sense of being possessed by a desire or bundle of desires. "Desire" in a project devoid of the prudence required to recognize the sustained effort turns out to be wishful thinking, not genuine passion. Whether in the authentic setting (in the smaller sense—who the person really is), this concrete development is good or evil, beneficiary or reinforcing. What turns out to be a disastrous course of delusional action is another ultimately fundamentally determining question. With the help of an example, let us look more earnestly at what this central role of "passion" in the sense intended reveals.

Imagine a young person genuinely inflamed with the idea of becoming a physician, sufficiently motivated to make the many sacrifices, day in and day out, for the next eight years. But suppose this passion is very little mixed up with a genuine love for the knowledge he is gaining (suppose he is simply after the prestige) or appreciation for the opportunities to be useful. Could the whole affair be an instance of puffed-up self-importance? Can ambitious pride alone (provided the person brings with him some disciplined character) be enough to provide an enduring motivation? Pride is self-centered. One is tempted to say that from the beginning of self-awareness, an element of pride manifests itself.

The Self is, we acknowledged, a space of personal struggle, inner *polemos*. We are "drawn out" toward the other, attracted because a loving person or a beautiful animal or a landscape can beguile us, yet at the same time we tend to be self-protective, timorous, possessive. One may be sufficiently selfish as to rarely yield in genuine admiration for the other thing or person.

Let us consider a preliminary distinction between pride, legitimate self-love, and love of others, whether persons, things, or even settings (one can love, for example, his home and his town). Now, both the interior struggle and the *polemoi* with others in various settings could be the effect of the different loves being separable and ambiguous, fragmenting the space-time of the moment.

English has two very different senses of *pride*, whereas French has two different words: *fierté* and *orgeuil*. An Anglophone can say "I am proud to be an Englishman," meaning he has a legitimate *fierté*. He is proud of his country and its traditions and is happy to be formed by them. *Orgeuil* (an ugly-sounding word) means pride as destructive of love. It implies desiring to use one's powers to control others. This distinction helps us understand what "love" means. It is the capacity to reach out beyond oneself, offering freely to the other admiration and generous gifts of what one possesses, be they interior strengths or things one can offer, given with the intention of helping or enhancing the other.

But that description does not quite fit "self-love," in the benevolent sense. What is implied in genuine self-love is our mysterious spiritual ability to step back beyond the whole of ourselves, to take up a self-critical view, making possible appreciation for everything positive and healthy in what has been given to us, first, genetically, then culturally through the love, care, and education of others. As well, there are treasured things that we may love innocently—a garden, a lovely painting, one's home.

There is in us always a mix of good and evil; we are ambiguous. Only theoretically can anyone who is touched by sin break through all obscurity about the self. In Christian revelation, for example, we are informed there have been only two pure saints: Jesus and Mary. In the case of all other individuals the following meet inevitably at the center of this one self: the inconsistencies, ambiguities, competing passions and genuine loves, possessiveness and generosity of one and the same human being. This bespeaks an ongoing interplay of many dynamic "inputs" that are not wonderfully lucid. In that center of conscious awareness meet not just clear vision, insight, pure gifts offered to others but also all the vague impressions, deceptions, suppressions, pathological denials, insecure grasping onto possessions, and so on that are plagues interfering with the effort to be wise.

What is at issue is not just the question "What are your loves?" nor is it just an issue of the conflict of loves within you, but more profoundly the drama of the self struggling to give over oneself to the beloved—"the greater reality," finding the courage (whence indeed does it come?) to sacrifice the kind of CONTROL that comes from our being too afraid to let the genuinely OTHER into one's world "appropriation," or ourselves into his ("ex-propriation"). (Both of these questions will be considered later.)

Making oneself voluntarily vulnerable requires great strength. Why anyone should ever risk vulnerability, of course, is a fundamental ontological question that can be dealt with only in the authentic context. In the large sense of the widest horizons and most profound depths englobing, illuminating, and founding human being, the searcher of wisdom has his task cut out for him.

I am leery of the term *values*, for it is subjective and hence tempting to relativism. In comparing "values" it is essential first to be clear about the *metron*—the measure, the criterion according to which relative worth is being judged. And then, according to what is at stake, pains need to be taken to situate in larger worlds with broader horizons distinctive criteria relative to one another, as demanded by authenticity, onward and outward to the largest discoverable horizons, embracing objective reality as much as possible to avoid "values" founded in nothing more than my happening to want something. The question lurks in the background: "Am I justified in wanting this thing now?"

The finite valuing of ambiguous and partly ignorant human wills should, one may hope, give way gradually, beyond all *polemos* of "my" and "your" values, to absolute receptivity to reality in and of itself, free of arbitrary "valuing" based on a whim. Further reflection in this transcendent vein must await the defense of an authentic vision I have promised to present later. (The indulgent reader has the right to smile.) Until then the word *value* whenever used in this text is introduced with its ambiguity in mind.

My fear regarding such narrowing, deadly to the project of wisdom, motivates my coming back once again to the ideal of authenticity: authentic critique of the narrowness of one's horizons alone allows one to build the self in the unique adequate context. That is nothing less than the whole of life, so far as we can be called into the fullness of Being. From roots sunk deep into the traditions that found us, some fruitful since birth (including its cosmic foundation), and the traditional roots of the ideas that cooperatively found society come the political and religious "ruling considerations": we struggle to allow the whole of life to reveal its feeding and molding us.[4] One's vision, so rooted in many foundational traditions, stretches forward to death, and includes whatever future, if any, remains for those creative accomplishments achieved during earthly life, even after one's death.

"Critical appropriation" demands facing the question of the destiny of all human accomplishment, but not forgetting the likelihood that the universe itself will sink into informationlessness. If it is fated that nothing will remain after the demise of all life in the cosmos, what case can be made for an altruism that would see us generously working for future generations? And if some realities might be preserved for eternity in a domain transcending finite time, then a wisdom should be built around those relationships. As opposed to becoming obsessed, achieving appropriate "distance" from different kinds of reality is not, then, just a matter of deploying horizons in ways that allow some kind of objectification or intimacy for the moment. Just as important, authentic distancing in order, paradoxically, to presence appropriately requires keeping in view the ultimate real context so far as we can know it.

4. See my *Tradition and Authenticity* and *The Catholic Tradition*, published by University of Missouri Press.

4

IMAGINATION

Thus far, I have examined two fundamental aspects of what it is to be human. I have tried to show how our fundamental experience of human being is conditioned both by our relations in various worlds and by how such relations are animated by our freedom and our character. Given that we are situated in the world and given that we all have characters and dispositions that yield a certain ethos in the world, how do we appropriate and come to understand the meaning of such complicated and inter-related realities? I wish to suggest that imagination and understanding are vital in that they permit us to make both our own situatedness and our characteristic modes or ways of being in the world. Our imagination is not merely individual; it is also collective and spans recorded history. We see traces of it everywhere in the legacies of art, music, science, philosophy, religion, and more. It is a particular facet that typifies human existence and human being in general. It is also a vital tool for us in order to understand and imagine what a more general sense of human being entails. This chapter focuses on imagination and its role in helping us appropriate ourselves and our world as constitutive of human being.

IMAGINATION, INTERWOVEN WITH UNDERSTANDING, IS INVOLVED IN THE FUTURE OPENING OF EVERY PROJECT

Any form of human presencing in whatever compartment of life, and whatever the "frame of reference," demands imagination. Imagination makes its appearance on the earth before the human. At some level in the rising, evolving complexity of animal life, evidence of imagination appears. I am not knowledgeable enough about zoology to hazard a worthwhile guess as to species and era; I have no idea at what point the degree of "spirituality" is reached that could sensibly be recognized as "animal imagination." The wiggly alarm signals sent by the earthworm eager to dig back in when I turn him out of house and home in my mulch pile do not offer us clues as to what he sees in his mind's eye—he has no eye, and he has no mind, not at least in the sense of critical reflection.

I recall the little dog who feigned the presence of an enemy by barking out the screen door only to sneak a few bites from the bowl of the big dog who was duped into coming also to bark into the empty night. Like all these difficult borderlines in biological evolution, one can confidently acknowledge imagination when it clearly presences beyond all fuzziness. (In a cat, for instance, we see clearly feline wiliness—but in a worm? The huge information flows in every living cell are mind-boggling, but what evidence is there of single-cell pro-jection or primitive self-consciousness?)

The elaboration of impulses and the embodiment of thoughts in images are dimensions of every aspect of human consciousness, with two stark "transcendental" aspects: "the not yet" future is always imagined in some way as we push onward and outward, and the imagination embroiders the presently palpable object with information and images stored in memory, reworked in projecting the future dimension of a field of cognition.

Pro-jection always has an element of will, whether what I am going after is perfectly achieved or turns out to be "pure unrealizable fantasy" ("I was presencing to a phantom"). When my dog on a leash stubbornly insists on sniffing this tree trunk, while I want (and tug) to get him to move on, do we not witness a clash of wills? "But the dog has no free will!" Really? Would it not be more accurate to acknowledge that, lacking the full range of human imagination, the vision entailed with his present stubborn insistence is less free than my wanting to move on because I have a schedule with much to do yet this afternoon? The pooch cannot explain to me the urgency of his keeping up to date on the neighborhood carryings-on. In any event, my superior strength and my determined will prevail. I am freer both in being able to set the affair in a richer context and, in this case, in possessing superior psychological and physical power: Mr. Dog is dragged along.

Although the popular notion of "imagination" tends to be dominated by certain kinds of images, we shall see that in fact we imagine, for instance, emotions ("At this moment I would like to cherish and treasure you, as the Lord invites, but, somehow, I do not manage it"). While accompanied often by "pictures," a moment's reflection recalls that the emotions are not pictures. "Image-ination" is, then, not only about "images" in the narrow sense; memories of feelings, for instance, are not pictures. As we proceed I shall sketch some of the varieties of entities we imagine. The significance of that will become clear, including the various kinds of powers with which these differences of imagination endow us.

As I develop here a view of the role and kinds of imagination, I cannot avoid giving a large place to the tasks of intellect and reason as well. But only in a later chapter's synthesis of the uses of our cognitive capabilities will the full role of intellect in the midst of all our imaginative cognitive capabilities become a central theme. There the following principles will reign: "No intellect, no human freedom." And this: "No cognitive content, no image."

I am deliberately postponing a major reflection on the extent to which we are not just minds in bodies but also agents able to commit ourselves in free response to the world through will. "Human presencing" is more commitment (hence will) than thinking. Later, I shall single out human will, showing it to be central and essential to the human act as such, hence distinguishing it as best I can from will in the higher animals. I hold back from going at that all-important issue until I have offered some idea of what good will come about with all its reflectivity and, hence, its freedom. (The code name for this level of will at its most positive: "love.")

Being ourselves bodies, we encounter the world mostly in the forms of other "bodies out there," from stones and trees through dogs and human bodies to planet earth and planetary systems, galaxies, and (with much help from the imagination and from elaborate scientific reasoning) the universe as a whole. The variety of ways these different things can presence plays a critical role in invoking the ways we can re-spond. If certain kinds of things never enter the world of a given individual, he will be called to no corresponding *ant-wort*, understood as an answering to call, a responding. But when a new kind of thing is suddenly confronting me in my field of meaning, there will be a spectrum of possibilities of how I shall re-spond, and hence varieties of ways of presencing to that object, with many possible "frames of reference."

The entire panoply of ob-jects and *ant-worten* is presented to our cognition in the form of images in various degrees and kinds of elaboration, which most of the time we take largely for granted and think about in terms of the function of some use we have for them right now. Even atoms are still frequently imagined (inaccurately and out of ignorance) as little definite planetary systems, from which molecules are built up (recall your images back in high school of atoms as little balls tied together by rods), or expressed in formulae with letters and attached little numbers. If we desire to know "what is out there," we hoi polloi have to learn how to presence to these subatomic particles and energy waves as the cognoscenti do, and how they imagine, as well as understand these things—an altogether new way of presencing.

The relations between all of the various kinds of things, from particles through federal government regimes sending Hubbles into orbit to study galactic clumps, tend to be imagined by commonsense man with the respective institutional paraphernalia (for example, federal buildings and books of administrative law) in steady state, providing the anchors for even the most dynamic relations. The finitude of our "intentional" capabilities—our ability to know and to decide how to use—entices us to crave dependable fixity. Especially in the sciences, these elaborate images that we manage to build stably often include aspects we know about but have never been able to sense, yet we are still able to discover in some way and then to fix on an image that the imagination fabricates. However inappropriate we may ultimately recognize our construction to have been as representations of real things, we know that they nevertheless helped us deal with certain dynamic processes. The imagination can create images of the dynamic, such as a picture of water cascading over a waterfall and dwindling in dry season. The musician has to mold stabile forms he puts down on music paper to give anyone access to the rollicking music he has just imagined into existence. Savor the paradox: Images are rather ethereal forms of stabilized incarnations of our cognitions, projected into the future, based on a past we are further elaborating!

We are clear about the fact that the universe itself and all the life seething from the earth and winging its way above its surface are not a set of reasoned phenomena. Rather, the inhabitants of the universe, while being things and relations between things capable of being reasoned about (only humans can do that reasoning), are not products of either our reason—yours, mine, or mankind's collective reason—or our imaginations, nor are they products of our wills, with the exception of human artifacts (including what each of us has made of his body) and human disturbances of natural processes. From this challenging exclamation follows a basic fact we all acknowledge: the dense things and intertwined relations and processes of the world yield only partially to patient, constructed human rational investigation and willful intervention. Some believe in the GUT (General Unified Theory) as not only a live possibility but THE key to our understanding everything. Most thoughtful people would probably agree there is no reason we should expect there to be no ultimate mystery.

In our construction of theories about the world, imagination throughout the ages has employed and continues to invent various methods, of different degrees of appropriateness, for achieving whatever it is searchers may at the moment have wanted to accomplish. (There is no method that leads to a successful and complete GUT.) Most who think about it today judge many methods to have shown adequately their inappropriateness—for instance, astrological methods are generally inappropriate for what they are purported to yield. But then particle physics is not likely ever to be the most effective way to deepen one's resonance with a great piece of music, nor does it do much for our musical appreciation to learn that computer studies have revealed that the number of basic musical forms turns out to be not just finite but rather small, nor will particle physics likely help us to understand the human imagination in its central significance.

Those cavalier reflections should at least help us appreciate this truth: imagination, while essential to our knowing, is by no means just for the sake of knowing. At this moment (literally, this is the case), I look through my office door and happen to see my four-year-old grandson kneeling in front of a plastic spaceship-control console, gesturing and making impressive noises of jet flight. (He is musical, and so makes the best explosion and jet-engine noises I have ever heard.) He is having fun: immersed in an imaginary world, he is conversing with himself, pushing buttons and steering vigorously. He is obviously on no reliable flight path.

Much use of the imagination is not about increasing our learning at all but rather for enjoying human imaginary worlds. We all want to have fun. (The most committed Christian monks seeking to deepen their "friendship with God" acknowledge the legitimate humanity of having a bit of fun. And their use of imagination in their efforts to be in God's presence is a subject of anthropological interest, with both pain and joy generated.) So the will too is not only about serious commitment. In its most grotesque follies, it is treasured by some.

The reader will by now probably appreciate my point that imagination presides far and wide over our lives. The many uses of the imagination evidence the life of the spirit groping beyond the constraints of the methodically developed intellectual structures of our science and our sober practical organizations, as we enjoy in many ways—innocent and not so innocent—our sheer powers of imaginary world construction. As we bring out into the sober world of daily action our loftiest intellectual constructions and our most narcissistic imaginary playback, we sober philosophers are still in need of images of the thing we are going to deal with next, however simple or complex. In the form of vagaries of human imagining, this includes, alas, imagination's capability of serving desires that want hard realities magically transformed or wished away. Active denial as magical transformation reminds us never to underestimate the joys of carefully cultivated airheadedness, or the perversions of destructive souls.

For a contrast, jump a moment from the vapid to "the exalted mythological": it would be meaningless to talk about a religion (whether in the narrow exalted sense or in the wide sense in which everyone "has a religion" ruling considerations of one's natural faith) without exploring the dominant imaginative element in its symbolism. As with sex play, this symbolism reveals some fantasizing around a core of emotion, which images help one to believe in and to hang on to what are thought to be certain ultimate but admittedly elusive realities. These "ultimate considerations" are often thought about in the fashion in which they are imagined. In part, it is because that imagining responds to the way some of the creative founders of a religious tradition wish things to be ultimately. Other times it is because the elaborated, part-imaged, part-conceptual formulations of ultimate realities are simply what a tradition, struggling to express the inexpressible, has managed to elaborate, passing down a prophet's vision. (For example, think of Karl Marx.)

Without clarification of the notions of image and concept, my previous comment is not too helpful. I shall come back, when the way has been better prepared, to the challenging issue of how (narrow-sense) religious traditions are born and then proceed to be elaborated over long stretches of history. Meanwhile, what I have pointed out about fantasizing around a core of emotion is just as true in science as in religion—more so in the soft sciences as in the mathematical sciences. This is certainly true of Marx but also of Heisenberg, for even in physics an underlying vision is driven along emotionally. In medicine, for instance, the physician imagines therapeutic interventions in function of the best theory of the affected system or organ he has been able to learn. The complex systems with which he is dealing have to be imagined in some way, so he can grasp from these working images the most appropriate scheme of knowledge imaginable.

And he has to learn to live with the obscurities and even the black holes in his knowledge.

All symbols, including the most unequivocal mathematical ones as wishful fantasies, are imaginary forms with a core of intelligibility. We can, with effort, say something conceptual and abstract about every sort of imagining, if the occasion calls for highlighting the core insight that the symbol is meant to convey. When important matters of wide range are at stake, the adequacy of an imaginary form as instrument for expression about things and relations, and those ideas themselves, should be put to the proof of our total thinking ability's capacity for grasping being. Honest critical judgment demands no less: it requires authenticity, really, our thinking being driven forward into the "not yet" by an attitude of wanting "the whole truth and nothing but the truth." But given the travails of finite human freedom, such full seriousness sustained remains rare.

When a talked-about project turns out to have been well grounded in a sound analysis of the situation, imagination will be seen to have been at work, hand in hand with reason, fruitfully, as the responsible person intelligently pictured what was yet to be done, and so was ready with the effective actions at the proper moment. (The authentic wise person will generally enjoy the benefits of the best-thought-out field of possibilities for those matters that fall under his re-sponse-ability.) In all instances, even in the most irresponsible fantasizing, reason and hence concepts are part of the picture. They do not just help the projector of the future to distinguish mere dreaming from sound creative imagining, but provide all sorts of cognitive content for the images, even when they are intended to be pure fantasy, not leading to any external action. Even my grandson's spaceship fantasizing showed signs of ragged conceptual content, although the ideas involved played a very minor role in the pleasure. Even as the most creative artist is weaving the purest fantasies about a core of recognized objects, themes are being drawn from past and present experiences of real things about most of which, if he is articulate, he can discourse in conceptual terms.

When in a subsequent chapter I shall focus on cognition and analogical reason we shall discover more about the essential contribution of the imagination in the "coolest" scientific enterprises. The emotions of lived temporality are at work in us, and this in many different forms of imagination. The symbols used to express whatever can be expressed will reveal both insight into formal relations including the dynamic and the ineffable beauties of form. The elaborate forms developed in physics are beautiful in both their lucidity and often their great sweep.

With cognition the emphasis shifts to intellect and reason and to the truth of its foundations. But in the most earnest scientific enterprises those gifted mathematicians, the quantum physicists and the superstring cosmologists, are troubled that they cannot always imagine (and thereby relate to commonsense experience) the "weird" (a particle physicist's word, not mine) phenomena discovered at the "quanta" level. While using imagination, our feelings and our understanding can also transcend imagination: there are things we can understand beyond what we can adequately image, and things we can feel, as expressed in the common sentiment, "Words cannot express the gratitude I feel." Yet even the "purest" mathematician always has to imagine where he believes he is headed in his musings; he has some notion, partially still merely imaginary, of "what a solution may look like" before it takes definitive shape in a "demonstration."

Imagination, because it is thus transcendental, in the sense of accompanying every human cognition, even those who in turn transcend it, again like emotion, and for that matter the entire operations of finite freedom, is impossible to encompass; there can be no adequate description of it. Eugene Boylan, the Cistercian author of *Difficulties with Mental Prayer* (1943), points to the unconscious realization of the inadequacy of any feeling or emotion to satisfy the deeper needs of our soul. As we continue to explore the dynamics among emotion, intellect, and will, this claim that faith, considered truth in intellectual form, is the highest reality within us should eventually, when the pieces are in place, be confronted "head-on." As the next step I shall wrestle with imagination in its own right, although intellection and reasoning will be invoked at points to make sense of how imagination works. But the human imagination's creations, both in the individual and even more in the accumulated results deposited in all the world's artifacts and institutions, are too vast and varied (and too imaginative!) for us ever to be content with the most elaborate description.

THE INTERPENETRATION OF IMAGE, CONCEPT, AND SYMBOL

Are a thing, an image, a concept, and symbols ever separable from one another? To be sure, each of the following transcends the other:

the experienced thing "out there" (or welling up inside my soul); the image with its mysterious, suggestive tentacles and depth in the restless and mysterious realm of the imagination; the concept with its soaring abstraction and its peculiar lucidity; and the symbols that become the instrument for expressing all that can be in any way ex-pressed. Symbol, thing, concept, and image can all be to some extent ex-pressed, pressed out *(ex)* into cosmic time and space through "incarnation" in a gesture, or a sound, or a word written on paper, or in musical notation on a piece of ruled paper, or painted on a canvas. The symbol that stands for something else that is not a symbol can itself be talked about, which requires symbols to express what a symbol is and how it functions. Through symbolization the things we have come to know are conveyed (and stored away in the soul's treasure house of symbols, my very soul, through the mediation of the symbol, standing over against me). When written down and stored in a library or on a "floppy" or in a museum of paintings and sculptures, these things are accessible, perhaps centuries from now, including all that inspires my "ruling considerations," natural faith. In terms of human being in general, symbols play a crucial role insofar as they are the vehicles by which larger, more complex, and more enduring visions and accomplishments of human being are sustained in collective memory.

With that question in the background, consider again each step in strengthening our sense of the impenetrable otherness of the thing. (Some aspects of what follows will be further elaborated in the next chapter when we concentrate on cognition.) First, the "thing" transcends all our efforts to see, taste, feel, and hear it once and for all, and to penetrate it exhaustively with insight, to measure it and capture it in image and symbol. No thing, not even the cultural object, not even a poem, is completely the product of human work. Even the most "stand-alone" thing reveals, upon closer examination, that its standing is due to a set of infinite relations, and that it is disturbed by our efforts to probe it. You need not descend to the particle level of the Heisenberg uncertainty principle to see this. Think of an example where the resistance—the otherness of the ob-ject—is very human, very psychological . . . and very stubborn. Second, the image retains its suggestive connections to other images and through them to many other things, to concepts and to symbols, especially through the evocative (and usually pretty murky) depths of the imagination; our minds partly involuntarily tear around the circuit of these relationships, illuminating the image at the center of attention. Third, concepts are those insights and mental and spiritual realities that we grasp through imagination, intellection, and will. The concept displays inexhaustible luminous connections with other concepts. Examples of concepts include time, space, human being, science, and so forth. Finally, the symbols, which not only are our instruments for holding on to all the others—things, images, concepts—themselves belong in suggestive systems of language. These systems move the poet along lines of imaged tentacles of that special, indescribable linguistic world. Each language is a realm of immense "stored-up" artistic creativity, constituting all the grammar and vocabulary of common, specialized, and esoteric languages accumulated since man began to speak, held in libraries since he learned to write. Human being is incarnate in language.

Can a painter really grab hold of an image emerging in his imagination without beginning to sketch it on the canvas? Can he work out his feelings for the appropriate colors without trying them from the end of a brush? In the process he does not, of course, have to form any verbal symbols, for he is developing painted forms as media of expressing what is developing imaginatively deep in his soul. I do suspect, however, that many an artist converses with himself silently—and I mean in words—about what he is doing and what is emerging. Some talk out loud to themselves while painting. My artist friends are all willing to talk about what they are doing in a particular work, and seem eager for others' suggestions about what is going on in the work. They are accustomed to translation, indeed appear to welcome the challenge!

I have trouble imagining what is the properly conceptual dimension in listening to a beautiful theme in music. Suppose I am being swept up by Samuel Barber's addictive *Adagio for Strings, Opus 11.* Upon reflection now, I see that it mysteriously evokes for me a peculiar ("puritan" I call it) sadness I find in the American soul. Also my mind's eye sees there an obvious formal structure, including how it relates to the emotions Barber is arousing, rising in *Liebestod* fashion to a gentle climax with no loss of dignity, and fading away peacefully. Upon reflection, I was just now able to find some words to express concepts (*sweeping, addictive, mysterious sadness, American soul,* and even *adagio,* which, although it means "slow," has taken on a second sense related to the Wagnerian sexual arousal climax and rapid decline, classifying the piece within familiar musical forms). Each of these notions relates the work potentially with concepts in different departments of life, just part of the relationships in which the work and my experience of it are caught up in a many-colored interweave.

This linguistic prowess enabled me to communicate to you some idea of what I feel when following in a sweet melancholy the reinforcement of the two (occasionally three) voices of the *Adagio*, all this burden carried in the original quartette from which the string orchestra piece is taken, by just two violins, a viola, and a cello. This exercise offers an example of how one is able, with an effort, to discover some conceptual potential in what was heretofore almost entirely an emotional experience. I shall return later to the question, so important for understanding the dynamics of human freedom, of why all words, indeed all symbols of whatever kind, presuppose a basic act of intellection: "to see if they fit"—why there are then necessarily concepts behind every image and every symbol.

The root meaning of the word *symbol* strikes a note of wisdom: the Greek word connotes bringing together two parts of a whole that has been broken, to prove that the two "friends" are in harmony . . . in other words, "It fits!" Most things are represented in the imagination as existing outside of our mind (my bicycle, for instance, and, indeed, Samuel Barber's *Adagio*, which, once he finished expressing it on lined music paper, came to exist outside his soul, whereupon the question arose, "Does what is written down capture adequately what he was imagining as he composed the quartette? Does it fit [*symbolein*]?").

An error, or a delusion, may take the form of one's believing that something actually exists "outside" that in fact is only in the mind. Or one may mistakenly believe an incomplete copy of the musical text of the quartette is the whole quartette. But these kinds of questions keep suggesting this larger question: is any imagining ever "only in the mind" in the strict sense? What we have thus *far* seen hints that it is not, that even the "purest fantasy" is chock-full of knowledge, much of it derived cognitively from and hence potentially again relatable to realities outside the particular imagination in which it occurs. Much of that reality is ultimately reattachable to a reality that lies outside of the mind—to real cultural objects and natural things and social, intersubjective "states of affairs."

In this relation to a reality greater than what my mind can create imaginatively lies our hope of keeping our imaginations under some critical control. Do not forget how servile the imagination can be in "doctoring the records" to fit what we passionately desire. Often, when the larger reality comes crashing disastrously into the fantasy world—"nature's revenge"—it is only then that we begin to be saved from distortions built into our own constructions. Try this experiment: Invent a nonsense verbal representation of something that could not possibly exist. Write it down.

First, you will discover that it is difficult to invent a plausible nonexisting thing, worse yet one that will for sure never be. Now try to describe this "purely imaginary" creation better, reflecting on all the verbal symbols, one by one. Take note of some of their references to things or states of mind, or whatever, that lie beyond your imagined scenario. Try to see where they came from, especially where they originated in experience, and hence how they refer you back to "the outside world."

I hope to avoid all confusion between *imagination* and *consciousness*, despite their intimate interpenetration. Consciousness involves some degree of explicit awareness of incoming data of many kinds. This can be freshly arriving sensory data and freshly minted combinations of data to form creative new images. Or it can be recall of old images stored in memory that I may be surreptitiously altering as I recall them. But in all instances, recalling, deforming, re-forming—insight into the meaning of what that data presents, image-forming is involved. Consciousness transcends imagination. All imagining requires consciousness, but not all consciousness requires imagination. Insight, admittedly, always depends on the imagination to provide images drawn from past experience to "flesh out" the present sensory contact, the grasp of conceptual connections, and the present looking toward the future. But an insight penetrating to the significance of the image or images alone allows for the possibility of any correct relationship between images, the concepts and the symbols chosen to ex-press the object.

Suppose an artist beginning to evolve an image of what he thinks he wants to say: he begins to mold symbols to give that sense a first bit of cosmic time-space existence accessible to the other. This is so whether those emerging symbol constellations take the form of a sketch, a melody, a poem, an essay, a "beautiful" mathematical demonstration, or something else. Throughout the process of *poeien* (to make), which results in the imaginative object's unfolding, a complex dialectic of developing insight, emerging image, and mobilization of symbols is taking place, a silent interior discussion is going on in the "artist," with attention riveted now more on one rather than on another aspect, but usually rapidly skipping from one to the other as the process of their mutual "in-forming" goes on. As the image begins to be ex-pressed, the artist may see better what he is driving at. His motivational feelings profit from his reflection on what he has already molded into whatever matter he is using. This is suggesting further development of the "graven" image as symbol or, if he is improvising in a discussion, as his now partly expressed thoughts take verbal form and so on. To the extent that he is intent on the image's capturing some thing or state of affairs, which itself is not only an image, he will keep working on his sketch or his verbal description to make it more "faithful" and complete.

Only purely natural events come out of the future without passing through a future-anticipating human imagination, often indeed crashing into the present with a jolt of utter surprise for us, like the sudden opening of a crater in my garden or a tremendous thump on the roof that causes the house to quiver. "I can't imagine what in heaven's name that was." But to begin my investigation I try to summon up from past experience at least one hypothesis, and failing that I go after empirical data from the crash scene, wondering what the force of gravity has pulled from the sky.

WHERE DO WE BEGIN TO DESCRIBE THE RICHES OF IMAGINATION?

So, confronted by this *embarras de richesse*, the cornucopia of images streaming from human imaginations, and frustrated by the dynamic complexities of imagination's relations with our other cognitive capabilities, where might we begin our glimpses of imagination at work in as many areas as possible? We need at least enough to fashion a responsible view of the large place that imagination should enjoy in a philosophical anthropology. Simple answer, difficult execution: basically, begin in ourselves! Guided by the few indicators I am about to offer, the reader will, I hope, enter into his own interior life to capture phenomenologically, as it happens, aspects of imagination at work. Integrating these riches into the dynamic complexity of human being will prove a never-ending reflection.

As there are many quite distinctive kinds of imagination, you should try to observe "as it happens" the unique contribution of as many types as you can personally discover. If you are "tone deaf" to certain basic forms of imagination, my advice, to be blunt, is to work to find the ways that exist to help people get in contact with an important aspect of human being. People "lacking imagination" are as dangerous as superimaginative people with poor moral principles or psychic disorders. Is it possible that, like literal tone deafness, the physiology of the brain plays a part in the hopeless incapacity of some individuals for certain kinds of imagining?

Now that the point has been made that imagination works in dynamic interrelation with the cognitive and emotive powers of the subject, we can move on to discuss the different kinds of imagination. I tentatively propose the following catalog of genera of imagination:

1. The conceptual (accompanying every perception and all thought)
2. Model building (including root metaphors, as used by the philosophers to represent the whole of being)
3. Action-oriented and future-anticipating
4. Fantasy, of which I see four species: mythmaking; artistic (verbal, graphical, and musical); fantasy for fun and escape; and dreams
5. Prophetic revelation and its relation to and contrast with dreams
6. Self-imaging, with dimensions of mythmaking, building a picture of who I am in function of what I want to be and what I believe I have already achieved, and what I believe is our common human destiny.

There will often be found in a single complex act of cognition several genera of imaginings. Best to start, however, with a preliminary glance at each of these uses before we examine intertwining capabilities.

The Conceptual Imagination

Conceptualization is a joint endeavor of insight and creative forging of imaged forms to represent the content of the insight. Looking at each in turn, I shall distinguish perception from image making, and then reflect on the interaction of insight and imaging.

What would incoming sensory data amount to if I could find no categorization that would allow me to hold on to it? It would certainly not constitute a perception—indeed, it cannot be "given" at all; it would not even add up to an irritation, for to be irritated is to know where, by what, and, to a degree, why I am being scratched or from where comes the mysterious rumble.

That very thought gives me a feeling: I feel suddenly confident enough to risk being blunt with the reader about the issue I am raising. In fact, I feel coming on nothing less than a fundamental transcendental claim of great significance for understanding human being, one that will destroy the whole "positivist" endeavor—quite a heady and triumphant feeling!

How is that for imagining! I now attempt to paint the insight in words: There is simply no "sensory data" isolated from conceptualization. No one ever sees "blue," but only a blue something—the shimmer of blue-silver light on the surface of the lake agitated slightly by the breeze, or the blue light streak in a spectrum that always fades over into the adjoining colors on each side, both purple and green. Recently driving through a dark night under a cloudless sky I saw an intense blue flash at a low level on the horizon. I awaited the sound of an explosion. I cannot imagine what it was. Retaining the image of an intense low-level blue flash, like an explosion from a center, I am able to describe the phenomenon for you, but I still cannot imagine what it was. The other person in the car was baffled. Note that in the description I employed the familiar concept "a flash," I attributed a generic color to it, and I centered the whole description in the concept "intense flash," with the added specification of "explosion," the illumination moving suddenly in all directions. The form weaves sudden happening, expansion, illumination, color all together into a coherent descriptive whole.

Supporting our ability to interpret an event like that is our silently operating body. A massive exchange of information is going on in the body all the time, between parts of each relevant cell, and between cells to the level of organs, including the most complex organ, the brain, most of which information exchange, at all levels, is as such never "sensed" by the person. Yet his cells and organs have built into them abilities "to know" what to do in the presence of the data that are relevant to our knowledge because it unfolds in consciousness, data received, for instance, by a cell and "interpreted" by it according to the capabilities of its receptors and the centers in the cell that "know" how to switch on whatever is programmed by the imposing event to be next, given the "information" going through these processes. All this information exchange is proceeding without even the smattering of reflective awareness required for the operation that interests us here: perception. These vast intercellular and interorgan information flows all occur without conscious "conceptualization," without awareness that we are involved in these corporeal foundational processes. But, as in a computer, in-place recognition structures filter, select, and transmit impulses to the required next set of receptors that, if the circumstances permit perception, then flash in the brain a sight in the eyes or a feeling of warmth on my fingertips, or other perceptions. I have repeatedly pointed out that much of the sensory data I am receiving at any given moment remains on the margins of human consciousness,

at those famous "horizons" of my attention. From experience I am programmed to pay almost no attention to much of the sensory flow so long
as my memory continues to instruct, "Such-and-such is most vaguely in
the background but is not relevant just now." Still, the fact that I am not
for now alerted or otherwise motivated to pay closer attention nevertheless does not interfere with my "horizonal" cognitive powers. Aided by
memory, they are constantly, at a low level of awareness, reassuring me
that none of this data requires a higher degree of attention but most of the
time will "pop into view" when needed.

Just now as I am writing I was distracted by movement of patches of
lively color visible through the trees. Almost at once I interpreted (correctly) that it is the noisy boys from the house behind who are skating on
their ice hockey rink, and at once the thought occurs to me: "Thank heavens it is below freezing, my double windows are shut, and even as loud
as they scream, I cannot hear a thing, thank goodness!" The rapid conceptualized interpretation: "the boys playing hockey" was easily verified,
and the thought about my seasonal problems of securing silence surged
from a particular segment of memory. On top of all that, I recognized a
good example for my text, and voilà! You have just read it.

Cognition is founded in re-cognition, imaginatively stretching the old
concepts as far as possible to accommodate something "really new." If it
is a real "breakthrough," even just a very small advance in understanding, the perceiver will have to create insightfully a new concept, with
an element of the totally new included (most often new only to this perceiver; breakthroughs for all of mankind are rare). If the breakthrough is
of wide significance, at that point the perceiver had better really have the
touch of the poet, as he will probably have to create a brave new symbol
to ex-press it.

I mentioned earlier that a concept like "tree" or like "overheating
economy" captures an "intelligibility" that, being an abstraction, exists
not in the cosmic world "out there"—there is no "tree-in-general"—but
only in the "virtual reality" of our interior space; there is no economy
as some sort of thing, only human minds weaving together certain processes of manufacturing, services, purchase, and sales. In the cosmic
world, on the "macroscopic" human commonsense scale, our concern is
largely monopolized by individual things and concrete relations between
things, especially concrete settings. "Why have prices for clothes risen?"
So, obviously, the concept, produced by an act of intellectual insight, is
retained, and exists only in the memory, and is called up imaginatively.

Every remembered concept is accompanied by an image, sometimes not totally appropriate to the intellectual form. "Negative number" may be accompanied by a "-2" sign, or an image of paying back a debt. How do we represent the concept "magnetic field"? Try to think with no accompanying image of what you know about magnetic fields. Now note the accompanying emotional charge, however feeble. The interaction of concept-image-symbol and now emotion (part of the key to why you are thinking about whatever it is in the first place [presently to illustrate a noetic process] and part of whatever is now revealed—everything carries with it in the human encounter an emotional charge) holds implications for how human beings live out their lives. What the concept captures may be an aspect of extramental reality—for example, a resemblance between all those things we symbolize by the term *tree* that is founded in their real "in-themselves" shapes, their being deeply rooted, their having trunks and branches with a "wooden" consistency, and so on. Sometimes those resemblances are founded in causal relations we are able at least partially to explain; sometimes they turn out to be simply "look-alikes" that lead us into believing "brother" things that are not even "distant cousins." The "wolverine," for instance, is misnamed because of just such a resemblance. Instead of the smallest of the wolf family, he is in fact the biggest of the weasels.

Recall the inflation concept once again. There is no thing "out there" corresponding to the concept "overheating economy," but, we acknowledged, there can at times be situations in a particular world of production and commercial exchange when "demand" (another wide-sweeping abstraction) is outpacing supply, setting off "inflation." (Note the image— what do you see, a balloon expanding? And note the emotional charge: when will it go "pop"?) An "overheating economy," then, is an abstract, structural representation of a vast complex set of trillions of real actions and relations between concrete people—treated in the aggregate, caught up in an immense network of processes—some of the outlines of which, like the human agents' actions of buying and selling, we are able to perceive.

The building of systems of mathematical concepts and relationships has been a fundamental dimension of the advance of civilization. So basic is it that until the beginning of the modern age, with the discovery of the notion of "function" and the development of a mathematics of dynamics, religion and mathematics were intimately interrelated. An adequate anthropology must pay attention to the mathematical dimension of the human mind. I shall probe further into this and several other aspects of cognition in the next chapter.

Model Building

The concept "overheating economy" cries out for construction of a "model." Models are complex imaginative representations of certain aspects of systems, often vast ones. They can be of various chosen scales and "grain," that is, "fine-grained" all the way down to the effort to measure or perceive and accommodate into the model every kind of particle, and all the way up to a very selective "coarse-grained" model (or "universe," if one is working in quantum mechanics seeking to secure an understanding of the cosmos). One perceives only aspects of these systems, one "profile" at a time, from a point of view in which the perceiver is centered. Often, we build up a model from a sequence of perceptions, direct or mediated through measuring instruments, chosen to provide data germane to the question that motivates us to take the trouble to observe and in observing build the model in the first place. In other instances, from a platform of acquired wisdom about a region or level of reality, a genius, in an incredible leap of imagination, will capture in a brief set of equations a highly compressed expression of a set of relationships of vast range. This will send bright minds to create possibilities of measurement (or even of optical or audible perception) that were previously undreamed of to prove out the compressed vision.

Note that a model may stand either for an individual system, such as this cosmos, "the expanding visible universe," "this overheating American economy," or for the type, like a kind of complex organic molecule or "characteristics of economic overheating in general." But as a structure, whether static or dynamic, which has been assembled imaginatively, it must be the subject of an insight into the sense of that structure (when dynamic, then vectors; when static, fixed rather than evolving relationships).

In *Being and Truth* I defined *structure* as follows: "any perceived or imagined or conceived whole, into the sense of which the mind enjoys an insight, that is, can grasp the characteristic way in which the parts of the whole belong to one another." Because of this insight into an intelligible belonging together of essential parts (that is, without that part the structure would be a different kind of thing), the mind is able to abstract the form to stand for that type, leaving behind many particulars (which can change without voiding the essence—for instance, the model can be very "coarse-grained," or it can be "fine-grained"): for instance, the type of the expanding high-tech mixed entrepreneurial–social welfare economy (there can be many similar economies to be compared in keeping with the form [in this case structure] of the model; given what he is trying to do, the model builder leaves behind for now zillions of details characteristic of different subtypes and even unique economies). Or one can consider the type of "expanding universe," of which there may be only the one exemplar, the universe we in fact inhabit (unless, as "string theory" suggests, there may be an "infinite" number of "universes").

To help clarify further what is involved in model building I shall contrast the way we build up images of individual persons with how formal model building takes place. Concepts are at work also in such personal image building, but in the kind of concrete cognition involved in elaborating our view of a given person, the relevant concepts are usually not very critically reflected upon.

Everyday Elaborating of Images of Another Person

If I think of one of our daughters, at the center stands an image of her as she is now, not a "still photo" but animated by present "outtakes" of her in action, in situ, in her house, perhaps making her guests feel at home, sternly reprimanding one of her little children, laughing at jokes, being very open and communicative or, in the case of another daughter, hard to know what she really thinks. As the four sisters in our family are fairly close and I am aware that a good part of the life of three of them is wrapped up in their professional activities, but as I have seen very little of them in action in those settings, I must draw on a small impression gained from one visit to factory or hospital or law office, then upon anecdotes to fabricate an animated image of what each must be like at the office or in the operating room or dealing with other social workers and "clients." If I continue my reverie about one of these persons, I may pull a snapshot out of my mental album and see her as the round-faced, energetic baby shouting for the hound next door, "Chips!" I know certain important facts about each of my daughters' professional activities, domestic life, hobbies; I compose these with the dynamic style—the personality—of each of them, as I represent each person to myself. These facts gathered from here and there, by chance and perhaps suggesting what I believe to be important, or for some reason at least "striking," nevertheless require some understanding of what each does with her life, some insight into what it is to be managing a large high-tech manufacturing plant, or operating on the human heart, or insight into what is required to force advanced math into the reluctant heads of Toronto seventeen year olds, or what it is to help sad Natives through the social support system in Anchorage. I know many anecdotes about each of my four daughters and one son, all accompanied by highly fabricated but vivid images, mise-en-scènes in settings I have seen in the lives of all five of them. Had I not seen them, my imagination would fabricate as best it could some sort of picture built out of conceptualized generic impressions based on experiences from elsewhere, adapted to the cause.

Now why would it be misleading to term *model* this elaborate knowledge with its incarnating images I have built up of a particular person? It is perhaps wiser to reserve the term *model* for a more explicit, more intellectualized concrete image of a methodically analyzed system. I term it "methodical" because it is worked out with a clear motive with an intention of clarity measured by a practical end, far, for instance, from the fuzz of family reveries in dotage. What I enjoy of each person is an elaborate, shifting, growing (both as the result of new experience and of additional, undisciplined, emotionally based reflections) image. It is much less analytical, much less intellectualized than the explicit model of a virus, with much less critical reflection involved as over time the elaborate image alters for me. I may "criticize" that daughter without being, in the scientific sense, "critical."

Methodical and "Mathematical" Model Building

The contrast between casual elaboration of a notion of some individual and methodic model building is best seen in the case of "scientific" reconstructions of historical events and processes in the quest for some sense of what really happened. The careful "critical" historian is dealing with key individuals, but his scientific intentions make his endeavor much more like model building than either the casual ongoing elaboration of one's notion of a given person or of mythmaking (which I shall consider in a moment). To start with, the motives are different in all three types. In historical reconstruction there is a drive to find sound evidence of the events that actually occurred, and a desire to know the personalities involved as they actually developed. The goal in historical research is usually to be less primordial, less sweeping therefore than what the great myths seek to make present, and much less fanciful than my undisciplined ongoing building of an elaborate image of my daughters. Unlike the mythmaker's exploration of meaning, the historian's is not usually motivated by a desire to soar into the not-yet, the could-be, the transcending ought-to-be, or to recuperate the forgotten that has been at the origin of it all. Nor is the historian just casually dreaming of an intimate—a family member or a friend about whom I may be for the moment concerned. Rather, the responsible historian (or the scientist) seeks to remain humbly submitted to the already-having-been facts, which, only because there is good evidence of their being true, deserve a place in the model.

The emotions, reflective of what one wants, are different in the three cases: emotions drive the reverie-dominated elaboration of one's image of a given person; as the historian's careful reconstruction of a life and a social setting laboriously unfolds, both are different from the emotional thrust of the myth soaring with grand ideals (and threats of disaster . . . the historian offering diagnoses of why historical disasters have actually occurred). The inspired mythmaker's soaring vision contrasts with the often breathtaking intuitions of the mathematical model builder. Both can be sweeping, but the emotive tonality is very different—for instance, "fear and trembling" (Kierkegaard) versus purified, consolidating, and reassuring lucidity of the well-founded model.

The historian, concerned with the infinitely subtle and complex weave of human motives, unique in their combination in any one dramatic act, cannot begin to diagram anything more subtle than movements of companies and battalions in a large four-hour battle. One is more likely to get the feel of a platoon patrolling in the Vietnamese jungle from a novel than from a history of the Vietnam War. Already at the most basic organic level, it is difficult but not impossible to capture in mathematical statistical formulae dynamics at the molecular level. But when evidence of "information-processing" operations very close to "intentionality," lacking only reflectivity, manifest themselves, the researcher will often be mystified: "This kind of cell knows how to counteract in the following steps the invasive presence of such-and-such a pathogen, but just how it 'knows' we ourselves do not yet know." The more "judgment" is involved in deploying from a panoply of possibilities certain combinations thought to be effective in a complex defensive operation, the further the biologist is from mathematically modeling the reality.

Action-Oriented, Future-Anticipating Imagination

The future is not yet, but "the real future," that which will actually happen (which we shall only know for sure, of course, when it has happened), is always already being formed in part by what already exists. I shall elaborate the obvious for a moment, requesting the reader to think of examples that will help him grasp how the deeper, more stable elements of the "already having been" interact with less predictable dimensions.

Because of what we do not know of the processes presently at work, we cannot predict beyond a certain degree of probability what will develop, but after certain events will have occurred we can then look back and recognize often how far in the past certain dynamic elements were already at work, shaping step by step a future state or phase that, subsequently having happened, is now already partly past. Some of its effects now partly continue, and are very likely, even in some instances certain, to continue for a while. For example, the improvised hockey rink in my neighbor's garden came into existence on one freezing day when, I deduce, water was sprayed to provide a smooth surface, and given the present weather conditions, I can anticipate will remain for at least the next days. Their house is likely to remain largely what it is long into the future, although the possibility of the owner parents adding an extension, given the dynamics of the neighborhood, is not to be overlooked. The house is too high-quality to be a candidate for demolition to make way for a new house, in decades to come. Although Toronto is rarely menaced by tornadoes, and severe earthquakes are not likely, both can happen, but they are sufficiently neglected such that they do not affect real estate prices.

Every real event has some "roots" going all the way back to the origins of the cosmos. This is especially easy to see as we reconstruct ongoing processes and project them imaginatively on the basis of what we believe as of now to be their dynamic structures: something of their vectors are displayed and can, because of the "visibility" of certain roots, be extrapolated with varying degrees of certitude. Processes display various degrees of probable stability, and our knowledge of them is affected by various degrees of imaginative projection. Some vectors reveal themselves to be determined—when I throw a ball it is fated (and in this case we know why) to describe a ballistic curve unless some interfering force, like the solidity of a tree trunk or a violent wind gust, interferes. That example is a product of my imagination directed by the intellect's grasp of the intelligibility of these processes. As we move toward the future we take for granted the most reliable vectors. As I walk out into my garden I know I shall spot the house of the neighbor. But imagine the shock when I return from a week out of town to find not the neighbor's dependable house but a newly excavated hole in the ground.

Fantasy

I pointed out that higher animals show signs of fanciful projection, dogs and polar bears, for instance, roughing it up without injuring one another. Even rather primitive insects and animals somehow have ways of "imagining" where they ought to go. But only man builds interiorly vast imaginative structures of meaning, employing images and narrative to widen, deepen, and complicate a vision of great sweep, and even of the Ultimate.

I shall set the scene for discussing fantasy by invoking the mythmaking that allows human beings to establish some intellectual and emotional control over the largest scene we can embrace. With that context sketched out, I shall focus in on the human capacity to create works of art of all scales. I shall call attention particularly to our creation of symbols of all kinds that form the fabric of every scale of imagining, right up to those greatest myths and the struggle to find a language not totally hopeless for allowing revelation to speak through the prophet.

Mythmaking

Images are rather ethereal forms of stabilized incarnations of our cognitions, pro-jected into the future based on a past we are further elaborating. A myth is a story about personages and events that is meant to capture the sense of certain paradigmatic relationships that have meaning for our lives, transcending the world of the everyday obvious. Myths are sometimes about persons who actually existed, who may become archetypes for our emulation ("mythically embellished heroes"), and events that actually happened but are treated as material for the story ("mythically enhanced history"), intended to have meaning far exceeding the concrete historical limits of the event itself. Sometimes myths are about what I would like some real person, or persons, to be. This is not to be confused with sheer fantasizing. As the term is meant here, the myth is intended to be about truth. When the story veers off into the irrelevant or the merely fanciful fluff of a "fairy tale" it ceases to be myth and is just fiction, perhaps a story told just for fun or to vent certain emotions. Myth, properly speaking, is serious business, a way of exploring imaginatively what is in the mysterious depths of the human, and in the human-divine relation.

Reinhold Schneider described the role of myth in forging our historical understanding, and he understood how history itself generates such powerful images. Sometimes history forms images that stand above the ages with the power of allegories. They have a deep meaning; indeed, they are as impossible to interpret exhaustively as is the word of one endowed with grace, almost like a revealed word. If we penetrate more deeply into history we shall find that it is very rich in such images, which use the means of earthly reality to express the reality that lies beyond this world and make visible the substance of an epoch in its relation to eternity, often anticipating this; perhaps it would be possible to summarize the history of peoples and the salvation history hidden in this, in such images, out of which the directing spirit itself seems to speak.

Paul Ricoeur considers the great myths as necessary for full global expression of human consciousness. They can be "pre-history within history," capturing primordial experiences that peoples may have first performed as rites, celebrating the people's experience, before a story is extracted and perhaps embellished by a poetic genius. So profound and exalted can these myths be, they entice some critics, such as Schneider, to speak of "revelation," expressing a primordial human need for the infinite ground to cross the gap to lead mankind where it wants it to go.

I shall insist that dream, myth, and revelation, while closely related in the imagination, need to be carefully distinguished. Myths seem to uncover the structure of man in the original experience of creation and redemption, of origin and destiny. In these great myths we discover the element of commitment on the part of interior man, applied to the body through which man opens onto all reality, expressed in pregnant symbols. Signs, corresponding to original needs (we only sign because we need to), move us to something other than themselves. Myths are about truth. So verification is here too an issue: myths are verified by being integrated into the whole of one's natural faith. Their truth is to be discerned in terms of authenticity: one's maximum openness to reality allows the myth to speak in its own terms, as a return to "primordial experience."

The decision to embrace the myth ought to be based in "original experi-ence," what Luigi Guissani calls the nucleus of original needs, especially the need driving the search for authenticity—the need for truth.

Reason requires understanding and judgment: "This is how it is with reality." The claim to prophesy or genuine revelation adds a singularly important dimension: belief that God has taken over, that the divine is speaking, using images formed in-spirationally in the mind of the prophet as his language. I shall go further in a moment with the crucial question of verification that I just raised again; we shall contemplate image and logos meeting at the profoundest level.

The poetic license of the mythmaker allows him to elaborate and embroider the dramatis personae but only to the end of bringing forces into confrontation and illumining their possible, credible relationships. Even a story woven just for fun, so not worthy to be called a myth but just a tale, normally has to have some degree of verisimilitude, but its "real-ism" can be pretty thin if that serves the aesthetic purpose—for instance, comic exaggeration. Or at the extreme it might even be "dada," deliberate, provocative nonsense (which usually hides and reveals a sense!). Serious myth, in contrast, gains in credibility by making sense through illumin-ing realities the listener can discover in his own experience. Images are completely open, unlike the fixed symbolism that understands them as something ultimate; they are as open "as the wound of existence from which they flow." The concept (as its very name indicates) is something that closes; the image is something that opens, because it points to the network of dynamic relationships that constitute the living reality that is depicted in the image.

Invocation of the wonder term *authenticity* should always remind us that the self *(autos)* stands in the middle of our struggle to see. A self-image can be a myth, a dream about who I am, want to be, and perhaps even could be. This is the sense in which a myth is not meant to be sheer fantasy but more an illumination and projection of possibilities. The young woman who is slaving through dry undergraduate introductory science courses because she sees herself someday a pediatrician loving little babies is living out a dream, one that may be a myth in an entirely healthy sense, illumining the sense of what she is doing.

The enormous modern ideological constructions as myths: the Puritan City of God; the Revolution and Dictatorship of the Proletariat; the Aryan Reaffirmation incorporated in the Third Reich; the People's Republic of China (based on that stirring vision, the Little Red Book); the Islamic

Republic of Iran—the list is long. Some of these are founded on belief in a revelation (the Puritan vision, the Islamic republic), others on claims of science (the dictatorship of the Proletariat, the People's Republic), others on purported great insight (Aryan superiority, which most people always believed to be errant nonsense and today is held only by a few marginalized individuals but for a brief moment in history helped mobilize armies and lead them to mass destruction). The false elements in a myth that can mobilize a people can be devastating. An anthropological principle: Never underestimate the power of myth!

Now, today, there is clearly insufficient evidence to settle the *Gigantomachia* of development myths. In contrast to this, Einstein's initial proposal of a theory of "special relativity," then a few years later fleshed out as "general relativity," was never a myth because, wide-sweeping and revolutionary as it was, the hypothesis consisted of a lucid mathematical demonstration of coherence making sense of all that was known on the level at which it is couched and providing indicators of where further research for verification could be directed. This has subsequently been carried out, successfully verifying the theory basically if not absolutely perfectly.

I do not mean to suggest that the fertility of these conflicting scientific myths, all three of which deserve to continue guiding searches for evidence, if they can, either invalidate or somehow justify patience with stories claiming to make sense out of human being as such. A different kind of evidence is claimed by the traditions of revelation. And a different, nonempirical level of thinking from a base of internal meditation is at work in the surviving natural religions, the most influential being Buddhism.

The student of human being should ask how belief in such stories can be responsible. I shall show a distinctive dimension in this regard in the Abrahamic traditions of revelation, one that goes beyond the mythologized, even in the ideologized forms they have displayed. This is necessary for anthropology, not only because the Abrahamic religions have changed the course of mankind, and the Christian core has influenced the birth of the powerful liberal democracies, but also because those prophetic traditions of revelation continue to be an intellectual challenge: they offer, I shall claim, the most significant—indeed, unsurpassable— teaching concerning love and its place in the human adventure.

Those kinds of accomplishments of the theistic traditions are due to the radical and self-conscious nature of their claim to transcend the merely mythological in their teaching. They claim to be compatible with genuine science, a foundational claim of utmost significance, if true. Mythical dimensions and elements in those traditions are in tension, but claim their most thoughtful proponents, not mythical at the core. In any event, it is a moving claim, still driving the *Gigantomachia*.

Artistic

The human being shares with the higher animals the quality of being essentially not only ex-pressive but, what is more, theatrical (meaning we are "show-offs" (Greek *theo*, to view). Since every intersubjective world is based in theater, let's go there in search of the artistic creation of very greater and more nuanced demonstrations of this showing off to one another.

Every act of expression is a little (and most of the time even banal) artistic creation, in the higher animal more constrained by his narrower built-in focus, in the infant human still very typical but soon blossoming into a wider gamut of gestures and, after experiments with unintelligible sounds, the uttering of meaningful words. From then on the treasure house of gestures and words—especially words—fills ever more rapidly. Every scene subsequently draws from the actor's personal treasure house of symbols, applied with more or less creativity to the situation. This can be done either with the intent of steering the unfolding drama in a desired direction or just "venting"—but in all cases with an intelligible content at the core. "What a rotten damned mess this is!" shouts the frustrated chef de cuisine who has just ruined the main dish. He is not intent on bringing new light to the situation but rather enjoying some emotional release.

When the intentional expressive act involves a "making"—the forming of some matter to achieve a cultural object that will display a sentiment or provide an instrument for completing some desired process—then we are likely to be more aware of its artisan (not just its artistic) reality. Would the reader kindly undertake here another experiment: Watch just for one day how much (often mediocre) art, requiring (mostly routine, banal) imagination is at work in managing the little scenes of everyday life. Catch your and the others' expressions at work trying to point you in some direction or to achieve a soothing, or whatever. Notice gestures, especially body language, as well as words and other symbols. I believe you will be astonished by just how rich, if largely banal, is the vocabulary of words, gestures, and psychological maneuvers. Note how dynamic their use. These "performing arts" situations of everyday life are not *ars gratia artis*—"art for art's sake"—but are in the service of something transcending "mere art." "Art" apt to show forth even the divine? But certainly too the moral evil of sinister manipulation.

The Fine Arts

In some cultures human beings have been able to seize on the matter of everyday drama and build it into grand works of "the fine arts"—religious theater from the Greeks and Romans, including magnificent temples; medieval religious drama; modern psychological soul-searchers; and, more recent in its invention, the novel. (A few great novels preceded psychiatry. The late arrival of the novel raises the question of what there is about "modernity's" discovery of subjectivity that called for these radical inventions, novel and psychiatry.) A novel or a play can be admired for the beauty of its language, and its story can be just fun. But if the artist is serious, the story will bring out intriguing possibilities in certain human situations with earnest implications, showing forth mysterious depth of penetration into human being, both the interior psyche and the rich implications of the social. (Recall, the early religious myths started this.) The novelist and the dramatist will dynamically create images, from an instinctive feel for the dynamic, the twists and turns of development the story could take. He can show us how the cultural objects that "orchestrate" a scene—not just the tones with which lines are delivered but how clothing, furniture, artistic objects, and the light and air of the day all work to provide a theatrical setting. That is why I have mentioned fiction first among the "fine arts"—because it is so close to the art of the present era's self-conscious, everyday social encounter. Poetry in this larger sense, embracing prose fiction, lies closest of all works of artistic imagination to the foundational in man, both his corporeal insertion into the social on the "cosmic" plane and his interior life. Poetry in this large sense reveals, more than any of our other methodic endeavors, how the corporeal and the spiritual interpenetrate. (Music, as we shall see, can achieve insights from motion, "voices," human and instrumental, but does not have the definiteness of expression of verbal or written language. (Poetry expressed through music is another story.)

"Phenomenology," as it has flowered, had to be preceded by the achievements of the post-seventeenth-century novel and "psychosomatic" poetry. Both came out of the "subjectivist turn," so apparent in

Montaigne and then distorted by Descartes in the seventeenth century. Was it the rapidity of social change introduced by the surge forward of the bourgeois class—recall the rise of "humanism" already in the fifteenth century, contributing in the sixteenth to the Protestant Revolt—that led to ever more intense subjectivist introspection?

The sagas of old and the great tragedies and the archetypal novels unveil worlds created by the mythmaker, each a realm of being with its own interior dynamism, able to draw us in, making of us dwellers in a new socio- and interior reality with its own peculiar radiance. These poetic explorations of the emotive interiority suggested and nourished a more dramatic and sweeping form in music.

Every display of great beauty in whatever form produces an *"Aha! Erlebnisse"*—a sense that here stands revealed something transcending the language of its revelation, something exquisitely, accurately, and penetratingly observed. This is so true that the very language crafted for the revelation of the newly discovered, which has become a joy and a power unto itself, plays in, through, and perhaps to some degree in rivalry with the being in itself of the object described. Consider two examples: Once again this morning I marveled at the small still-life painting in our dining room, illumined by the rising sun: a cluster of fat wine-dark grapes, a wedge of Madonna House cheese sitting on a carefully arranged piece of stiff folded parchment, partly turned in a way that added movement. I asked my wife, "Why do people like Dona Surprenant spend their precious time doing things like that? It's not original—an imitation of Chardin." "It's beautiful: that's what time is for, to see and to teach others to see," she answered without looking up from the morning paper. That little painting ought to teach people to contemplate the beauty of things, natural and man-made. The language used in the painting is a joy unto itself—how those grapes can exude reality—realer than real, and how the tan stiff parchment could be executed with such necessary crinkles and with tiny suggestions of green showing through the predominating yellow. I never tire of looking at that little window onto reality revealed in its depths. The second example is the insurmountable apparent contradictions in certain important details within the five gospels (five if you include the works of Paul). This can be taken as inconsistencies warning us that these accounts are not strictly exact, or they can be seen as a device through which the divine sends us beyond the finite to the incomprehensible infinite, the very tensions created by differing approaches emitting sparks of meaning. (Henri de Lubac wrote three tomes on the paradoxes

found in the holy texts.) In the most splendid works the display of beauty
is achieved with a balance between the means, each of which may be
tempted to become "show-off," and between the means and that which
the expressive devices have actually allowed to be revealed.

Since writing the above comments on the little still-life, I was invited
to an exhibition of the Hermitage collection around Catherine the Great.
I was surprised by the technical perfection of the artists. But every work
was so loaded with things and spectacular displays of the persons por-
trayed, it was overwhelming. The ontological difference between those
large, rich canvases contrasted with the little still-life shows very different ways to admire very different things. The outrageous Empress of All
the Russias and Miss Surprenant's cheese chunk and a few grapes demonstrate radically different views onto reality.

Observing the tensions in every work of art, from an intense conversation to the theological reconciliation of the gospel accounts, we
can see interacting the two fundamentals of human being, "the cor-
poreal-cosmic" and "the tending-to-transcend." At every reprise we
should recall that human being strives to transcend, reaching horizontally again and again into the past and pushing out toward "the yet to
come," to embrace all created reality, and vertically, either striving to
climb upward toward the Transcendent Source itself or receptively responding to the call of those who claim to be prophetic, opening beyond
the merely cosmic.

Sometimes a genial mind will "blast open a hole," like the famous
"bubble" cosmologists hypothesize happened in the explosion of a
"supernova": by blowing away most of the obscuring gases the explod-
ing star opened a "hole" of relatively slight obscurity through which we
can receive the revealing data of the greater universe. Of all artistic fantasy the least "ballasted" by the demands of surface realities is so-called
abstract painting and sculpture and instrumental music. Even the most
"representative" "realistic" painting and sculpture abstract a certain form
from the inexhaustible richness presented by visual perception. But the
so-called abstract arts are more abstract than that: in the "most abstract"
arts, only minute aspects of natural form and color are selected to have
recombined their dimensions and textures, so that they glow in ways
different from anything in nature. (Recall the frank assertion of primary
colors by Picasso, Miró, and Chagall.) In inventive ways the artist opens
new vistas of the possible. A sense of freedom prevails—a freedom that
can give us the shivers by its closeness to "liberalism's" deformed notion

of freedom as "freedom from . . ."—freedom from the ineluctable constraints of reality. The most abstract art (including instrumental music)
makes it appear that "the sky is the limit."

Music, which does not stop at appearing to move (on the music paper
fixed symbols guide performance, and when performed the music is
dynamic), is the most emotional of all man's artistic creations. I am assuming here that poetry and theater are essentially musical. The unfolding of
the dialogue or the movement of the melodic line, the surges of "dynamics" (as crescendos mounting to the strongest [fortissimo!], actors shouting, then diminishing to a whisper [pianissimo!]), and the changing
cadences of rhythms evoke the profound emotional surges of our experience, resonating with our living *Ek-sistenz* as we push forward through
time and space, polemically seeking to domesticate tense in-flooding and
upsurging forces.

The creative musical imagination working with the text of a song, having interpreted the meaning of the words and the emotions they evoke,
translates those sentiments into sounds that go beyond a traditional language's music. As with each kind of imagining, we notice the unique
ways in which sound enwraps us in reality—for instance, the rising and
falling of a strong gust of wind, the quiet, almost purring sound of a voice
cajoling one, all the rhythms of various beats transmitting the chuffing of
a steam engine, the rum-rum-rum of a four-cycle diesel, contrasted with
the accelerating whine of a jet engine revving up. Music cannot transmit the textures of touch, but it can weave textures of sound, drawing
on different exquisite instruments lovingly developed to deliver sounds
indescribably interesting and vibrant, interrelating in all the ways the
great "orchestrators" (Wagner, Mahler, Stravinsky, Ravel) have invented.
(Highly colored music is very recent.)

In staging a drama the director chooses his cast with attention not only
to voice but also to *Gestalt*. (Bent on finding the finest voices, there was an
era when opera directors overlooked the improbable *Gestalten* of many
a great singer!) In an opera all the aspects of drama are enlivened by the
capabilities of music. Anyone who has sojourned long in the desert of
phonograph recordings rediscovers with delight at a "live" performance,
opera or only instrumental, that not only does one hear 250 percent more
"overtones," but the beauty of the instruments and of the movement of
the musicians playing provides a full experience. The "live" concert is
truly alive. Music unfolds in time, theme stated after theme, arousing
expectations of development, and development often followed, as in the

classic "sonata" form, by a summing-up synthesis, *polemos* ("climax" in the drama) ending in resolution, but sometimes in terminal explosion.

The dynamic structural forms that composers have invented suggest the vital processes of the organic kingdom. I recall my association of the Samuel Barber *Adagio* with the Kennedy assassination (recall, I was in Germany that night), or all the history that surges up with the triumphal blast of *La Marseillaise*, or examine the structure of the Gettysburg Address. The mysterious, pregnant, emotive, imaginative symbolic connections reveal some of the obscure rhythms and colors of human being when the artist sets them vibrating.

My mind's eye sees in a given work a formal dynamic structure, and dimly grasps something of how it operates, including its essential relation with the emotions the music is arousing. In the Barber *Adagio* example, upon reflection I was able to find some verbal symbols expressing concepts fixing the dynamics (*sweeping, addictive, mysterious sadness,* and even *adagio,* which classifies the piece within familiar musical forms). Each of these terms relates the work potentially to different departments of life via concepts that reach into nonmusical realms (a "sweeping" view provided by distant prairie horizons centers the movement in the all-around gazing observer). Was this extra effort of expressing verbally the effect of a piece of music a valid intellectual way to obtain a more permanent and "relatable" hold on the actual emotions? I raise this question as a means of reminding yet again that every form of imagination reveals not only its bodily dimensions ("reverberations") but also the potential intelligibility of whatever it presents to the mind's eye. This insight is there along with the peculiarity of the object's own materials—in the case of music, the wonderful world of sounds; in the music of the drama, the full human *Gestalt* in motion. A drama is not only music but also restrained dance.

Drama and the cinema, as I suggested, are like vocal music, but in the case of songs and cantatas and operas the music carries, expresses, and enhances the sense of the words, whereas in the cinema or the drama there may be for much of the piece no music as such but only the music-like flow and surge and ebb and polyphonic interplay of dialogue, and the physical movement of the actors and, in film, the considerable flexibility of the camera, able to paint atmospheres and backgrounds, including immense landscapes, like no other art.

It is significant that most cineastes demand musical enhancement. It comes naturally, and even the staging of most plays involves some music. It is also significant that the "canned" music accompanying our daily lives more often distracts us and dulls our general receptivity than enhances and orchestrates, as quality music well chosen can. In film and on stage the writer and director may take a page from humble everyday life and immortalize it. Early in one of Michel Tremblay's plays about Quebec working-class life, the scene, set around a kitchen table, rapidly degenerates into a roaring argument over the relative merits of "le peanut butter smooth" versus "le peanut butter crunchy." The very act of lifting the most banal of little tableaux from boring life and canonizing it by making it part of the rigorously insisted-upon bits of dialogue and direction in a DRAMA transforms into immortal ART a moment that in real life passes quickly. Believe it or not, GOOD art: through the most banal of the banal Tremblay can reveal the tragedy and the hilarity of human lives, allowing the face of love to shine through. The imagination is the great transposer. The mind's imaginative eye can feel out in little scenes and unpretentious things the incongruities that the critical reflection has yet to muse about explicitly, and then, by transforming them ironically to wildly different settings, bring us to admire them. From that point, more critical, more methodical, hence more philosophical thinking can move forward.

To drive home just how absorbingly human and divine music can be, I would remind the reader of the intertwining development of the Christian liturgy. The New Testament evidences the singing of psalms from the earliest Eucharistic celebrations. To this day the liturgies of the Orthodox traditions are sung from beginning to end, and the whole Christian life is built around liturgies, with the chanting of the monks providing the most thorough musicalization of human life one can find anywhere.

The art that is obliged to stay in closest touch with reality is architecture. Consequently, in no other art is the danger of "art by committee" so real, in no other "fine art" is the imagination forced into such discouraging constraints. That is in part due to the very limited physical, nonliving way a building sits in the cosmos. You can train a dog to do tricks; the building is just going to sit there unable to strive against the pull of gravity. But, nevertheless, the building is a work for social use, which the dwellers should be able to count on and enjoy. When the wife of the wealthy patron who commissioned Frank Lloyd Wright to build arguably the most glorious modern home ever conceived, Falling Waters, complained about the bright red of the salon, Wright shot back, "You'll get used to it!" The danger is just as grave that the architect will be so taken with his "statement" that the building ends up being uncomfortable to the occupants. (Or, as happened with Falling Waters, requiring millions of dollars of structural underpinning because the "anticommittee" Wright refused to listen to the structural engineer.) A similar tension inflicts *Gebrauchsmusik,* as Paul Hindemith termed works written not just to be played but to be used. *La Marseillaise* is an example of splendidly successful *Gebrauchsmusik,* as, I suppose, are all those cantatas J. S. Bach wrote for use Sunday after Sunday in the Thomaskirche.

At some point the artist declares the work finished, his once-and-for-all performance at an end. But the spectator or reader or listener now in turn becomes a coperformer: on the basis of what the artist has made available, the recipient has to imagine what the artist may have meant. Unlike a conversation, where the listener can break in and ask for clarification, the audience is for the moment on its own to make out what it can from the canvas or the printed page of poetry or the singing and playing.

With the performing arts the interplay of imaginations triples. The director, or simply the performer in a solo concert, takes the indications presented by the artwork as directions, but just as any interpreter of a nonperforming artwork has a sovereign freedom to twist his interpretation, ignoring clear indications on page or canvas, so can the director or performing artist. In all instances, from the little commedia dell'arte of a conversation to the vast Met performance of *Der Rosenkavalier,* there is active an interplay of imaginations with varying degrees of possibility for the artist to correct ex-press misinterpretation by the receiver.

All use of the human imagination is dynamic, future-opening, and most of it is intersubjective, some of that being dialogical. But in the quest to express and to receive meaning, an element of intellectual honesty must be at play.

Fantasy for Fun and Escape

Even to mention the greatest music and drama in the same breath with fantasy for fun and distraction is close to blasphemy. But the sad truth (I find it so, anyway) is that the entire popular entertainment industry (if you throw in tourism it is the largest industry today!) lives off just that, fun and distraction. Play and recreation are essential to *Homo sapiens* because he is essentially also *Homo ludens.* Re-creation! As with everything else essential to human being, how and at what, and when, one plays affects health, physical and mental: play can be wise or unwise.

The new media have swept onto the contemporary scene, bringing staggering effects. Beginning with the daily newspaper in the mid-nine-teenth century, this happened so swiftly, the flowing in of exponentially greater quantities and new qualities of data and information, that it continues to escape anyone's ability to sense the extent and complexity of its impacts. Take an example: who can measure the extent to which "organized, professional" sports absorb relatively peacefully bellicose tendencies in certain kinds of people?

Privileged to discussions with Marshall McLuhan for two decades and since his untimely death, reading the prophets of the high-tech, virtual world to whom he introduced me, all the while observing my children and students struggling in the Brave New World, I find it frustrating to reflect in the midst of one of the great "state changes" in all of human existence. The *poiein*, at the heart of all that, is without precedence in vitality and variety in the history of mankind, imagination run rampant. Some exalted pundits insist our best option is to get clearer about what we want and then use our creative imaginations to spin a satisfying fantasy. That challenge gives all the more reason to appropriate critically, authentically, our intellectual capabilities. This lies at the heart of education.

Ursula Franklin has often commented on the fact that technology has a double effect. On the one hand, it facilitates communication, making it easier, more accessible, and more rapid. On the other hand, the way in which technology is delivered and the way people interact with it as an essentially anonymous interface alienate people more and more from one another. Younger people, for example, are often lonelier because the face-to-face community that is necessary for human well-being is compromised by new computer technologies. Consequently, when educating people with new technologies, one must become aware of their shortcomings, but one must also be active in trying to stem the alienating effects of technology, which eat away at a society's social and cultural fabric.

The elaborate distractions of our high-tech, virtual world have reached grotesque proportions, threatening human well-being. For example, the extremes of virtual reality found in films using computer-generated "special effects" offer the supreme case of artificial nonnarcotic titillation generated to distract. Putting it in that sour way suggests a connection with sex used for the same purpose.

How do we describe in a general way the margin separating justifiable, needed relaxation, with its element of restful distraction, and the "denial" involved in gutless escape from the reality one should be facing up to? For instance, those fanatics ("fans") who neglect work and family through obsession with following sporting events or frequenting gambling casinos provide the summit of the absurd. Playing a game of tennis for exercise, of chess for mind exercise and change of scene, or games that invite creative use of the imagination, and all of these nonobsessively, all capable of bringing friends together, each in its proper place and time, is obviously healthy. But virtual reality effects (not just violent impacts of video games but the recorded music pounding savage beats and violent lyrics screamed through iPod earphones) invite to escape.

Dreams

If one defines the imagination as that cognitive power that, in conjunction with the intellect, and to the extent it is fully human, at least partially directed by the will, produces images, then dreams may not belong in the category "imagination" at all! Although also made up of a stream of images, and although, as we can see when we struggle to remember what we have experienced during a dream state, showing signs of a strange contribution of intellect and a bizarre sort of reasoning, the awakened dreamer realizes he has been taken over by the dreams rather than being in any way master of how they have unfolded. Generally, we feel quite unresponsible for them. From there to go on and assert, however, that we have no responsibility for them whatsoever would be wrong. We recognize that our reactions to past experiences, some of those reactions containing a voluntary dimension, can contribute to the dreams. We see that our dreams are revealing something about what is going on in us emotionally (and hence with a cognitive element), however slight may have been our voluntary contribution to the building materials of the particular dream.

Dreams vary not only in emotional intensity but also in richness and suggestiveness of content, and in credibility in this sense: some dreams grab us as though they were reality itself, but others as we recall them seem to us to have been unbelieved all along. Many persons have reported dreams of incredibly rich symbolism. Some have further insisted that some such dreams were genuine prophesy: inspirations received in dreams. At the other extreme are dreams with almost no hold on us.

Recently, I reported a simple dream to my wife because it appeared to have no relation whatsoever to anything I have done or would ever likely do: a simple overseeing of the preparation of a culinary dish. Two weeks later I do not remember what the dish was, only that it seemed totally uninteresting—not actively boring, just banal, in a word meaningless. But it seemed to me the dream had been clear, although of almost zero emotional intensity. Even the dream's apparent monumental irrelevance does not seem to be a point of interest! I do not believe it was about "irrelevancy," or "boring," or anything at all! I would hazard the guess that some of this nocturnal playing around on the part of the brain is related to some sort of physiological release, and its "transcendent meaning" is of no further interest.

A person will sometimes go to sleep having wrestled for days with a problem and awaken to find that he has dreamed a solution. Most of us, most of the time, find it difficult to remember our dreams very well, to the point of philosophers wondering whether the remembering at the moment of awakening is not in fact all there really is to the dream. When that memory is clearer than usual, we will often be astonished by the bizarre conjunctions of themes, personalities, and events, and the jumps between them. We may be inclined, perhaps erroneously, to believe the struggling dream went on for an hour. It remains puzzling that sleep allows the brain to engage in activities, aspects of which we are some of the time more or less clearly aware, different from "daydreaming," which tends most of the time to be far more coherent and explicable as to content than "night dreams" when sleeping.

The Role of Imagination in Prophetic Revelation and Its Relation to, and Contrast with, Dreams

As I pointed out earlier, many thoughtful people in our time do not believe that genuine prophetic revelation exists: they are convinced there are no inspirations originating in a divine initiative. But most of the honest skeptics, of course, do acknowledge there are many phantoms of thought that have their origins in the involuntary carryings-on of our brain in the sleeping-dream state.

Those who believe in the authenticity of certain revelations may reject critically other purported revelations in their own tradition, and often all the revelations of other than THE one true tradition, if they are so inclined. Since the issue I am raising here, unlike in dreams, is centrally truth, criteria for discerning genuine revelations (if any) should be well grounded in reality and the experience of somehow palpable things. For nonbelievers in "revelations" and "prophesies" per se, these phenomena are nevertheless readily acknowledged to be indeed most imaginative—the imagination of pure fantasizing is at work, moved, to be sure, by meaningful emotional needs. Some of the most interesting studies of ancient myths and prophesies are the work of archaeologists and literary critics who share no transcendent religion.

This brief survey is not the place to launch a debate about the possible existence of genuine revelations, whether in the dream state or while awake. But given the importance of the Hebraic-Judaic roots of the civilization that has contributed in spawning the present world, the Church's carrying forward and outward the fruits of Hebraic, Greek, and Roman culture into that modernity from which we now spring, with due attention to the origins and interactions and the historical role and the present vast challenge of Islam (not to forget the vitality of Judaism), there are many reasons in an anthropology stressing the effect of changing worlds on human being. If we are going to make sense of human being, eventually we have to take up certain of the most significant challenges posed by the purported revelations of the great traditions, instead of dismissing with a wave of the hand the whole vast reality of "revelation."

Romano Guardini explores the critical difference between dream and revelation using a concrete instance of purported revelation. To stake out a place in a discussion of the imagination for the important issue of the discrimination of dream and revelation I shall paraphrase a passage from his classic work, *The Lord*, where the theologian is introducing the Book of Revelation, the vision of Saint John the Apostle, the text with which the New Testament ends.[1] It is by far the most dreamlike element in the entire Bible. Revelation, Guardini declares, is "a book of consolation," in which God, instead of suspending the hard realities of history, offers the ultimate hope, the transcendence of this world, which alone renders bearable its pain (which includes for all of us death). At the end of this anthropology I shall recall that fundamental to the profoundest human yearnings is the desire for peace not to be confused with oblivion: *Dona nobis pacem!* rings out the cry just before receiving the mystical risen sacramental body and blood of Christ at the mass. The "consolation" sought is not the everlasting thundering silence and disintegration of the tomb. The suicide is seeking not consolation but annihilation. The peace revealed is the fullness of life as the person rises to live in the balanced dynamics of the Trinitarian life of Father, Son, and Holy Spirit.

1. Romano Guardini, *The Lord* (Chicago: H. Regnery, 1954).

The consolation of the Book of Revelation is rendered neither in theological argument nor in summaries of future history nor in practical maxims but in images and symbolic events. These can, of course, be approached intellectually, digging into the secrets of numerology (the significance of seven, or of four-and-twenty) or into the symbolism of gems (of jasper and beryl and onyx) or the meaning behind animal forms (lamb and dragon). But that would be to ignore what John tells us at the start, that he has been "transported in the spirit": the images are visions.

How, asks Guardini, can a slaughtered lamb live? How can it have seven horns and seven eyes? It helps a little to say this is a symbol of Christ: He had died and was resurrected; was dead, therefore, yet alive. He who sees all things has seven eyes, because seven is the sacred number of entirety, and the seven horns represent perfect power. Guardini comments, "All this is correct, yet remains lifeless and non-essential. Where but in dreams do we find in our experience such strange things?"

We could encounter such a being in dreams, and though the mind protested, a knowledge deep within us would be satisfied. Why? Because in dreams the substance of things disappears, a profounder vitality emerges, seizes the forms of things, and transforms them—and not only as the artist's fantasy, always conditioned by ambient reality, transforms, but so that the very limits of the possible and impossible cease to exist. Critical reason is silenced; the ebb and flow of the inner life hold sway. The hidden will of the senses, the intrinsic meanings of existence to which the waking consciousness pays little attention, prevails. All this labors with tangible forms, reveals itself in them half-veiled yet shimmering through the veil. Somehow initiated, the "inner man" of the sleeper feels the message of the image even when he is incapable of expressing it.

So much for the dream. Something similar happens in a vision, but with the essential difference that it is determined from "above," from God. It is not the product of sleep's relaxation, in which the mind and its criticism, the will and its control, are suspended. Here the spirit of God seizes a person, lifts him out of himself, and makes him the instrument of something beyond the reaches of human judgment and will. Everything—the raw material of general existence, the personal life of the prophet, things, events, images—is utilized by the divine spirit as means of expression.

In dream, man's imagination functions in the service of some obscure impulse. In the vision, the spirit of God transforms the shapes of earthly existence to express a divine idea. Such images stand in an atmosphere, are of a quality, move in a manner as different from those of human existence as the state of sleep is different from that of wakefulness. The images in a vision emerge from a stream of omnipotence; they fluctuate, merge, and sink back into the flow. What they reveal is the mystery of an unutterably holy life of fulfillment beyond all measure, of an inexpressible coming, a transforming and perfecting through God: the completely "new."

In dreams the barrier between here and beyond, between self and others, falls. One vitalizing current streams through all things, and the dreamer feels both intimately related to all that he beholds and a stranger to it. In his dreams he encounters, startled into recognition, his profoundest, most intimate, and unknown self. What he beholds is a book that holds the whole meaning of his life and its integrity, or perhaps a lamp stand (both images, the book that cannot be unsealed and the golden lamp stand are used by John), and someone says: "That is the person you love. That is your happiness. If the candlestick were to fall, your joy would be shattered!" He would not say, "The candle's flame is a symbol of your happiness, because happiness is bright and warm and vulnerable as the flame," but rather, "The flame is your happiness!" For the visionary it is much the same, save that he does not experience in dream but "in the spirit." And what streams through him and the images he beholds is not natural life with all its instincts, hopes, and terrors but the new sacred life from God. To understand the Book of Revelation one must free oneself from the notion of the rigidity of things; gradually animated, they must mingle and flow, and the reader must surrender to their movement. He must entrust the things of daily life to its power, quietly following its course. He must learn to listen, to be docile of spirit, accepting the images as they come, opening his heart to their meaning, harmonizing all his being with them. The degree of understanding willed by God will be his.

If genuine revelation exists, then, obviously, there would be no more important question confronting man than how one comes to discern genuine from pseudoprophesy. At the heart of wisdom lie these two challenges: Is there genuine revelation? And how does one discern its genuineness? If not, does one then dismiss as fairy tales all the "prophetic" foundations of the civilization-forming theistic traditions? Or even then, do they contain glimpses into the depths of the human soul that are valuable for us to recover?

As wisdom itself will be the theme of the next chapter, dedicated to an overview of the entire gamut of our cognitive capabilities, and as wisdom stands at the center of this study, that chapter will be pivotal. Before turning to it there remains one more form of imagination to be accorded a place, a very important image, rightly reserved for the last, and tied to the question of our criteria for distinguishing sheer fantasy from sound creative imagination: self-image.

Self-Imaging, with Dimensions of Mythmaking: Building a Picture of Who I Am in Function of What I Want to Be and What I Believe I Have Already Become

With the search for wisdom situated at the desirable focal point of human activity, it can be argued at the same time that there is no more central part of one's natural faith than his self-image. One integrates into the image he keeps updating of another person much of what he has been able to observe about the other. But into my own self-image is likely to be integrated an important part of all my experience of everything, to whatever extent and for whatever reason I have come to believe it important to me . . . to who I am, to my personal world, to where I want to go, a vast and complex affair, much of it not subjected to sufficient critical scrutiny.

The self-image is unique, not only because it evolves constantly, parts of it growing intermittently hot and cold all day every day, but because even our dreams of who we want to become do not leave us alone! What is felt at this core of who I think I am is experience more intense and complex than any other. Only our images of those with whom we are most intimate—one's wife and children, and, for the seriously prayerful, the image of God—are in any way comparable. We are not "detached" about any aspect of our self-image, as obviously it motivates and molds our emotions more than any other image.

I suggested a moment ago that a self-image can be a myth, even a rather floating, almost entirely uncritical dream about who I am, want to be, and perhaps even could be. As a myth should not be sheer fantasy but more an illumination and projection of possibilities, the closer I am to the truth of what I have been and the more realizable the dream of who I could be, the vision calling genuinely for serious growth, then with all that comes the sounder myth.

But does it really make sense to say I imagine what I want? Something that can be, as wanting, is both now (I do want right now to stop my writing to go get a glass of water) and future-oriented (I do not possess now that specific something, but if I really want it, then I should be taking steps to obtain it, launching processes I can imagine, like walking out to the kitchen and opening the tap). If I only fantasize that I want something ("Oh, how nice to become a saint") and go on living in ways that are incompatible with the dream, then there is something confused in my self-image, a discrepancy between "levels" in my being, an imagining that in its fantasy is unhealthy, in a word inauthentic (in the narrow sense). Consider an example of a rather typical and serious failure of one's image of himself to jibe with the facts of his life, past or present: for convoluted reasons a person may believe himself to have been a neglected child, while everyone who knows his past is convinced that, on the contrary, his mother showered him with too much attention, inviting him to remain very self-centered. Later, when it was no longer possible for her to lavish so much time and attention, he reacted by inventing (and believing) the neglected-child scenario.

Obviously central in psychology and psychiatry, self-image could well be the pivotal symbol around which to elaborate an entire anthropology. However, that would be unwise. Development of the theoretical sense of self should involve not only reflection on concrete intersubjective human interactions but also explicit expression of the philosopher's belief about the truth of authentic (in the large sense) ultimate horizons so far as he is able to glimpse them. We are talking about human being, recall, not just the twists and turns of particular lives. Reflection on being requires a direct approach to the challenges of the claims regarding vertical transcendence (if only to assess the sociopathology that generates belief in ungenuine prophetic vision in various great traditions) as well as the horizontal horizons of *ek-sistential* time. I hope the reader by now understands that structuring our lives are these two transcendental sets of horizons: vertical and horizontal. It can scarcely be denied that most of mankind bathes in a fog of mythical creation, so the critical philosopher needs at least to show to what this leads in the human tragedy.

Obviously, there will be much more about self and self-image in this study. In the present chapter's discussion of imagination I have offered a brief catalog of kinds of imagination. I have also tried to show how imagination operates in various human undertakings, informing the way these undertakings have unfolded throughout the history of human being but also in individual human beings. Individual persons create and contribute to the larger reality of human being, but they are also informed by it. There is a reciprocal and mutually informing and conditioning relation between the individual and the larger reality of human being that is developed, collected, and advanced in time.

5

ANALOGICAL THINKING AS A TOOL FOR UNDERSTANDING

In *Being and Truth*, I outlined an epistemology necessary for the appropriation of being. Here, the emphasis is not so much on a model of cognition that typifies human being in general. Rather, I wish to look at a specific cognitive tool that allows us to understand the being of multiple worlds and the beings in these multiple worlds, including human being in general and an ultimate Being, namely, God. Here, I wish to examine analogical thinking to show how it is that we experience the real unity of various worlds and intersubjective relations. This unity is foundational in order to begin to be able to understand ourselves as human beings but also to comprehend the larger legacy of human being through the ages. Analogical thinking is also important in order to grasp questions of ultimate meaning and purpose, which are central for the unfolding and development of our own individual human being but also human being in general.

WHAT WE NEED TO KNOW

In struggling to illumine the *appropriate use* of our human cognitive capabilities, we are confronted by an existential paradox: on the one hand, "appropriateness" can be judged finally only in light of what we know of the ultimate context, but, on the other hand, most of our judgments are made in narrow contexts, that "artificial isolation of partial aspects of wholes" that Karl Stern laments is unavoidable as we go through each day dealing with one practical concern after another. The pressing demands of practical concerns most often justify "specialization": a little local problem, simple conceptual analysis, quick and limited action in a context we commonsensically take for granted. Moreover, these are familiar contexts furnished with familiar things, providing a sense of being at home.

Allow me to formulate again this central truth: one of mankind's most urgent needs is fostering attitudes of authenticity that motivate the wise to move beyond narrow horizons in one's construction of ultimate contexts, subjective and objective. Those attitudes are genuine only when accompanied by the disciplines of research and contemplation. In the throes of action, we are so absorbed in the immediately presencing objects that we are oblivious even to issues "just over the horizon." The rest gets consigned to "philosophical issues" that belong to the academy, and meanwhile will have to wait for a rainy day. The "man on the street" wonders how the philosopher can suppose anyone ever has time and talent enough to deal with those vast questions, issues such as the implied ultimate "in itself" objective structure of being, the subjective outer limits of my own personal wisdom, or the potential contained in the stored-up collective memory of mankind.

On top of all that, there is the gravest of problems, the one raised by thinkers like Karl Stern, of the inadequacies, perhaps catastrophic, of what functions uncritically as our personal practical "ultimate context." The ambiguity hidden in the notion "the ultimate context of the true" adds to the dilemma with which we must now wrestle. Does that mean the ultimate context "so far as I know it," with emphasis on my field of meaning fueled by my limited expertise, or does it mean that "collective human memory" stored in libraries and data banks, or does "ultimate context" mean the very fact that a given human act (including the act of thinking a thought) is, and so manifests, a part of reality, which then logically invites our gaze to look into the past? Does this partly account for the event, further forward to what can be glimpsed to be coming deeper into the cosmic foundations of whatever the reality with which we are trying to cope?

It will prove helpful to pull the dimensions of the ambiguity together: each human act, by adding to reality, reveals yet more about the objective reality of either or both the cosmos that made it possible and one's "interior life" within which knowledge of it happens. Every act has the potential of enlarging the person's and, therefore, humankind's understanding of reality. In this subjective-objective bipolarity, there hangs not "the tale" but the difficulty of taking hold of "the practical tail" of "appropriateness."

LURKS THERE "AN ULTIMATE MEANING"?

Most human beings never reflect deliberately on the concept of being, but implicitly they can take for granted that it applies to every manner of entity. This suggests that a network of all kinds of relationships between things constitutes some sort of all-inclusive reality relevant to, and having to do with, the sustenance of all things. What might account for the ultimate meaning's unity and its contribution of relationship between every thing and every person who is, or ever may be, or ever will be? Even though most people never make these kinds of questions the object of serious, explicit contemplation, still the challenge of "the sense of it all," or of the ultimate goal, or even of the nature of the path I am in fact following—"Where am I going? My life is meaningless. I am just surviving"—"lurks" in the background, offering itself clearly enough to be unmistakably there the instant one is willing to attend seriously to any issues of "ultimate" meaning.

As we inch toward the question of ultimate meaning, is it advisable to go one step further and assert that all mature healthy human beings have a need to attend to the question of "the sense of it all," of "the ultimate context," of "the path," of "the source of unity," expressing the implication, the feeling of, *the unity of being*? That question is inevitable once one raises the issue of the appropriate use of our cognitive faculties. Are we, by virtue of our extraordinary natures—the sweep and creativity of the human being—meant to raise explicitly the question of "the sense of it all" and, hence, the question of "how are we to know that unity"? If that were to be the case, assuming the vast majority never plunge into ontological speculation, then the need to contemplate the whole is perhaps almost always suppressed. We may be enticed from moment to moment to give into other more pressing, narrower passions centered on "compact" objects in narrowly focused ways.

Concretely, realistically, how often do you ask critically, searchingly, "Just how does the path I am following relate to the very different path being followed by another, perhaps a fervent Muslim or an atheist cosmologist-physicist or a neo-Freudian psychiatrist? Might the sages of those traditions know something important about "being" that I have been ignoring, or, perhaps, to which I have had no access?" Protest: But are we not just "too busy" to spend much time "on the big picture"? Or is this mindlessness in the form of a moral failure, a refusal of the call of Being? What influences the reality of "who needs what kinds of fields of meaning when"? Obviously, the question implies balancing tactics to achieve an ultimate strategy.

I shall now put the strategic issue in its most demanding form: all mature human beings ought to be methodically drawn out toward *(e-ducere)* an explicit conception of *a fundamental, all-englobing, rationally, and in terms of genuine human needs critically founded ultimate field of meaning, a vision that inspires to ever wiser founding of "the sense of it all."* This would be an explicit context of contexts never to be allowed to get too far from our contemplation as we struggle to find the very sense (both direction and overall significance) of human life from its origin to the death of the individual and the final disposition of all human accomplishment. Reciprocally, the vision would be constantly nourished by new factual discoveries and by creative efforts to expand and render more responsible the ultimate horizons of meaning.

This proposition is obviously (in the "large" sense) religious, but not inevitably theistic. Someone who has long since decided, for instance, to throw his life into particle physics and cosmology may tend to center his most serious contemplation on an expanding universe, displaying a hierarchy of constructions, from vibrating "superstrings" to the proteins that construct the cells and so forth. It may give him pause when he considers the theory that 92 percent of the cosmos's composition is the mysterious "dark energy" about which we know nothing except that some kind of energy must be posited as repelling the exceptional clumps of matter (which themselves overcome its repulsive force sufficiently to form galaxies and stars). Still, he is likely to believe all levels of the development of the cosmos to be essential parts of the meaning of the most wide-sweeping fanciful constructions of the most complex things at the top of the hierarchy: the human beings who are reflecting back on and acknowledging (perhaps giving) a sense to the entire development. Such a vision fulfills the description given in the statement of my platform: *an explicit context of contexts never to be allowed to get too far from our contemplation as we struggle "to put it all together," to find the "meaning of it all," the very sense (direction of development) of human life.*

Any further discussion in this book of what it means to be "religious" will be joined to reflection on the criteria for judging whether one is "mature and intact." By what criteria might one reasonably question the wisdom of leaving out what certain great traditions have for millennia argued are essential to reality? Or turn that around: By what criteria do you judge that the wisdoms of all great traditions should be respectfully interrogated, on the assumption they all have things to tell us about human being, if only the significance of what glimmers forth from mythology? How, for instance, can an educated person justify ignoring the enormous advances of scientific knowledge of the universe and of man himself?

Your time and resources and mine are limited. Perhaps society as a whole and I personally would be best advised to concentrate on the explosive new developments of virtual time. But if you are going to justify ignoring traditions continuing to form vast populaces, perhaps because they are "ancient" and, therefore, presumed "fanciful" (and continue to ignore those populaces themselves—a large anthropological reality), you had best be sure your criteria are indeed "mature and intact," not arbitrary and displaying indolence, even ideological intolerance.

THE ANALOGY OF BEING

A concept of "being" must be able to find a place for, and "make sense of," considerations as varied as a "down quark," a peanut allergy, a human being, a dollar, maybe even a euro, an economic meltdown, a nervous breakdown, and an infinite transcending Source of the whole universe, be it pure fantasy, pregnant myth, or evidenced reality. You cannot expect the concept of the *analogia entis* to be simple!

For authenticity, the following question is today inevitable: has a given great tradition been driven by a credibly expressed Ultimate Reality, or is it a splendid myth, or not splendid at all? ("Splendor" equals a brilliant shining forth of reality itself. The Hubble's peering into the heart of galaxies we did not even a century ago know existed reveals new splendor.) Does maintaining an ultimate framework for one's ruling considerations today constitute a dangerous illusion, or are aspects of all three—credible reality, pregnant myth, and silly illusion—at work in every one of the great traditional religious visions? Maturity, health, and reason demand the most serious response to this question.

Fundamentally, in "the analogy of being," "being" enjoys its significance from the "source of unity" itself. It is that causal source that accounts for our ability to call all the particular entities and the relations between them "beings," that is, factors as different as the material, cosmological, relational, imaginary, spiritual, primordial, foundational, even teleological, getting their sense from one all-englobing densely relational, foundational reality.

RELATIONS AND THE TRANSCENDENTAL
PREDICATES OF BEING

Today, environmentalists probe the difficulties of designing a future for mankind on a planetary scale, for a planet that is rich but necessarily of limited resources. When, earlier, I promised to illumine "the analogy of being" as a conceptual instrument for this work of wisdom, it was already clear that even taken as a spiritual challenge, the problems of humans on this planet need to be contemplated in the still larger context of universe and ultimate meaning. As a necessary step toward this I propose to prepare here a more developed understanding of "the analogy of being," interpreted in light of what we have learned in our high-tech epoch, from contemporary physics and biology up to a spiritual stratosphere. I shall start with a brief reflection on "what is said of all being and every kind of being," which will carry us a step toward the goal of relating all beings under analogous being. In preparation, I shall describe the different "transcendental predicates" in the terminology used by Saint Thomas, a description I find not just of use but compelling, a necessary building block for "the analogy." The unsurpassable vastness of the unique analogical, ontological concept will help us hereafter recall that from the smallest moment involving the most banal everyday activity to the widest and most profound sweep of scientific and theological visions, we shall be encouraged to look more searchingly at the human cognitive capabilities that make such vision conceivable. Only in a later chapter will the significance of the *analogia entis* become clear enough to merit the reader's agreement to the need for long and serious contemplation of "being" as such.

"Being" is one of those "transcendental predicates," that is, "said of all things." Beginning with "being" I shall move on to the other such predicates: First, "being" *(ens)* can be said of every individual thing, every kind of thing, and every sort of relation between things. In this way, as being, all things are ultimately relevant to one another, whether they possess no freedom, like an atom or a boulder, or one enjoys the infinite freedom of the supreme and infinite *ens*, God. Second, each thing, regardless of its kind, forms a distinct unity: it is *unum*, a coherence that accounts for its being what it is and an aspect of its being that which it is. Third, all things are "something" *(aliquid)*, that is, they all possess their unity in distinctive ways of being with their own particularity—one kind of "essence" (which may be only an abstract idea, or an essence with only one particular, or one shared by many particular entities of that same kind) and an existence unique to just this individual, which is reducible to no other: this hydrogen atom may contain the exact same number of subatomic particles as another, but is not that other, though they may be related in the same water molecule. Fourth, the inherent intelligibility of all these unities with their distinctive whatness (*verum* [true] what makes every thing relevant to cognitive capabilities, and integratible in a larger structure or setting). Finally, the attractiveness of every being to will ("goodness"), by virtue of being something, and being, as I like to put it, is therefore "relevant." (The disorder of an evil thing does not yet destroy the good at the foundation; most evil is misuse of what is good in itself.)

Implied in this analogic analysis is the notion that every *ens* gets its being and meaning through relations to other entities—through the things that cause and sustain it and through the things it in turn affects. Understanding that things are both "their own thing"—this unity—yet get their being and their meaning in relation to relevant others (causes) does not at once require embracing belief in an all-founding Infinite Being.

Any cosmologist who reflects on the implications of wanting to derive from the "initial conditions" all things that later evolve should realize that he faces difficulties: first, that the all-pervasiveness of these "transcendental predicates" is difficult to dismiss from enlightened common sense, and, second, that accounting for leaps of evolution to higher levels of being constitutes a daunting intellectual challenge. I have already been pointing attention to the fact that in human affairs an element of "leap" in the form of creative opening of new meaning is a mysterious aspect of reality. The creative insight is followed by work to fashion new kinds of cultural objects to occupy a place in the cosmos.

THE ANALOGY OF BEING AND THE RELEVANCE TO EACH OTHER OF ALL COGNITIVE REALITIES IN FINITE FREEDOM

The relevance of the cognitive realities, "the transcendental predicates of being," to our finite freedom entails the following: In the preceding chapter we saw the importance of imagination at work in our endlessly developing self-image. The personal limits—the boundary of their natural and culturally acquired capabilities—of each individual human being obviously play a familiar role in every situation, indeed in every aspect of every situation. Those personal limits reveal already existing relations between things and persons and possibilities of going forward into the future.

No matter how "eccentric" the personality of a given subject (imagine the "uniqueness" of a given capability on the part of the high-wire virtuoso of the Cirque du Soleil), those specific acts are intelligible, are illumined in a framework of familiar being and typical relations, even when "pathological." They are meaningful only because the human mind is always able to relate them to other acts, events, and forms, dynamic or abstractedly fixed in "formalizations"—for instance, the whatness (aliquid) of an essence.

At the limits of our present knowledge our particular cognitive acts lead "in all directions" to the unknown, perhaps to the profoundly mysterious, but we confidently continue to search in all that for coherent meaning, drawing on all the intelligibility that is already at our disposal, and hopeful that little by little "all will make sense." Everything we deal with "out there" in the larger reality, transcending our present grasp, may strike us as "saturated," but at the same time it seems infinitely illuminable. But on this condition: as ours is an attitude of "authenticity" in both senses—so long as our research and reflection is moved along by our conviction that *verum* is a necessary predicate of all *ens*.

THE ANALOGY OF BEING REMAINS USEFUL EVEN WHEN DESIGN IS DENIED

The notion of design did not trouble the Fathers and Doctors of the Church: The Infinite Source is supreme Light, and mind-boggling artist. Agreed, we have to wrestle with some notion of design, for ourselves: on the human level of being at least, it is obviously active. But whether below the human in the evolutionary development and "above" in a divine source, if any, design can be seen at work, though a most important question, is not, in my understanding, something that must first be settled for the concept of "analogy of being" to prove useful. I shall explain why that is so.

The reason this conceptual scheme I am putting forth takes the form of a unique kind of "analogy" is because the meaning of the term *being* is obviously able to adjust to all the radically different kinds of beings and relations between beings of which we have any cognizance. Humbly, I would point out that recognition of this very human capability invites us to take seriously the enormity of human cognitive capability: in some limited sense my mind and yours can embrace the entire universe, even leaving a place for multiple universes, and every kind of thing, and every particle, can find a place in the mind's light. Contemplate that awesome power! What are we meant to do with it?

Whether we believe a creator designer God exists or not, the notion of an infinite being is intelligible to us, intelligible but not easy to understand. One can easily see that when he calls it "a being" and even source of Being, the sense of "being" is both different from what would be meant by calling a pebble also a "being," while denying the obvious: the pebble is not the possible source of unity throughout the dynamic set of relationships that make up the cosmos and all things, nor is the most powerful of human beings. "Being" in this analogical sense is a concept unique as accompanied by the small number of "transcendental predicates"— what can be said of all things and all their kinds and all relations between them. We have had a glimpse at the very small number of such predicates that go beyond all limits, "transcendentals": "truth," "goodness," "something-ness," "unity," and "beauty." By contrast, consider a term capable of very wide predication, say each of which can be said ("predicated") of every thing and kind of thing. Take composite, for instance, but it is not a "transcendental"; all finite things are indeed composites of essence and existence, all material essences are composed of finite form and limiting matter. A "quark" may be simple (we cannot yet be certain), if not, then perhaps a "superstring"; nevertheless, both figure in the "analogy" as having a particular kind of form (there are seven types of quarks) and a materiality that means an individual quark stands in concrete relationships from a position in the universe, although in "quantum" ways different from atoms, and so on up the scale of complexity. Only the notion of an Infinite God refers to a unique and simple all-englobing reality, in no way "composite"; not even the triune aspect of God is composite, according to mysterious Christian theology. Human intelligence diffracts the simplicity of God into an unending list of qualities; the quark, if it is indeed simple, cannot be diffracted.

Once again I ask: How is it that it makes sense to call by the same term everything that was, that is, and that will be, whether a quark, a granite boulder, a thought in the mind, or an all-creating God? A gross and common error needs to be dispatched at this point: *being* does not mean "that which is known in the mind." All that you or I know is, to be sure, "known in the mind," but much of what we know clearly evidences "being" independently of being in our minds. To be known, things must "be in the mind," but to exist, to leave behind "nonbeing," does not require human minds. When a human mind comes across something new to that mind, the person recognizes that this thing existed before, unless it is the mind's innovative creation.

In struggling to understand "the analogy," the first aspect to keep in mind is that Being is all inclusive, hence indeed "grand"—a "transcendental predicate," "going beyond" all distinctions, embracing every kind of being. This symbolizes the clear distinction in meaning between particular things with their peculiar and characteristic limits ("beings") and whatever it is ("Being") that unites all under one meaning—and hints at least at the possibility of a network of real relations from which nothing escapes. (Before the reader sighs, "Ah, there you are: God after all!" the reader should recall that physics would not ignore this requirement.) To be a "being" means to participate in Being,[1] and Being is necessarily "the Being of beings," the term having sense only in relation to the many things and kinds of things, and their "participation" in the intelligibility of "Being," in a weave of real relations. That latter consideration requires some explaining.

Commonsensically, we talk that way without difficulty: Something that once existed can be said "to have gone out of being"—only here I capitalize the transcendental (going beyond all limits) "Being." One could say that a thing that earlier enjoyed the being of a material thing existing in cosmic time and space, having ceased to be in that sense, now takes on a different sort of being: that of a memory; it has been reduced from being a cosmic reality, becoming an *ens mentis* only—a being in the mind. There may be current evidence in the cosmos of something's having been, but in the meanwhile it disintegrated, leaving enough fragments behind to allow later explorers to discover the evidence. If my notion now is "There never was such an oak in the garden; it is a figment of your imagination" and in fact there once was, my *ens mentis* (a being of the mind) has additionally, unbeknownst to me, the being of an error. The oak is an *ens mentis* and as an "oak that never was" is an error, for (suppose) the oak

---

1. Individual human beings and human being participate in Being. Please see my *Being and Truth*.

did exist! (If I know that it existed and I am denying it, because I stole it, cut it down, and sold it, this is not an error but another kind of "mental being": a lie!) The idea I have formed in the project of building a house is at first only a mental being, in this case the mental being of a real project, for I genuinely intend, as of now, to carry it out. But getting from dream to cosmic existence will require real work, efficient causality in this case assembling materials into the desired form. The coming into being of my lie about the stolen oak requires a kind of spiritual efficiency to produce the mental entity, the big lie. Later, I am trapped and so might as well admit it: "Yes, I told a lie, I stole the oak, I am sorry." (Efficient causality in a spiritual-social mode.) Hard work! "Coming clean took a lot out of me." This new event puts in motion the law, and I end up physically in the slammer for six months. Yielding to the threat of legal physical force, I go off to trial and to prison willingly. There are many forms of "efficient causality."

Now once again the question in the background that keeps haunting the God-shy reader: for such unity of all under one concept (even all these different forms of efficiency), would there not have to be in reality something that somehow explains every being's being so relatable, every thing's being so meaningfully a "being," implying its having some kind of place either in nature or in a mind and a most significant relation between nature and mind? Yet more bluntly: is the foundational reality represented by the notion "Being" itself, if it is not merely "whatever mind can accommodate," something in some way really constitutive of all beings? Obviously, I have not yet succeeded in exorcising the ambiguity. The "really constitutive" can be understood in two ways. First, it could mean that the overarching unity that allows the term to be applied to every thing of whatever kind, real entity or image or concept or "bright idea," derives from all these notions of things having occurred to a mind. The "whatever is or can be" would then really mean "whatever has or might occur to a human mind." All "beings" then would get their Being as moments of content in human minds, thus taking their place in history. The mind, of course, may at the same time accept evidence for some of these beings' showing themselves to be extramental realities as well, whereas others would be recognized as purely imaginary, convincingly "only in the mind," some so contradictory in their meaning that they could not both be and not be in extramental reality. In this way the possibility remains open that the "merely material" gives rise, at a certain level of complexity, to what human beings experience as the "spiritual," which would then be understood to be entirely a product of the organ called "the brain." The brain through that of its activities we call "the creative imagination" directs human work to produce new structures in the material. (Many thoughts and reveries have been forgotten, and there will be no way of knowing they ever existed, a pity in the case of a great "insight" that was told to no one.) The second possibility is that while agreeing with most of what has just been said, one can intend a larger claim. Here are the factors that need to be brought together: the network of causal relations between "objective" things, the network of relations between things and the ideas to which they give rise when encountered by a human mind, creative ideas, and the work that brings something to be in keeping with the design in the mind. Do not forget that these factors interrelate in complex ways, the networks of relationships stretching back, and out, and forward from one's center of awareness as a dense weave.

Now, if we seek to throw light on this great complexity, would we not have to push further in experience to illumine an underlying network of "efficient causality" and to penetrate more deeply into the formal structures—the essences of the kind of things that can produce all the factors listed above, their complex relations contributing to the makeup of other kinds of things? The Latin Aristotelian tradition of the medieval doctors chose this term for the cause "which effectuates *(efficere),*" which brings something into existence. They stressed the need to identify all the sources of the "objective" being with which they may be endowed, all the capabilities required to account for this new thing's having come to be when and as it is. Here at last is a first principle that can guide us through this labyrinth: All beings reside on an objective base endowed with a reality-producing element of "to be" *(esse).* The *esse*—the "to be"— is the existence of this thing with this essence in these concrete circumstances unique to that thing, including all the relationships in which it is caught up. The *esse* is therefore the source of the characteristic powers of that thing to affect and perhaps even to participate in bringing to be corresponding "other things," and to be itself affected in ways characteristic of its kind and its present situation. Would this not imply that all things, including ideas and imaginary forms, ultimately derive from real things and relations but also, in the case of human artifacts, from desires known only in the mind? Even the latter, the most imaginatively soaring above existing realities, are related, some immediately to certain causes, others remotely. All our knowledge of things, whether "material entities" occupying a natural time and space, or images, or abstract concepts, ultimately derives from real things and relations and our knowledge from experiences of those objective realities and through human brain functions. (The strong realistic statement of Saint Thomas comes to mind: "Nihil in intellectu quod nisi prius in sensibus" [Nothing is in the intellect which is not first in the senses].)

That "pure opposition to nothingness" *(esse)* that is manifest by whatever establishes itself as having some kind of reality would be true even of an *ens mentis,* a notion the being of which is only in the mind. Images exist by inhering in, and requiring, mind in order to enjoy *inesse,* existence in that mind. *Inesse* (or in-being, literally that being-in-something) expresses the derivative entity's dependence on the existence of a freestanding thing (substantia). The "free-standing substance," too, reveals its causal dependencies, but its *relatively stable* "standing alone" allows the mind to treat it as more permanent and more independent than it is. (As every thing enjoys *esse,* objective, somewhat independent existence is nevertheless itself dependent. A free-standing human being, for instance, depends for its nourishment on other things without which it would die. A mature adult person is probably 98 percent beholden to other forces than his own pure creativity!) So there is a definite relativity in these notions. The infinite *esse* of God (or Source of the universe) is itself conditioned by nothing exterior to itself; the *esse* of what Aristotle called *ousia* (substance) is an *esse* that is not absolute; it is dependent on a cause, *inesse,* aspects of a substance that depend on that more freestanding thing to survive. Nothing lasts forever in the created universe, and nothing is without its ongoing dependencies. As an aspect of the particular form of its *inesse,* the idea or notion occupies its own mental and logical space in the mind, it relates logically to other notions, and it even has a history, its past and its intended future. "I never thought of that until this moment, but I assure you I shall never forget it." Every idea, image, notion, or concept enjoys complicated relations with the *esse* of real things known by the mind to lie outside the spirit.

STARTING AT THE BEGINNING . . .
BUT ARE THERE TWO BEGINNINGS?

Now that I have raised the issue of an overview of a conceptual scheme for accommodating the widest and deepest contexts, be they open to an infinite first cause or rather to the still mysterious Big Bang, I can start our discussion of *appropriate use* of cognitive faculties from the beginning. Without a way of accommodating conceptually "the ultimate"—beginning, present widest scope, and (teleological or just disintegration)—had we no way to deal with "the beginning and the end," what could "the proper" in "the appropriate" possibly be? I have acknowledged an ambiguity, and I have suggested how to deal with it. There are two proposed "beginnings": first, the start of the universe, whether "a creative act" or a Big Bang that, as the physicist Tyson said, is just one of those things that happens from time to time; and, second, me, in the sense that whatever my reflection, it takes place in me, it is centered from the start in my own little world that reaches out (ex-sists) to embrace all that is, both within and beyond me, and you, as we acknowledge that every healthily functioning human being is his own "center of a world" (which he is tempted to believe is THE center of the world).

There is yet another ambiguity: it lies in that phrase "from the start." It means both that from the present center of my reflection I look out on larger worlds, the access to them is from my interior outward, in every cognitive act I start from my center. And second, that "beginning" refers to the deepest roots in the past of my history, cosmic and cultural. That "subjective" reality conditions all one's knowledge, all one's wisdom, everything, including, of course, the construction of a great concept like that of the Big Bang universe or of the Analogy of Being.

The appropriate use of our cognitive capabilities requires, among other challenges, staying alert to the tensions caused by the interaction in us of the subjective and the objective. If there is a most central concern of not only this study but all my volumes, that is it. As we shall see, the ultimate framework for unending exploration of the subject-object dynamics should be the analogy of being and within it our critical appropriation of what we are able to learn about the becoming of the universe, cosmically and historico-culturally.

In continuing this reflection on the appropriate use of our cognitive faculties, I choose to start now with the second (and Johnny-come-lately) of these beginnings, little me. That is because I am inevitably the center of my every reflection; I shall concentrate on the dynamic structure of my present interpreting, resolutely avoiding neglect of objective reality.

I am some 13.2 billion years late for direct experience of the cosmic singularity, but nevertheless I remain my only access to the traces of it through attending to those who report on the special radio receivers' picking up the fossil background radiation of the explosion. Here I am, then, this small little concrete being, an objective thing born of two other like beings of different sexes, married for the occasion of launching a life-long family structure. From the moment I grasp that I am not the unique center of reality, I am in the process, whether I am yet aware of it, of discovering myself to be a speck of the Big Bang universe, one of many human centers out in the cosmos, all of them that we know about being the 6.4 billion on this planet and its lonely earth-orbiting space station: each of us is a moment in, and a distinctive perspective on, the universe, a clump of organic tissue and bone located in a given place, this unique instantiation of what we recognize to be a "species" made up of 6.4 billion living individuals of extremely similar forms.

As this particular individual of the kind we recognize as "human beings," I am intensely attached to and immensely involved with some of those of my own kind—particularly with the persons most important in my life. I hold on for dear life to certain things—my social status, for instance, and my wealth. Anyone can see, however, that none of these beings, including the event of the singularity, is Being itself (until the appearance of man there is no evidence of anything—not even the dense network of all kinds of relations between them; indeed, not even I, center of my universe of cognition, am Being itself). All my knowledge of Being is rooted in my particular set of cognitive faculties and experiences stored in memory, but I, though cause of some things, see clearly that I am not the cause of most beings, or of Being as such. Neither finite thing nor aspect of the cosmic unfolding, including human critical intelligence that comes along 13 billion years after the Big Bang, is Being itself or the source of Being. Yet there is no being unrelated to any other being! (Even if there is an Infinite Source of all being, it is forever related to all that has poured forth from its creation. The mere thought of it alerts us that the question of the possibility of an Infinite creative source is a "notion" to be dealt with, even if one aspires to show that it is a phantom of the human mind.)

THE EXPANSION OF THE CULTURAL WORLD

As down through the ages human beings struggled to imagine the englobing reality, each epoch of history has stretched horizons ever further. The notions of ultimate objective foundations of the whole have developed, often in tense competition with one another, in the clash of philosophies and theologies within same cultures and, once they were in serious contact, between cultures. In our present epoch the planetary scale of cultural encounter and the historical depths of inquiry have imposed unmanageable demands. Consider the relevance of one of the demands on human being that has become especially pressing today: the need to manage. We now include in that demand the need not just to store and access efficiently unimaginably huge treasures of information but to manage better our cognitive capabilities. Sharpening our sense of the needs imposed by the search for wisdom, we restructure and rein-spire the methods of education.

Imagine for a moment the vast knowledge institutions that have developed since the founding of the Muslim university of al-Azar in eleventh-century Cairo and the European universities that grew in the thirteenth, giving birth to sophisticated methodic, scientific knowledge and research institutions, libraries, professors, guilds, and so forth, over the seven hundred years of development. In the course of this develop-ment creative expansions of our cognitive capabilities (more in cultural content than in organic power, new habits of research and analysis, not organic growth of the brain) have been achieved in order to grasp new possibilities that man has opened to himself.

The question asked by a recent book, *The Ingenuity Gap*, about our cog-nitive capabilities in the present setting is relevant indeed: "Can we create ideas fast enough to solve the very problems—environmental, social and technological—we've created?"[2] The author, Toronto's Thomas Homer-Dixon, is not optimistic. Significantly, intelligent and well informed though he is, he saw no necessity in his study to cast the question in the context of Being itself. The religious dimension in the large sense is totally absent. That interesting study shows how withdrawal into spe-cialization turns the gaze away from questions of ultimate meanings and the source of intelligibility itself. Many of the brightest and best educated do not know where to go once they have stared into the Ground Zero of the Ingenuity Gap.

2. Thomas Homer-Dixon, *The Ingenuity Gap* (Toronto: Vintage, 2002).

COGNITIVE CAPABILITIES FOR WRESTLING
WITH THE FIRST PRINCIPLE

The Great Divide in the disagreement among the thoughtful as to what man is runs through the question of deciding between one of two possibilities at the center of the *Gigantomachia:* either there is an infinite God or we are each little gods. If there is no conscious design apparent in the foundations of the cosmic complexification or revealed from a Source, then cultural design and human meaning are ultimate dynamic superstructures achieved by human creative cognitive capabilities. If that is the case, we intelligent, well-educated humans alone are responsible for whatever "sense" is to be made out of the world. Be this as it may, an overarching complex concept like the *analogia entis* remains an indispensable cognitive tool for building the least-inadequate vision of the all-encompassing reality. (Ultimately, this will come to nothing, of course. Unless there are conscious creatures rather like us elsewhere in another universe, when mankind kills itself off, or cosmic forces do it for him, the universe will revert to being an unappreciated furnace of material process.)

What cognitive capabilities, able to stand up to the postmodernist criticism of our virtual times, do human beings possess for keeping responsibly alive the question of what then is "the ultimate reality"? Consider first this challenging possibility: if a transcendent sense-giving source of all beings were to exist, it would be the "unique of the unique"; beyond the narrow limits of every manner of thing, indeed beyond the vast but finite dynamic processes of the universe, it would be the only absolutely unique, "outside of which nothing else can exist," in relation to which all "have their being," and so there can be, in this strongest sense, *only One.* This monism has the advantage of making a certain sense of foundations for the "analogy of being": the Infinite *esse* would be source and foundation of the entire structure of Being, the key, "the primary analogate," as the philosophers call it—"Being without qualification," one might say. "God!" Everything else, all finite things, is inevitably "a being of this or that sort," set over against all the other possibilities, all sources grounded in the one foundation.

But if there is no infinite source, in what sense would the material substrate that manifests itself in the "singularity" of the explosive expansion-complexification of the cosmos be "source"? (If there proves to be more than one cosmos, perhaps myriads, the substratum of being would be physically all the cosmoses in different phases of development and eventually perhaps of collapse.) Be that as it may, we can still say this: humans are "more unique" than any other species, being the only one (for sure on Earth, and so far as we now know in the universe, although that question remains open, as it does also if there is an Infinite Source). For now, the only kind of entity to recognize explicitly and reflectively the differences between the species is the human being. That gives us a kind of "one-uppance" as definers of the "unique." For this reason, that we discover and dispense "meaning" in ways exemplified by our discriminating of species, we are also unique in being the only species to produce a "who": we are the ones who name ourselves and who react in (limited, to be sure) freedom to all others, and hence stand at the center of their being recognized. This truth is related to the fact we can do with the other species what we will; faced with our intelligence they are "game" or "lunch," while each of the other species is very limited in what, if anything, it can do with us besides rot us out as "disease," or, if wolf or bear is center stage, eat us. We are the least eaten of all species, and the one that most progressively fights disease! And we are the only species about whom the question arises of whether *we ought to do all that we can*. We are the only moral species so far known. As finite, reflective freedoms able at least to think up a God and often capable of thinking we are gods, we are the only species to worry about our *Stellung im Kosmos*, our place in the cosmos, as Max Scheler put it: our position in the scheme of things, a sovereign character to our unique position; to be a "who" is to be a king.

We are unique then in being up to now the real, empirically encounterable gods who, to meet our needs, invent the mythological gods and accuse ourselves of having invented the myth of the One infinite absolute "creative God," whom, if we follow Nietzsche, we then subsequently and sovereignly (Nietzsche is not so sure it was "wisely") put out of existence. *Gott ist tod!* In the fullness of time, and with the greatest imaginable sovereignty, we killed him, remember? Zarathustra told us, after all, reluctant though he had been to shatter with the terrible news the wise Old Man who emerged confused from the contemplative forest.

Depending on what side of the Great Divide one's faith falls, cognitive capabilities will be put to certain different uses, in distinctive modes. I shall take the case of the Zarathustra-ignoring theist first. He is easily tempted to respond to the fundamental question "Who are we?" thus: "We are whatever God has made us, as he intended that we should be (which includes intending our capability to revolt, and the possibility of

God's "trumping" our revolt). Who we have become insofar as it is positive depends on our cooperation with his grace; our rebellions have only held us back. What cognitive capabilities are implied, working on what kind of evidence, to know such things as that? If the relevant cognitive capabilities turn out to be in significant part the ability to fabricate fancies of the imagination, humanly created images with thin rapport with reality, then, like all art, they show the wonderful (and often sinister) human capacity to create and then to propagate art to move multitudes. It is a bald fact that whole civilizations have been formed by these images. The question "How do we invent these things (and why, and why do they work)?" is tantamount, as we shall see later, to asking how a human being comes to believe, how particular sources of "evidence" are accepted as believable. This remains as central a question in today's "philosophy of science," in anthropology, as any that can be asked. It is a question to be critically judged in a way appropriate to it.

What is that appropriate way? It is not fundamental enough today to respond, in the case of the question of "the origin": "to find out more about what God intends of us, we must pore over the teachings of his revelation, and contemplate his presence in history." True enough, but not adequate. From the start of any receptivity of evidence from any source, one must have been led somehow to at least a beginning belief in the source as in some way meaningful and reliable for establishing the appropriate kind of meaning, that is, one's fundamental attitudes about *what is* (or at least how I would have it be!). This belief basically influences the choice of objects for the believer's study and contemplation, and the perspective he will take on the now identified things seen as having some importance. Someone who is theistically inclined may develop methods of theological contemplation, of reflectively living liturgy, of reading sacred texts of his tradition, and ways of transmitting effectively charity. A contemplative enterprise of this kind leads fairly easily to discovery of the sense of the "analogy of being" with a clear embrace of a sense-bestowing infinite foundation rather as I have been describing it.

Now for the other side. Those who see no compelling evidence of any Being or beings superior to us tend to agree there is a responsibility to use our cognitive capabilities to study, "from the ground up," the traces of our having evolved within the context of a still unfolding universe. For these serious thinkers too, while remaining atheist, the world itself is mysterious and wonderful. But atheists are frequently confident that with the appropriate development of our cognitive faculties and the instruments we produce with it, more of that mystery will be dispelled. But many others see new mysteries taking the place of old. (The theist can share this sense—some mysteries are partly cleared up but replaced by new wondrous considerations in cosmology.)

6

WHY ARE WE SO WEIRD AND WHAT CAN WE DO ABOUT IT?

Whenever, with a sigh and a face of Jeremiah, I say, "People are weird!" I receive universal agreement. Never once has anyone responded, "How can you say that?" Upon more reflection, however, some of my friends balk at the word. *Strange*, maybe. How about *evil*, though they would condemn few persons as simply evil—Hitler, Stalin, serial killers (mental cases rather than pure evil)? Most of us will admit to having done bad things, but to having "a streak of evil"? In any event, what *evil* usually means is something narrower than our general weirdness. All evil is weird; our using the great gift of our freedom to ignore and distort and to destroy reality is, without contest, the weirdest phenomenon in the universe.

I am convinced that, at the last gasp of our vast subject, we can all fruitfully reflect on the fact of our being the weirdest creatures of them all. (No animal species has systematically planned and worked for its own possible total destruction.) So profound is our weirdness, the rabbis of old were inspired to elaborate the brilliant myth of "the Fall." The reader who has not pored over that text should see what a treasure of wisdom about the psychopathological it contains. Underlying it is this simple theistic conviction: *An absolutely good God could not have wanted us to be like that.* The entire redemption story that has been unfolding ever since is an elaboration of the belief that he has saved us from our own perverse self-destruction. The whole dynamics are weird, but they reflect a true human state of yearning.

There are many aspects of human weirdness that are not sufficiently disturbing to merit being called "evil": Think, for instance, of the "harmless eccentric," like the learned eighteenth-century lawyer Philip Neri, who wore clown shoes when meeting distinguished Romans in order to humble himself. That is weird indeed but surely not, as far as that eccentricity goes, "evil." His eccentricities did not prevent his canonization. (The publicized weirdness of many canonized saints is a sign of the Church's wisdom!) The pathologically irresponsible wreak destruction, but, "because they know not what they do," their interior disposition is not necessarily evil. Moral evil, however, requiring responsibility and accountability, is not just "puzzling" but so incomprehensibly counterproductive, so mean-spirited, so stupidly mindless when it is not "diabolically" insidious; it opens a mysterious abyss of strangeness that reveals something approaching the absolute in "the analogy of weirdness." At least so it strikes the person who has struggled to base his wisdom explicitly on something he experiences as fructifying, and calls for constant combat of evil, destructive temptations.

The English word itself is . . . well, weird. According to the *OED* it originally appertained to divine fate, to mysterious powers. In *Macbeth* it clearly relates to its roots, "wayward," but that itself is obscure in meaning. Today, it has come to mean "unusual," but in a troubling sense. The student of wisdom can readily see all that is weird as having the potential of seducing us to wander off the "straight and narrow" (that is the biblical term) that is "the Way," and finds there is something troubling even in Philip Neri's clown shoes. Confronted by the amusingly weird, we do not know what to do; it pulls us from the rational path, and we wander as we wonder. There is something here that just isn't right.

The German word for *weird* offers a further hint: *unheimlich* (*Heim* means "home"); human beings, caught up in all manner of polemics, have trouble being at home in this world. We saw that the Bible even says bluntly that our home is to be found in our origin and end, with God and his angels in heaven; our home is not in this world.

Restless, not all of a piece, a tissue not just of paradoxes but of contradictions, much that the human lives and much that we do is uncategorizable; we can rest for long nowhere. It is not just lack of knowledge; the most significant forms of human weirdness are not awaiting solutions from better psychoanalytic techniques. As the myth of the Fall suggests, it is as though there were a flaw in humans, as though something has gone wrong basically.

It is weird that alone of all creatures man should consider himself strange. But then man alone is capable of sophisticated self-consideration. That is central to what we mean when we think about the human being's "interior life." We take our weirdness for granted, but we should not. *Au contraire*, it is weird that we should be so weird. Why should there ever be people like those described so brilliantly by Hervey Cleckley in *The Mask of Sanity*? The fourteen cases of patients diagnosed as instances of "psychopathic character" (the terminology has since changed) fit poorly the accepted categories of psychosis. They are often intelligent and resourceful people who in important ways do not fit in, and often simply do not care to fit into, society. "Max," the first he describes, impresses Cleckley by his intelligence, but long experience with the tiny Viennese former featherweight boxer convinces the physician that Max is, yes, "intelligent," but intelligence itself is "an inherently ambiguous term"; in other words, it is itself a weird phenomenon. Throughout the 452 pages of the fifth edition of Cleckley's work, fruit of lifelong reflections, the physician is seeking clues as to why human beings can be like that, how they can develop into "psychopathic personalities." Hovering in the background of Cleckley's fascinating (and frustrating) investigations are the questions: What can and should we do in the face of such distortion, given this striking, indeed socially unbearable, weirdness? What are the limits of the psychologically possible and the morally required? "We" here are the "wise" individuals, the scientific leaders who know we have some kind of an especially challenging role in seeking to guide society toward a more fruitful existence, in particular key roles in education and in expending societal-financed research resources.

There are among the wise voices of hope. Cleckley himself, though not optimistic about treating "psychopathic personalities," at least hopes for more realistic handling of them, with increased compassion. I am sure he would greet the progress being made in understanding a little something of how the brain works. But I wonder if today he would be satisfied with psychiatry's penchant for dulling the activities of "psychopathic personalities" pharmacologically.

This would be a good moment to recall the words of hope of psychiatrists Stephen A. Mitchell and Margaret J. Black: "Clinical psychoanalysis is most fundamentally about people and their difficulties in living, about a relationship that is committed *to deeper self-understanding, a richer sense of personal meaning, and a greater degree to freedom*."[1] How the relevance of "spirit" and "brain" interaction fits in not only remains full of unknowns

---

1. Stephen A. Mitchell and Margaret J. Black, *Freud and Beyond: A History of Modern Psychoanalytic Thought* (New York: Harper-Collins, 1996).

but is mystery at the interface of meaning and what cosmically supports and is necessary to human knowing.

"Self-understanding, personal meaning, and freedom" are not per se weird. What we do to impede them and to distort them is, indeed, very weird. Taken by themselves "self-understanding, personal meaning, and freedom" are insufficiently authentic in the sense developed in this book, too "self-centered." Recall that the *autos* in *authenticity* is not the petty self-centered self but that taking responsibility for the whole of reality insofar as our projections can embrace it—*Eigentlichkeit*, in German (*eigen* means "one's own"), in the sense that I am responsible for the overall knowledge that founds my personal wisdom. What we have been able to discover and appreciate is not for manipulation but for admiration.

True, penetrating self-knowledge is a necessary component of authenticity. But authenticity remains closed to whomever is still seriously emotionally blocked in ways that stunt interest in "the larger reality," the vast dimensions of Being that do not always serve immediately my personal wants. That "larger reality" is the authentic framework for genuine freedom. The self is not really understood without sound reflection on the origins and what we can divine of the destiny of human being. Finally, "personal meaning" is reliable to the extent one is correctly understanding what he owes to other persons and how he is dynamically connected to them; in a word, the wise and prudent man plunges into the realities of re-sponse-ability.

THE WEIRDNESS OF FINITE CREATORS

I am not introducing this issue of weirdness to recompense the weary reader with an element of humor. The mystery of our weirdness matters enormously, as becomes strikingly obvious from that point where we leave the merely quaint to enter into the perverted. There people are no longer simply amused but, as happens with all evil and with the psychopathic blocks to truth-revealing feelings, damaged. (The implication is intended: I am suggesting we ought not be that way.) We are all a bit weird in this quite unamusing fashion for this reason: we are spirits capable of creation, not completely ex nihilo—we must make use of the previously formed "matter" and the treasury of symbols we inherit—yet the genuinely new element in what, for instance, an artist does comes from beyond "the already having been." The creative element in our daily activities may be less obvious than in the making of an artwork, but our every act of interpretation introduces a bit of newness; every creative act adds to "the essence" of the object with which we are dealing.

We are spirits capable of creation but so limited, our every godlike creative act generates another *polemos*, potentially tragic but most often only comic if successfully massaged to keep the party going. What a supremely paradoxical notion: an act of finite creation! The paradox reaches in a reverse way even to God's infinite act in unfolding the entire cosmos, for from the Boundless comes the bounded; no boundaries diminished the lavish flow of being from divine Person to divine Person. Now, because of a decision of the Infinite, boundaries, expanding, yes, but limits, nonetheless, have been set. Given the limits of human perspective, the notion of the Infinite revealing itself within the limits it supremely set seems to us transcendentally weird. But Judeo-Christian revelation explains that the Infinite Creator did this so his human creatures could learn to love themselves through loving their Source and End.

However our relations to the Source and End strike us, a philosophical anthropology must face the two most essential and hence most significant negative aspects of man, or it will have essentially missed the phenomenon an anthropology sets out to study. The first negativity is what I would call "a limited positive," essential to the paradox: our time-space situatedness, with birth and death and present physical location as the known ultimate but still shifting limits. That finitude is not per se a source of moral evil. The second negativity, going beyond the paradox of finite creativity, is humans' use of creative power in acts of destructiveness, their ability to abuse their freedom in perverse ways.

An anthropology that does not confront head-on our weirdness misses not only the nature of man but an authentic gaze at Being itself. Through our limited knowledge of evolution we remain stunned by the weirdness of nature. We understand really very little about how evolution works. The leaps, the dead ends, the lavishness of species, the violence and the delicate designs, the power packed in the genetic codes, the codes' having come to be in the first place, and so forth, leave us in profoundest wonder. I am an avid reader of the debates between the neo-Darwinians and those who say we must not ideologically foreclose on the apparent evidence of mysterious design. I am convinced that the present state of our scientific knowledge in no way authorizes closing off that complex field of debate.

Among the realities we do know with certainty is this important truth:

whatever the complex processes involved, they managed to achieve the present summit, that finite human being who, while capable of the most disconcerting acts, is the one also capable of responding to gifts, capable of genuine responsibility through a legitimate autonomy, and equally talented at achieving the nadir, fleeing responsibility into mindlessness and what philosopher Walter Kaufmann calls "decidophobia." Deliberate refusal and purely destructive aggressiveness are ontological possibilities at the very summit of known creation!

That every finite thing bumps constantly up against its limits is no paradox; it is just part of being finite. If one has limits, he can be assured of what I shall call "local frustration." If he dreams only mythically of an ultimate fulfillment, the cynic is right. But whatever one's hope ultimately, the fact that a creature would deliberately use his creativity for meaningless destruction so disconcerts us. Many are blocked from believing that the source of the evolutionary processes could be something wholly good. To counter that block, the believer in the infinite goodness of the Source is called upon by revelation to reach to the bottom of his own creative possibilities to come up with some understanding that makes credible the mystery of an infinite love: needed is a glimpse that the Source not only allowed challenging finite freedoms to come into existence but also knew how, out of the evil that would result, to bring supreme good and to manifest literally unimaginable love, something most non-Christians find, as Balthasar said, too good to be believable. Balthasar was convinced that, since the spread of Christianity, mankind stands before a stark either-or: either acceptance of "the revelation"—the assuming of all evil by God himself in and through the sacrifice of his son on the cross, the sublimest glory of love, the absolute triumph of freedom, the only pure "autonomy" ever able to occur in history—or, a pitiful alternative, face the increasingly unnuanced struggle of masses of human wills seeking to prevail, ultimately globally. If I were to propose to contemplate this either-or, I would go on to suggest that it can lead toward the depths of what can be described as that "deeper self-understanding, a richer sense of personal meaning, and a greater degree to freedom." Read "life."

Those who, knowing of this claim of an either-or that is at the center of the greatest civilization-creating force in all of human history may in rejecting the "either" feel themselves relieved of any responsibility for explaining the particular kind of weirdness that has been introduced into the world by the great religions, especially the one that most likely will strike them as the weirdest of all, Christianity. In any event no one should think it is just an accident that the present global "War on Terrorism," centered for the moment on combating "the axis of evil," pits the least un-Christian of large nations, which is also, just by accident, of course, the one "hyperpower," allied (uncomfortably) with the tiny Jewish state (8 percent of which is Orthodox, and probably 80 percent thoroughly secularized), against the most consequent of Muslims (by a certain reading of the history of Islam and the Holy Qur'an, a reading rejected by many Muslims). Sigmund Freud, in my view, was right in opposing such an intellectual *laissez-aller:* he courageously offered an explanation in terms of sociopathology for the madness of just this kind of historical carrying-on rooted in religion.

Yes, this purported "central act of all history," the event of "the Redemption" is, like the sin the Redemption is supposed to have wiped away, itself the most *unheimlich* claim of all, the summit of pretensions of the human "spirit" (St. Paul says if Jesus Christ has not risen from the dead, "then we are of all men the most foolish"), while purporting to be at the same time the only thing that can make sense out of human being. "The War against Terrorism" will not end; there will be moments of quiet. China, which is worried by the Muslims of its southwestern-most province, and Russia, with vast Muslim problems of its own, will have to decide how far to go in helping militant Islam. (In June 2006 the Russian president proposed an alliance of Russia, China, and Iran to push back the great powers!) All of this—a part only, but an important part of the *Gigantomachia*—urgently requires more reflection. Even if purely mythical mystification, this planetary struggle throws fundamental light on human being, "the cosmic struggler."

Because the issue of our basic human weirdness englobes all of human being, I have to limit the discussion of it, a necessity for all the seemingly limitless themes of human being. So I shall build up my limited picture of the bizarre from a few comments on a few forms of everyday weirdness chosen to help us see better certain key elements of the complexities of our finite freedom. I shall not attempt to consider seriously as different kinds of weirdness the disorders obviously caused in part by neurological difficulties and severe psychosomatic damage. Instead, I shall remain in the domain of what might be called "our everyday strangeness."

THE WEIRDNESS OF EVERYDAY FINITE FREEDOM

My hope is to understand better what entices us to succumb to those forms of the weird that are evil acts, to grasp something of the destructive dynamism of those free acts of perversion and damage of reality that are the weirdest phenomena in all of creation, and found everywhere man is active. What is so weird is that it is obvious, upon a moment's reflection, that moral evil is exactly counterontological: it is strange indeed that Being should contain within itself the possibility of a twisted kind of abuse of creativity that allows a precipitous fall into nonbeing.

The collapses that result from abuses of finite freedom are not cosmic in origin. Indeed, when we compare them with the orderly dissipation of the creative Big Bang energy into the incomprehensible spaces of the run-down universe trapped forever in the ultimate "heat sink," there appears an orderliness to great cosmic processes in contrast to the confusion and rubble left by human acts. These free acts of annihilation are simply counter to the cosmic movement of evolution that, mysteriously, and for a while, and, I believe, programmed by something that is designed, appear to build inexorably toward structures of the highest complexity and grace. Man from his first appearance, as caught in the earliest cultural remains, and continuing until now, pushes "upstream," against the dissipation of structure, and meanwhile all of us erratically but knowingly commit free acts of disruption. Counterentropic building up, but all the while being sapped at the base by the primordial dissipation of energy, and in the midst of all of nature's opposition of cosmic movements, the highest creature participates in both the noblest acts of construction and the gratuitous acts of destruction. Such is the weird multidimensional opposition of forces and spirit.

THE PREMATURE PSYCHIC HEAT SINK

We can imagine without difficulty that within the enormous experimentation and complexification of evolution many particular forms would appear that strike man as weird in the sense of "quaint," "picturesque," that is, of no obvious utility for anything, perhaps simply "evolutionary failures." Much of that kind of weirdness may be an appearance of strangeness simply because of our ignorance. But all life in its evolved complexification, quaint or not, and despite every weirdness, succeeds in moving counter to entropy at least for a brief while. In the tense dynamics of an unfolding personal life counterentropically storing up capability, there is at the same time a staggering loss of potential sunk into what we might call "the premature psychic heat sink" of resentment, envy, every form of self-hatred, terror at making a decision, or taking responsibility for what we have done. Hiding from reality invites letting the undertow of the cosmic forces hold back the maturing development of the soul. Without such weird blocks to development, each of us, whatever our gifts, could be so much more than what we have become. Were it not for our weird reticences, we might even begin to feel justifiably "secure," and society could indeed be closer to "Paradise"!

On the social level recent experience offers an unsurpassably absurd symbol: Imagine the two leading military powers of "the cold war" spending more than two trillion dollars to achieve MAD (mutually assured destruction). A friend of mine, then "number-three man" at the arms control agency of the U.S. presidency, was the official who during the 1970s commissioned two in-depth studies of the probable effect on the environment of an all-out "mutual exchange" of nuclear destruction. The two groups of scientists working independently, naturally enough, given the complexity of the problem, disagreed. They both said that "nuclear winter" would occur, but while the one opined that human life would not survive at all, the other, wildly optimistic, suggested that perhaps human life might muddle through in the extreme South of the Southern Hemisphere. Now, I submit, that is a really *w-e-i-r-d* situation human beings, at dint of enormous effort and great brilliance, have caused. And also have become astoundingly adept at ignoring. Even the "wake-up call" of September 11, 2001, has not seemed to produce in the thoughtful people of our advanced societies much profound reflection on the fact that the event that occurred at Alamogordo at 5:30 A.M., July 16, 1945, changes the basic situation of this planet.

Modernity's rejection of the very idea of "sin," heretofore central in the tradition, is itself rather weird, dumbing down as it does the interpersonal nature of responsibility ("trinitarian," even in a natural sense: the object—or the other person—proposes a challenge, and the subject re-sponds, completing a mutual giving, which is reminiscent of the interaction of the mutual loves of God the Father and God the Son, reciprocally creative as "the Holy Spirit," here the new dynamic intersubjective bond). A patently personal rebuff, or a response in the form of a clever lie, is a sin against the victim. Not just a "fault, a "misfortune," a "slight": *a sin* (the word is perfectly intelligible and appropriate).

Like many other destructive processes that deform traditions, sin shows its own twisted logic: If, as libertarians passionately believe, the Absolute—the Source of all meaning—is me, the "absolutely autonomous," then obviously I cannot sin; I can just "realize myself" or "fail to realize myself" and be more or less clever in shaping "reality" to fit my comfort level, and more or less honest about it, reveling in the degree of Olympian autonomy I have achieved. My failure to be all that supposedly I might have become is nobody else's business, and anyway there is no criterion by which to judge. ("Honesty" in the abstract, with no sound foundation in being, sounds pure but is in fact floating, if not simply illusory.) And, finally, it could be that I was just predetermined (those genes!) to be no more than I in fact have managed to become. If there is no higher reality able to help us know the sense of our ultimate situatedness in the cosmos, then the only limit is the power of our imaginations, especially in the collective power struggles that go on as societies seek to function.

Suppose a very ordinary situation in which something I want is not what I should have if I am ultimately to flourish. Giving in to more immediate, or more insidious, desires, I trick myself into imagining reality to be just a little different from what it turns out to be. (More realistically, I suspected, actually, that might be so, but I failed to try to imagine just how horrible it would be when the time came to pay the bill! Lung cancer, for instance, turns out to be really rather unpleasant after all.) On some level, then, if I am not crazy, I vaguely recognize that I am "robbing the other eleven apostles to pay Paul." Oh, but I am just weak (fatalistic); I cannot give up smoking, but maybe I'll be one of the lucky ones who does not in the end suffer (not so fatalistic after all). Or I cannot totally deny that I am overwhelmingly ambitious, and that my tendency to roll over others is fed by huge pride. But that is just the way I am—that's me! (fatalistic). I am free to do whatever I can get by with (unfatalistic), but not free to address a disaster-causing basic aspect of my being. Walter Kaufmann in his pioneering methodic analysis of "decidophobia" investigates just about every trick in our arsenal for hiding the fact that we are continuing a bad decision. No matter in what degree of mindlessness we may be indulging, the fine art of denial has to be skillfully cultivated. A basically well-functioning brain is made, after all, to get at the reality of things we need to know.

Throughout this reflection I have suggested that when an adult "of sound mind" is mindless about what should be important issues in his life, it is very likely he is in some way working at not knowing. Something more insidious than mere "airheadedness" is on the prowl. That is the point of an important aspect of weirdness: perversity, an essential dimension of the abuse of human freedom, the perversity of us liars. "Dysfunctionality" of this kind I would define as "not seeing what, in the circumstances, should be seen."

Having just assumed for the sake of this reflection a "basically well-functioning brain," I must in the next breath recall that our contact with reality is not all that unambiguous to begin with. In a way, reality at the start of a human's experiencing is too overwhelming: reality equals Mom, who, in the good scenario, practically smothers. Weirdness seeps in when the child fails for whatever reason to get the closeness-detachment, and the intuitive-analytic, balances right. That is an art, in which we all seem to fail to some degree, the patients in for psychotherapy usually just more spectacularly!

Weirdness is almost everywhere. But I want to insist with utmost emphasis it is not transcendental: there are those wonderful human acts of generosity, perfectly targeted, unambiguous, producing good fruit, that reveal a sense of "being at home." Fairly rare, those "pure" acts, the cynic will say. I won't argue with that, but when they happen they are not weird. And rarer still, to be sure, are those saintly lives that shine with meaning and touch everyone who comes in contact with them, nourishing those who contemplate them and especially imitating them down the generations: I term these great souls, in a side glance at Heidegger, "the heroes."

MINDLESSNESS

It is weird that the only creature capable of thinking is so much of the time thoughtless. Mindlessness is both caused by certain forms of weirdness, those that prove to be blocks or disincentives to thinking (dimensions of decidophobia provide good examples—see Kaufmann's *Without Guilt and Justice: From Decidophobia to Autonomy*), and contributes to weirdness in general.

I shall not start with the world's best-known tradition for analyzing and talking about weirdness, the one that claims Freud as its seminal genius. I shall take my inspiration in further studying mindlessness from the first sustained reflections on it: Pascal's and Kierkegaard's. Their insights are brilliant and never reduced to a simple table. Walter Kaufmann's methodic analysis of decidophobia, on the other hand, provided good organized points to the following analysis, but his exaggerated, unrealistic notion of autonomy, a function of his resolute atheist faith, is not, as we shall see, altogether consonant with what follows. With gratitude for the insights from all three thinkers, I have humbly cobbled together what follows. I can see at least eight factors contributing to mindlessness: distraction; authoritarianism of many everyday worlds; misplaced desires, or obsession (control); lack of education; fear of the truth, which, to the extent we allow the realities of which truth is the revelation to enter our lives, adjustment to our programs is always demanded; failure to hear—hearing *(obedientia)* is difficult for a proud, busy man; lack of imagination; and lack of balance, attention too narrowly centered, no wisdom. (Later I shall ask, can one be too narrowly centered in choosing to focus his life in contemplating the Absolute?)

This dreary list grew out of the encounters with various forms of mindlessness that occurred in the course of this study. I intend now to pull together more systematically the causes and, then, after providing the needed context—the further examination of the virtues required to support a thoughtful (a "nonmindless") existence—I shall return to these causes to show how they may be methodically *(meta ton hodon* [along the way]) pursued.

Distraction

Starting with the massive reality of our everyday being swept along by the world, we have seen how the excess of demanding activities assaulting most persons in the developed world can be a major "environmental" impediment to any sort of sustained, wide-sweeping, carefully developed thought. Much that happens in a busy everyday life can be, and often ought to be, "thought provoking," but we are too hurried to be able "to stop and think." It is perilous to stop abruptly at a superhighway double cloverleaf to admire a striking vista. The air traffic control dynamic structures of our lives overburden our thought capacities, absorbing them into practical decision making "on the wing."

The problem here is the opposite of fear of deciding; rather, it is the apparent success of *"cool" "snap judgment,"* under the pressure of circumstances, "virtuoso flying by the seat of our pants." From that basic reality of flight follows inevitably a certain shallowness of commitment: it would be unreasonable to commit one's whole life to decisions he thought he had no time to consider carefully. Fortunately, the wealth of opportunity of the rich high-tech world always allows room to wriggle our way free from our old rapidly made commitments.

I spent two days with a friend who is a senior executive in a medium-tech company. On about ten occasions during our conversations I tried to draw his attention away from the immediate tasks of his job either to long-range-planning considerations or to social-political or religious issues not irrelevant to his role as leader (he is an active Catholic). It was painfully clear to me that this devoted man is suspicious of such reflection, which he seems to consider not only a waste of time but somehow an absurd diversion of energy—of which he has tons. His refusal to engage any theoretical issue was at times brutal. This from a good, bright, energetic, successful, courageous man, but of quite limited education. The relevance of that will become clear later.

Authoritarianism of Many Everyday Worlds

Most everyday worlds demand conformity—we are invited to knuckle down and do what we are told and to imitate the limited gamut of improvisations we see going on around us, treating as gospel the firmer structures. Kaufmann makes much of this, seeing it as a symptom of our fearing responsibility—we are glad to let the Church, or the Party, or the Movement, or the Company, or the Merchandisers decide for us. When you have not thought out who you are, there are only two choices: "going with the crowd" or becoming a wierdo eccentric loner, today likely to take the gestalt of just another "nerd" making one hundred thousand dollars a year as a computer whiz. The two choices of "being-avoidance" are equivalent in destructiveness of the person: obsessive concentration or *"Flucht vor dem Sein"*—flight before Being by stampeding with the crowd.

Misplaced Desires, or Obsession (Control)

Since we grow to awareness already having been integrated into and formed by the many worlds in which we live, we have always already learned to think in their vocabularies, permeated by their agendas. Much of our time and energy is spent learning and keeping up with the changes in that vocabulary and the situations that form it. There is both little opportunity and little desire to call into question the reigning assumptions built into their horizons. (Kaufmann develops this theme well.)

In the function of desires that themselves are narrow, absorbing, and often misplaced, we continue uncritically to be situated within those worlds. On the same uncritical basis, in the same desire-driven way, we place ourselves in new worlds with little examination of their ultimate implications. Giving into superficial desires, which can be at the same time intense, such as avidity of peer approval, feeds insecurity, because we really do not know who we are, and insecurity easily leads to obsession, as we latch on to something that provides a pseudosecurity. This is a failure to achieve the degree of autonomy that is legitimate and credible, a step toward authenticity.

Recall the earlier discussion of this form of the paradox of finite intellectual being: I am not a "law unto myself" (*autos-nomos*), because I am dependent and thus do not control much even of my little personal world, and at the same time I am a law unto myself, precisely in the sense of response-ability that has been explored throughout this book. The degree of well foundedness of motives for wanting to be "the best" determines the difference between the most mindless jumping, on the one hand, into a training that excludes almost everything else and, on the other, into playing in "a big game" that is also absorbing but because of what it involves—the richness of the reality—can be hugely mind-opening, if we somehow manage to leave ourselves time to think.

Lack of Education

From the start of this reflection I have reiterated this principle: sustained, broad-scale, and profound thinking requires education. One does not just think; one thinks "like a chemical engineer," or "like a Heideggerian lover of *Sein*," or "like an aficionado and performer of Renaissance music," or "like the CEO of an international oil company," and to some degree in all these ways of thinking. All serious, sustained thinking is founded in great culture, except that which mysteriously founds those cultures in immense intuitive creative leaps. A paradigm: a contemplative religious living in an advanced country has been painstakingly formed in the art of contemplation through a monastic institution passing on an explicit tradition.

Walter Kaufmann is so bent on "autonomy" he misses entirely the necessary dependence on a community of thought for formation and rich emersion in the insights and methods of a tradition. I believe he was too one-sidedly terrified of the negative aspect: the danger of such a strong ideological commitment to the tradition of one's own cultural formation that any salutary openness to the new is shut out. It is "high-level mindlessness" to fail to think through the implications of rich principles handed down by an old and honored tradition devolved into ideology.

It is easy to see the extent to which distraction interferes with the possibility of the long formations in thinking in various traditions that are essential to a wise life. Out-of-control distraction makes wisdom impossible. It is pathetic to observe unprepared persons trying to think their way through difficult and complex and most often fast-devolving situations. People have to learn to seek out and criticize the evidence for what they believe, and they have to be educated with a genuine security that allows them to be unafraid to challenge long-standing assumptions.

As it is hard work to discern, clarify, and test the evidence for anything complex, the incentive must be there to do it; there have to be *reasons that working to get at the truth is important; there has to be bred ("cultivated") a love for truth.* Kaufmann is passionate about our not allowing prejudice to stand in the way of getting at truth. What a pity that he is too quick to consign dependence on tradition to the dustbin of prejudice without seeing how genuine tradition and community are essential to the development of a truly free critical sense.

Fear of the Truth

"The truth will make you free!" But all truth new to us requires adjustments, and being creatures of habit, well settled into the patterns of our many worlds, saved by them from having to make too many courageous decisions of our own, we lack the will to find the time, the energy, and the courage—the leap into the "not yet"—to change. Kaufmann illustrates this central reality extremely well, but precisely there is where becomes tragic his underplaying of community.

Failure to Hear

Hearing is difficult for the proud, busy, and weak human. The tragic abuses of tradition, which take away responsibility, are no excuse. *Traditio semper reformanda.* Traditions are essential, and must always be reformed. Much of what has just been said about mindlessness can be summed up by pointing out that man makes himself hard of hearing, and dim-sighted.

Obedience (obedientia) is not a word in Kaufmann's vocabulary. What he does not see is that genuine obedience is founded in *a total commitment to the truth,* based on the faith that I am *always* better off accepting the reality of the real, and that the real reveals itself not just to me alone, nor even only to noncommunicating individuals, but to and through community efforts over time.

The unfolding of truth in time and space requires constant adjustment of past judgments. Every true scientist who slaves away to make a new observation does so because he is willing to hear (obey) the results, even if they trash six years' work. Every concrete failure to obey in this sense is an act of hypocrisy. It is a revolt against all authority (again a word that is negative in the mouth of Kaufmann).

The *"auctor"* is the originator: from *augere,* "to make grow," to foster, the source of what is real, the opposite of the authoritarian who says, "Do it because I say so." It is when a legitimate authority, suddenly lacking in genuine creativity, fills the void by sheer willpower and terror that we see the perfect, sinful perversion of the real, the corruption of the institution and the deformation of a tradition, which then requires reform.

Lack of Imagination

It takes a bit of imagination to find excuses for continuing to obey only one's own fantasies and distortions of the truth. But it takes considerably more imagination to envision adequately a complex situation, to see beyond the most obviously, most immediately given facts, and to leap beyond the present limits of horizons, vocabulary, principles advanced more with authoritarianism than with genuine authority.

See how creative imagination and imaginative memory are related. It is the same ability that allows both of the following: to hold on in memory to many facets of a complex, dynamic unfolding reality, to continue it into the future of one's attention as one contemplates it; and to see forward to what has not yet itself persistently presenced, which probably includes coming to see many connections already existing among the "already having been" facts that only slowly—and with creative imagination—dawn on one.

Leaps of the imagination as miraculous as Einstein's in the famous papers of 1905 are extremely rare, and so furnish inexplicable demonstrations of the power of creative imagination. They dramatize the pure grace of insight. We are so accustomed to little *"Aha! Erlebnisse"* (so the father of gestalt psychology, Wolfgang Koehler, called breakthrough experiences of insight small or spectacular), we fail to see how miraculous they all are. My eighteen-month-old son Marc recognized as we passed on the streetcar that a big power cruiser in a show window was a "bateau" just like the object in his experience with which he was familiar: an ugly little red plastic canoe in the bathtub. How can the brain possibly make such a leap correctly? For that matter, how is it ever able to create and recognize symbols at all? That is what traditions enshrine and pass on: the fruits of such leaps of imaginative creation and insight. Education develops the individual's imagination and understanding in contact with, and in order to be able to grasp, such cultural realities, one hopes in ways that prolong a sound creative process.

Lack of Wisdom

Lack of wisdom is *poor balance in our cognitive constructions; we are too narrowly centered, too restricted by our fears and practical imbalances between our many intersubjective worlds, and all not regularly enough re-formed through methodical criticism.* These effects are of course symptoms as well as causes of mindlessness. But the fact that one settles down as comfortably as possible within the little personal world he has constructed, by managing all his little worlds, individually and in their positions within one's all-englobing personal world, in a way that achieves a certain comfort level, requires remarkable inattention to the most fabulous realities. They have been pushed out and held from view because they are not immediately "practical," and because they require the virtue of a grand obedience. This unwise mindlessness comes without even trying, so absorbed are we within the interworld house of cards we have comfortably arranged in our personal world.

* * *

This brief treatment of weirdness was meant to explain an aspect of human being that is rather puzzling and counterintuitive. Weirdness has a profound impact on the way we live in the world and the way we view ourselves as individuals and the way we view human being across time. The weird is not identical with evil, although sometimes they coincide. The weird refers to that aspect of human being that is both factual yet strange or odd, even countersensical.

7

LOVE

An Example of "a Way's" Lighting the Path

Up to this point, I have discussed how human being is constituted by complex relations of different worlds where different persons with differing characters or souls dwell. I also discussed how imagination and the analogy of being can help us understand these worlds and ourselves. Part of this understanding must include an understanding of the weird. But there still remains a more practical question: what can motivate us to be more authentically human and help us appropriate all of the preceding dimensions and constitutive parts of human being? I believe the answer lies in love, but love is not something that is abstract. It is both cultivated and revealed within worlds and persons and within the dynamic relations that constitute our various worlds. Love can be understood only through the smaller and larger senses of what it means to dwell in the world as a human being, always driven to make authentic one's existence in the world. The next two and final chapters unpack the preceding claim.

THE HIGHEST FORM OF PRESENCE: LOVE

In my preliminary observations about human presencing, "love" was the name by which we called a person's opening to allow another—person or thing—to be present so the lover can know the object revealed, because the lover cares for whatever is presencing. If the other is a person, he too can manifest his wanting to be present, to exchange care. Benevolence ("willing the good" of the other) can be mutual, or it can be not reciprocated, one-sided.

Not all presencings are loving. An intense electrical storm catches one on the golf course; its presence cannot be ignored, so imposing is the phenomenon. What is the golfer to do to escape it? He seeks absence, not this frightening imposed presence. An officer of the law serving a most undesired summons is not lovingly received by me, although later, upon reflection, I acknowledge he was conscientiously carrying out a legitimate task, which he did politely and efficiently.

Why is it so hard for us to love? Everyone is for loving presencing; most are ready, indeed eager, to "fall in love" and to be loved. But in so many situations, we find it in fact hard to love. Often, we can be frightened by the real thing, with its insistent demand for response. We fear that commitment will be an "alienation." Suppose I become obsessed by stargazing, I have become so fascinated by the great luminous highways of our galaxy and by the nebulae that I have come to understand are other galaxies in their own right; I have become so fascinated by the reality of a cosmos unfolding before me that I cannot resist the attraction. Every dark, clear night, warm or cold, I am "out there" searching for the last three objects recorded in Messier's catalog, or I am so passionately fighting for time on the great instruments I have become unfit to live with. The heavens have taken possession of my soul.

If this obsession turns out to be a disorder in the person's life, resulting in his neglecting persons and things that should also be in his life but from which he has become alienated by the imbalance of his passion, he is not freely sacrificing himself to his astronomy; he is losing himself in the obsession. His giving of self broadens his horizons in certain respects, but the imbalance causes him to fail to cultivate other dimensions of reality to which he should be paying attention authentically. Taking possession of him, the obsession results in his ignoring other realities for which objectively he has a responsibility. In *Being and Truth*, I developed this notion of responsibility as related to responding; responsibility contains within itself a promise to do something, as the etymological root of the word *(spondeo)* suggests.

It is never easy to overcome pride so as to love the other—whether individual person or competing folk—in his or their very difference. Those differences may turn out not to be simple "correctable errors" after all. The differences may be elements challenging our respective treasured faiths. The alternative—crushing opposition by war (cutting off communications, mustering the authority of office, simply marginalizing people)—often seems more easily come by, but always turns out to have been in every way worse than the kind of considerate *polemos* that takes place between persons who genuinely respect one another even in their differences. Later we shall confront the daunting challenge of outlining "the wise way to go": abandoning unsound dreams of control as we sacrifice to love.

For the animal, the ultimate challenge is survival, leading to absorbing and often bloody *polemos*. Superficially, one might think that the closer man is to the survival level, the more his struggle is animal-like. That is not true, it turns out, for man, from the start, and at the most primitive, can allow spirit to reign. And we should all admit to selfish acts. I agree with Saint Paul in his alarm at not doing what he knows he should do and doing what he knows he should not.

Phenomenologist Max Scheler, in making something very telling out of the mediocrity of human beings—I refer to his wonderful study *Ressentiment*[1]—offers a stimulating perspective on love. For the Greek and Roman philosophers, logical form, law, justice—in short, the element of measure and equality in the distribution of goods and evils—are superior to love. Even though Plato, in the *Symposium*, for example, establishes great differences in value between various kinds of love, in Greek eyes, the whole phenomenon of "love" belongs to the domain of the senses. It is a form of "desire, of "need," and so on, that is foreign to the most perfect kind of being.

I agree with Scheler that this distinction is a natural corollary of the extremely questionable hard division of human nature made by the ancients—a division into "reason" and "sensuality"—into a part that is formative and one that is formed. Much that we have seen in earlier chapters points to the inadequacy of that distinction, because the two principles in reality interpenetrate. Why does Christian anthropology escape from it, despite the Platonic temptations of the early Fathers? Scheler's hypothesis is that in the sphere of Christian morality love is explicitly placed above the rational domain—love "that makes more blessed than all reason" (Augustine). This comes out quite clearly in the parable of the prodigal son. *Agape* and *caritas* are sharply and dualistically separated from *eros* and *amor*, whereas the Greeks and Romans—though they do acknowledge distinctions in value—see continuity between these types of love.

In explaining this, Scheler enunciates a principle that has come to the fore in our explorations, one to be kept at the center of our efforts to situ-

1. Max Scheler, *Ressentiment* (Milwaukee: Marquette University Press, 1994).

ate "love": Christian love is a spiritual intentionality that transcends the natural sphere, defeating and superseding the psychological mechanism of the natural instincts (such as hatred against one's enemies, revenge, and desire for retaliation). It can place a man in a new state of life. If that claim were to turn out to be true, it would give the most significant direction to our anthropology. To repeat: "A spiritual intentionality which transcends the natural sphere." "Intentionality" suggests direction: "tending in . . ." Scheler explains that the most important difference between the ancient and Christian views of love lies in the direction of love's movement. All ancient philosophers, poets, and moralists agree that love is a striving, an aspiration of the "lower" toward the "higher," the "unformed" toward the "formed," the *meon* (nonbeing) toward the *on* (being), "appearance" toward "essence," "ignorance" toward "knowledge," "a mean between fullness and privation." In the *Symposium*, Plato says bluntly, "We would not love if we were Gods," for the Gods need no fulfillment. The most perfect form of being—the divine, we would say—cannot know "aspiration" or "need."

Scheler contends that Christianity reverses everything in this way. He says that the Christian view boldly denies the axiom that love is an aspiration of the lower toward the higher and that the nobler stoops to the vulgar, the healthy to the sick, the rich to the poor, the Messiah to the sinners and publicans. One can certainly see here the influence of Nietzsche on Scheler's thought. The Christian is not afraid, as the ancient was, that he might lose something by stooping, impairing his own nobility. Now the very essence of God is recognized to be to love and serve.

One might protest to Scheler: but we are not gods. To acknowledge, as we have, that loving is difficult for human beings is the same as saying authentic human existence is achieved only with blood, sweat, and tears, a struggle upward. But that leaves this question before us: is this great difficulty just because we are not gods, because we are finite, or does it reveal in human being something more bizarre, perhaps a species-bound structural difficulty, something that might correspond to what we just recalled that Genesis describes, what the Fathers of the Church call "the effects of original sin"? In other words, is this an unacceptable fundamental deformity in our nature that retards the transcending, descending movement of generosity, something that might account for our difficulty in both receiving humbly and giving of ourselves generously, indeed "selflessly"?

The call to authenticity demands that the Hebrew and Christian theistic traditions' belief, that there is such a mystery of deformity about us, be addressed, if only to be demolished critically. The Hebrew with the Christian tradition grafted onto it throws open vast, ultimate horizons of significance. It is not just those formed by Judaism or Christianity or Islam who should face critically this aspect of ourselves that places such importance on our alleged "fallenness." The humanist who believes that "the Fall" is a misleading myth is likely to think it wise to dismiss the whole business with a wave of the hand. I suggest we hold seriously to the proposition that beyond the psychopathological there is something mysterious in our sometimes deliberately grasping the destructive when we could embrace the constructive.

Love requires being loved as a necessary condition for being able to receive and return love. I did not yet raise the question whether being loved, a necessary condition perhaps, may turn out, however, not to be a sufficient one. If not, what other factors than being loved are also necessary, for instance, to counteract traumas inflicted by acts of hate or of disordered passions? Is it possible that not just spontaneous but educative love is required to lead the young soul along a character-building path? There has to be a self to do the loving; a tiny infant gropes around, rather overwhelmed by reality. A child with a balanced, open temperament may learn more easily to love, but cannot all children be helped to build up habits of generosity? An anthropology that refuses to probe as deeply as we can into the question "Why is it so difficult to fulfill our nature and how can we best go about it?" cannot be adequate. Again, the more cynical kind of humanist (perhaps just reasonable) might reply, "There is nothing in our nature that calls for perfection; indeed, our finitude precludes it. We are called to manage as best we can a polemic world of power struggles. We have not evolved to be "love alone" (the latter the title of a wonderful little book by Hans Urs von Balthasar).

One can observe with the humanist, of course, that we simply evolved in such a way that what we popularly call "the good" is inevitably entwined with "the bad," and both are simply bundles of instincts developed during evolution, never destined to be "rationally" straightened out. Being selfless not only is obviously difficult but may not always be "wise," if by wisdom one means a wisdom of the world, where survival is the first demand. Selflessness may be, as Ayn Rand insisted, counterevolutionary.

Earlier I pointed to a natural structural difficulty that everyone can acknowledge confronts our efforts to love: our being born self-centered simply because we are constituted the center of our little individual worlds, with the instinct to survival a built-in, a "natural ruling consideration." Christians believe that if the God who is Love created us "in his image and likeness," that is, made us out of love, for love, then there must have been something in his plan from the start that could overcome this obvious structural handicap. That natural self-centeredness is the source of some ugly things if the little creature's development does not go right. Without overriding our natural freedom to respond, God might have provided some means to draw us out of self-centeredness, a response that would be lodged at the heart of love. That last point is based on the widely held conviction, shared by many humanists, too, that we are meant to be basically "free" even of the bondages we create for ourselves. Psychiatrists work very hard to help free patients from self-imposed limitations. (I am not including organic disorders that cannot be cured through psychotherapy. But I do mean the damage done to the psyche by others.) I have contended that common sense sees what that "something" is that can free us from the prison of our own selfishness. As to psychological disorder caused by neurological dysfunction or chemical problems, I repeat: that is another matter. Positively, it is all the loving others—the mother, the father, the friend, the teacher—educating us to love, to the extent they concretely and gradually succeed in drawing out our personhood, revealing to the young person the lovable reality transcending him.

That commonsense experience supports the hope that there is planted in our souls a natural propensity to respond to love with love. But from "propensity" to the actual creative breath of self-opening and self-offering love (on those occasions when we let love overcome ego demands), there must be something like a spiritual energy (which is what Scheler called "a spiritual intentionality") coming from the ultimate Source of our own spirits, deep down in our souls. As Gerard Manley Hopkins puts it in his poem "God's Grandeur": "And for all this, nature is never spent; / there lives the dearest freshness deep down things."

Recall this obvious truth: no lover is ever obliged to respond. Obligation by definition is not love—servile submission out of fear perhaps, but not love. "Martyrdoms" (*martyrein*, "to witness") can be sublime manifestations of a higher love but may also be witnessing to what you or I may know is a false god—the SS man giving his life for the führer. The witness of a misplaced martyrdom is powerful and most disturbing. Wasted or worse, it is expropriation by a false principle. Martyrdoms have taken the form of unbending refusal to obey a royal command—Saint Thomas More, Henry VIII's chancellor, comes easily to mind, witness to the holiness of the Church. Judging the legitimacy of the cause to which supreme sacrifice is offered is a vital issue.

Any genuine lover, including the Supreme Agape, freely puts himself into a position of vulnerability by extending his love to a free other, opening himself, among other risks, to the possibility of rejection. A gesture of genuinely allowing oneself to be "expropriated" by such offering to another risks an element of twisted pseudoresponse in the form of the other's appropriation, which would then not be really self-discovery by that other, not a growing becoming himself but just a power trip. God in his infinity cannot be overpowered, and he cannot be deceived, but the Old Testament shows him angry and upset by our twisted, ambiguous responses, our incomplete or inappropriate presencings, our refusals that lead to inappropriate absences, so upset indeed he seems tempted to destroy the whole order he has created. But then, like a vulnerable father, he relents easily to the prophets' pleading for yet another chance.

Conversion on man's part is humble, *humility* here once again being an analogous term. Humility should not be confused with the realism of recognizing the real limits of one's control. The Christian understanding of humility is located precisely in the utterly gratuitous divine initiative of God emptying himself to enter into the kind of reciprocal love relationship that can mean something to fallen man. Only the purely humble never disappoints—and that means the Infinite Divine lover alone.

My intention is not to back away from this reality: the tension existing between two lovers, whether both finite or divine, is complex and elusive enough for every poor man to get confused, even in a love affair with God, which retains ambiguity and mystery on the human side of the equation, an unattainable mystery on the other that cannot be plumbed.

Ontologically, it can be no other way; absolute clairvoyance and total "detachment" are impossible in a creature existing on his own. God's most beloved triumph seems to be working with a saint from without and from within that finite person to bring him freely to such perfection. Mary, conceived without the effects of Adam and Eve's sin, ready to accept the staggering demand of the Angel announcing that she was asked by the Father to be the Mother of the Word, accepted, puzzled but not hesitant: *Fiat voluntas tua!*

Since Plato's *Symposium,* so much has been written on love one is at a loss to know where to turn for help in reflecting upon it methodically.

To mine out a succinct but not totally inadequate vision from, say, Saint Augustine or Saint Thomas or Saint John of the Cross would be in each case by itself a hefty work of scholarship. I have been inspired for many years by a thin treatise, barely a hundred small pages long, which I soon realized invokes all the dimensions and dilemmas of love better than anything I could have ever hoped for in such a compact, clear form. The marvel in question is Hans Urs von Balthasar's *Love Alone: The Way of Revelation*.[2]

What I am wagering here is that the vision rooted in Balthasar's vast erudition can awaken in every thoughtful person echoes of realities that, though many readers may interpret them in non-Christian terms, can be integrated into his own ethics and wisdom with enrichment to his common sense. I am confident that readers most hesitant about Christianity will agree with me that many of the insights that I shall extract from Balthasar's text are illuminating for human being.

THE NATURAL REVELATION OF LOVE

At the start Balthasar reassures us that everyone can experience a natural revelation of love. It is in what we might call an experience of the fullest, greatest presencing. When a person encounters another freely, freedom engaging freedom, one learns this is not an invitation to master the other intellectually, to reduce him to being one's own object, to control him. One ought to recognize the total inappropriateness of all manipulative responses to any unqualified gift of self by the one who opens to him. Love granted to me can only be "understood" as a miracle.

The English translators included the word *revelation* in the title of this short work. The original German title, *Glaubhaft ist nur die Liebe*, literally, *Only Love Is Believable*, offers no hint that belief and revelation are related. But in a free gift by a person of a glimpse into his interior life, the "miraculous" nature of this revelation of self becomes apparent. The word *miracle* is not used here figuratively, "in a manner of speaking," but as a correct use of the fundamental sense of *miracle*: the bringing into being from out of the creative depths of a center of freedom. One can never account for it, either empirically or transcendentally, that is, by considering it a necessary constituent of the world, not even from knowledge of our common

2. Hans Urs von Balthasar, *Love Alone* (London: Continuum, 1970).

human "nature." A Thou meets me as an Other. Once offered, the gift of self can be accepted only in belief, in its acceptance as a reality genuine in its freedom.

Were I to believe I had comprehended the love of another for me, this love would be misused and inadequate, and there is no possibility of response. To com-prehend ("grasp in one's prehensors") something is in some way to take it into one's power. To the extent I believe I have understood someone, I am implying that he is not in that respect free to change, and, grasping now who he is, I can scheme and plot in function of that certitude. We encounter a similar miracle of gift when we experience startling beauty, whether in nature or in art.

This experience of necessity at the heart of things free is a fundamental ontological insight, an essential, foundational principle of wisdom: the "free" is anything but the merely capricious. Freedom as creativity is the fountain of necessity: that which, having been brought freely into being, to the extent it truly is, "radiates," manifesting that it is now necessary— it is what it is and cannot be other. So, neither love, in the freedom of its gratuitousness, nor beauty, since it is disinterested, are "products"—least of all of some person's need. We produce things; we scramble to make provisions to answer needs.

Artistic creativity, the radiation of beauty, and the love of the other for the other's sake have nothing to do with the power to command resources. I would add, is this not the very hallmark of "spirit"? The rose may be compelled by its nature to exude an attractive odor from its pollen, so that more roses can be produced as a result of the insect's pollination. But the gift suddenly offered me of an appreciation of its unique, necessary beauty (and the odor of a "tea rose" may or may not have something to do with material needs). Both beauty and human love always appear wonderful and glorious to us, this objective glory attracting us, an attraction that we live as some form of eros; we want to reach it and possess it. This is experienced as need fulfilling. But it is different with the glory of God, which is, as Scripture says, "beyond all comprehending": we cannot set out to find it, cannot call it down; its revelation astounds us.

We shall require considerable help to begin to appreciate the immensely important distinction of eros and agape, and the underlying reality here called, following Scripture, "glory" (*doxa*, as in "orthodox" [*ortho*, "straight"]: "You have got the glory right," or "This is the real thing"). In its Homeric context, the word *agape* meant "receiving welcomingly, graciously." But you can see from the New Testament's linking agape to *doxa*—the divine glory—that it has taken on a much more fundamental and profound significance.

Doxa-Gloria is the title Balthasar chose for the first part (seven volumes) of his monumental seventeen-volume unnamed trilogy. That first part, in German titled *Herrlichkeit,* confronts the reader with a triple pun: it does of course mean something like the radiance suggested by the Latin word *gloria,* but in German it contains the root *Herr* (the Lord) and the adjective *herrlich,* which means something like "splendid," as in "The party last night was *herrlich,* wonderful, glorious!" An aristocratic Lord, of course, is supposed to be splendid. Glory then means the primordial resplendence of being, which is wonderful ("miraculous") and noble. Hence, the erotic search for satisfaction is utilitarian; it is not the true, fundamental aesthetics of the free gift of Being itself, which is, rather, "glory."

Resplendence, we have just learned, is "necessary" and never "a mere product"—the necessary that is absolutely gratuitous! The reader should pause right here to look into his experience of beauty and love, contemplating that primordial truth of resplendence, the key to what "being" really is! No wonder Balthasar termed the first part of his trilogy "a transcendental aesthetics." What we often tend to call "an aesthetic thrill" may be only eros, the reaching out to satisfy an impulse or a need. *Doxa,* *agape*—nonproductive—is about creation of the new.

A hint that might help: the Easter vigil refers to the Fall of Adam as "Oh necessary fault!" A free (and disastrous) act that once committed is what it is, necessary, but certainly not resplendent. Once it has happened it cannot not be. God is not fated to respond; he need not; he has no needy eros. But in sovereign freedom he does respond, this time with the necessity that is resplendent, the most marvelous grace, the Redemption through the Incarnation, death and resurrection of his son! The noblest response to the utterly ignoble, the freedom (to destroy) responded to by the freedom (to create anew). This is all condensed into one aesthetic form: the horror of "the Man" pinned bloodily to a tree. This form has, paradoxically, miraculously elicited among the greatest of all human artworks. (Grünewald's tortured figure of the Christ nailed to the tree in *Issenheim Altarpiece* is in no way erotic, repulsive rather, but to the highest degree aesthetic.)

Once again: *Agape* is the term the New Testament employs for this gracious giving of himself on the part of the Supreme Source of all reality, the beautiful shining forth of the Creator in the creation, his glory *(doxa),* through which he freely binds himself to his creation, remaining faithful to it. Like all love it has to reveal itself by offering itself, but the divine *doxa* secures the total otherness of the appearance of the love of God, and prevents any confusion with any other love, however absolute and personal. The plausibility of this divine love is not illumined by reducing it to and comparing it with what man has always recognized as love. Its plausibility comes only from the form of the revelation itself. This form is so majestic that, without expressly demanding it, its perception exacts from the beholder the attitude of adoration.

I have stressed the centrality of "attitude," how the person "holds himself" *(verhalten)* in opening a future. Balthasar here points to a fundamental attitude, perhaps the most fundamental attitude to which we are called, through our response to the *doxa*: adoration. I shall struggle to give a first illustration of what Balthasar is driving at. When a man says of a woman with whom he has "fallen in love," "She is wonderful *(Herrlich!)*, and I adore her," he may in fact be expressing an erotic attraction. If he were to come to love her, however precisely, as an ever surprising center of freedom, in other words for who she is in herself, in the freedom necessity of her selfhood, he might then in and through her discover something of the ultimate reality, of the ultimate Source of all being manifesting its all-originating primordial reality, real and original source of all reality, ex-pressed analogously through the free creature. Then the frail human lover might rise to being able to mean literally, "I adore her!"

The reader can see the problem with this invocation of revelation for anyone writing a philosophical treatise on human being: if it is true that Love itself has reached down to us to reveal its glorious reality, and only through this can we hope to begin to plumb the depths of the mystery of our own defective human love, then this revelation by God of his glory would throw such essential light on our human experience of (lesser) erotic love that a philosophical anthropology would ignore it at the risk of avoidable essential distortion of the human reality! I might add, since this revelation has been the central continuing inspiration of two millennia of Occidental reflection on, and efforts to live out, the destiny of man, ignoring it would be anthropologically irresponsible: at the very least, its pretensions should be refuted, showing its (disastrous) distortions of reality (precisely what the powerful Sigmund Freud struggled to do).

It is a fact about human being that the most influential bundle of traditions in all of history, the "Abrahamic"—whether one believes their provenance to be in whatever sense a "revelation" or not—has unfolded with a vision of love at its center. Acknowledging that, I cannot responsibly avoid investigating here what light might be derived from these insights. Fundamental experiences vary dramatically: in the possession of those who reject any revelational claim, a purely human sense must be argued for the eros-agape distinction. Theists with different senses of how this revelation occurred will discover important nuances. We all can grow more sensitive to experiences of "love" and "grace" widely reflected within Occidental common sense.

A LOVE THAT IS NOT ALTOGETHER LOVE: THE LIMITS OF HUMAN LOVE

Love, Balthasar declares, is built into the foundations of all living things. In the higher animals this becomes unmistakable, as the unpremeditated play of eros becomes quite visible: the animal's dedication to its young; the individual's renunciation for the sake of the whole. In man this transitory relationship may extend into the spiritual sphere and acquire a meaning that transcends time: the erotic impulse may open the way to enduring faithfulness so that the natural relationship between parents and their offspring may be deepened into a genuinely spiritual family love; the dying consent of the individual to the survival of succeeding generations may give rise to the idea of self-sacrifice for the good of the community, the clan, the people, or the state—and a man's death may harvest the whole of his existence, binding it into an act of self-abandonment in which there is an intimation of the love hidden in being itself.

But this all implies a particular process, a way (for example, to species survival) rather than a completion. This is a key consideration. A process may be good in virtue of the aim sought, but at the same time it is not yet, not fully; it is on the way to becoming what it can be only when it is complete. Presencing is not the fullness of an (absolute) presence. Mozart is composing Symphony no. 41 in his head; he has not worked out the finale yet, nor has he written anything. Three weeks later he has written it all down. "It is consummated!"—all but for the first performance. Human institutions, I pointed out in *Tradition and Authenticity*, are cooperative, often hierarchical "being with" (*Mitsein*), evolved to acquire and keep control of certain processes in order to achieve collectively (but not necessarily evenly or even equitably) certain ends. Typically, institutions are driven by eros, not agape. But in their agreed-upon and consistent lasting structures—their "constitution"—they enjoy a presence more lasting and "higher" than the flow of processes they manage. There can develop a love for the institution that is closer to agape than to eros. The perennial problem for finite freedom is this: There are always other strong or weaker forces at work other than the erotic push forward, which limit or even paralyze the movement of erotic love.

Balthasar finds a good word to say about what he calls "the English Christian free thinkers," Hobbes, and more moderately, Locke, who saw the error of trying to make man simply into a moral animal, for he is first an animal, and remains limited by his roots. Any attempt to perfect man as a moral being runs into the reality of those animal roots. So Augustine and Pascal in their analyses of human existence got it right when they saw that concupiscence must be taken into account in any anthropology. It is that basic truth that has motivated throughout this present study a constant effort to remember our cosmic foundations, to see in every concrete situation the time-space limitations, and the incarnation of habit-molded influences on our free acts.

For the humanists, since human finitude means, then, that life cannot be explained in terms of a love transcending our nature, love withdraws into little islands of mutual sympathy: of eros, of friendship, of patriotism, even a certain universal love, a humanism based on the nature common to all men. This is easily the source of the great humanistic religions. The philosophical and mystical world religions all strive to achieve the "existential" experience of such an identity above and beyond all differences.

THE INELUCTABLE MYSTERY OF MAN

Love must be perceived. Recall the word of Karl Stern's professor: "We must be astonished at the proper moment." Astonishment (*taumazein*—Aristotle), awe, and adoration are different aspects of the same basic attitude: the preparation by which one is placed on the level of the thing revealed, by which one is attuned to it "at the proper moment," namely, when the beloved object offers to share itself. The coming to be of that moment is always a gift. If a geologist hiking with his family happens on an outcropping in which is imbedded something of great significance, the gift is typically twofold: there is the coincidence of his happening along here and the long-prepared reality of his relevant geological knowledge. Cultural history meets natural history at this moment. It may not be "proper" to ask his family to park their bodies at the foot of the cut for two hours, if that is what it would take. But if coming back for a long look another time is excluded by the fact that the family is leaving the next morning to fly home, a debate over what is proper at this moment may ensue, the research hanging from the outcome of an imminent inter-subjective *polemos*. The Christians became the masters of this sense of the moment because of the touching down into time of the divine, the ultimate in awesome experience: *kairos*, they called it. In the encounter between persons the attitudes of both are essential in creating the *Mitsein* that is an interpersonal encounter, a bi- (or even multi-) polar presencing.

Balthasar points out that the astonishment that is one's noticing that another really is other and fascinating is "a habit of mind," which he sees being strengthened by every genuine encounter. Every attitude is sustained through the reliability of the virtues of character. (Recall that bad attitudes can also be resolutely maintained, by well-practiced vices.) Now Balthasar challenges us further: the particular virtues that make possible all awe, astonishment, and adoration are "the trinity of faith, love and hope." These intertwined virtues must be present at least in germ for any genuine response of any kind to take place.

If my reader is himself prepared with the appropriate attitude, then he should be at least a bit astonished by that declaration. The claim that the condition for the possibility of a profound appreciation of anything is a commitment that whatever is at issue is worth the effort to contemplate is an act of faith, opening "a line of credit" to the other, as Gabriel Marcel put it, to every resistant other over which we stumble on our path. The other is truly other to the extent that I cannot control it, but I can have a well-founded faith that effort spent in genuine admiration of it will yield light. The hope invoked here is not much different from that confidence that the contemplated object will yield this something truly appreciable, worth the effort. The love is the engagement itself. The attitude, which combines in interaction the three virtues, faith, hope, and charity, demands building up, an education in the life of the spirit in which the person is gracefully (and often painfully) led out and opened up to certain kinds of reality. Together mature faith, hope, and charity constitute an attitude of mindfulness.

The humanist will have no difficulty acknowledging that something like the virtues of faith, hope, and love and are indeed in one sense "super-natural" in that they are a gift that does not come "naturally"— they are not the genetically predetermined natural givens: to appreciate

Chagall, for instance, I must have been motivated by something beyond me, something that cannot be expected just because I am born a human being with certain natural cognitive capabilities: I have been taught to look at complex paintings.

It is in no sense "natural" to want to contemplate seriously great art. "High culture" is a cooperative construction of free human beings called from out of a tradition to create "miraculously" (there is no explaining leaps of human creativity) "great" works—great in their complexity, their originality, the depths of their cultural roots. There is greatness too in the solidity of the institutions built to sustain them (think of the hard work that goes into keeping up an art museum or a symphony orchestra). As cultural, what has been given may be the result of a mother's cultivating through many free gifts, building up *(bilden)* in the young person a treasury of images *(Bildern)*, and drawing out from his nature a reality that goes beyond the basic human givenness that comes from every healthy gestation. It is a pure, long, and sustained work of love.

And, most basically and more defensively, I need the whole series of acts that sustain an atmosphere—a world—in which as a vulnerable child I am protected from damage. I must not ever be allowed to become so depressed that I despair of appreciating anything, which would mean that my nature had been (partially) thwarted. Some persons are so diminished by aggressions, coupled often with bad decisions they make in response, that they are unable to appreciate very much, least of all themselves. The tiresome notion "lack of self-esteem" we hear about all the time is, alas, a reality: it is a "libertarian" way of invoking a tragic situation—the destruction of the child's sense of his true worth.

The basic capacity to appreciate at all comes with the natural gift of human nature. But the gift of that which appears before us for appreciation, and the gift of knowing the appropriate way (and moment) to contemplate this kind of thing or that complex person, and the gift of having been guided away and protected from the damage we can do ourselves or that others can inflict on us, all this comes from beyond human nature and from beyond us as limited particular persons. When the presence that is offered is not just natural beauty or an artwork but is the being-there *(Da-sein)* of another free human being, there is obviously further complexity: that Other must open himself, freely offer himself, before there is any full human presence, two interiors revealed through bodily exteriors. That is the condition for the being-there before me that I am now invited to love, my love then being a responsive gift of myself. In both directions there is patently a gift coming most obviously from beyond the nature of each person, at the very least from the fruits of gifts of culture received.

INFUSION OF THE GIFT OF THE "SPIRIT TO APPRECIATE"

Being human does not entail inevitably, necessarily being loved by another human. (I know well a psychologically disturbed young woman who claims—and her stepfather confirms this—that she was never once cuddled during her eighteen months in an orphanage.) Nor do all gifts come "from the outside," through graces offered by other human beings. Rather, certain traditions claim, the Creative Source can infuse directly into the human spirit gifts of insight, light, love that transcend the normally, naturally, genetically given.

This anthropology is not the place to argue for or against such a claim. In *The Catholic Tradition*, I offered my reasons for believing a certain version of such a claim. Whether a certain genetic and educational preparation of the particular brain necessarily precedes every gift of insight is not an issue I shall deal with here. That "editorial" exclusion applies to this central question as well: if God infuses gifts of insight, are there any grounds for believing he eventually offers the super-natural gift of himself to everyone in one form or another, at one time or another in their lives, offers it directly, not just as foreshadowed in created things, the Church, or prophetically present in texts and works of art? That is an enormous question about which theologians speculate, one to which no one knows the answer. In his last work, *Was Dürfen Wir hoffen?* (What Dare We Hope?), Balthasar argued that "it is permitted to hope" that, in the end, God finds a way to win over every soul to make freely the decision of love, persuasion that does not fail (remember if God really is God, he can make himself quite attractive, even therapeutic!). The place of eternal desolation of those who have cut themselves off from every gift of love, while existing, as Scripture insists, would be empty! It is interesting to see how resistant to such an idea many serious Christians are; personally, I find it makes sense so to hope, if there is a God. Such a hope, if genuine, would achieve the opposite of presumption. But in the final analysis, Balthasar stresses, it is not given to us in this life to know. Our love here is based on faith and hope, not irrefutable, utterly controllable scientific evidence. But then neither is your evidence for your wife's love for you.

8

BALANCE AND INTEGRATION

Before turning finally to the ultimate foundations of wisdom, and the complexities of balancing loves, there remains a vast issue of overall ontological-authentic context, a tremendous challenge for formal education: presenting and helping the young learn to integrate the many different kinds and scales of time with which high-tech man is confronted. So recent and so complex is the progress in time consciousness, educators have as yet not even seen that authenticity requires a formal preparation for relating temporalities in tension. This is not the place to sketch an appropriate educational structure, even though in this study the various temporalities have been introduced and related. I doubt that we are ready now to undertake the full philosophical endeavor of building a sane curriculum.

The wise individual's personal time now enfolds what has recently been learned of cosmic time: the objective reality of the endurance and dimensions of an expanding universe, with earnest hypotheses of the possibility of the existence of many universes. Like the galaxies in our own universe, these other universes may be eventually found to manifest different phases of development, if hypotheses like "string theory" succeed in inferring such a reality. So the personal "interior lives" of those who know of these discoveries and hypotheses enclose the immensity of not just one universe but hypothetically a large number of universes, all in stages of development.

Paradoxically, it is significant how little the awareness that the Big Bang occurred 13.52 billion years ago seems to affect our sense of conducting our daily lives. If I am convinced by the recent measure that allows the accuracy of that figure, what effect has that on my scheme to cut five minutes from my itinerary to work this morning? For that matter, what effect

166

has it on my religion? Do I, as a believing Christian, not assume that the heart of "the drama of redemption" takes place within the continuity and awareness of a span of history (very brief in cosmic terms), and that my concern for my life and the lives of those with whom I share now this phase of the planet's development is where that which matters most is centered?

The same now well-established cosmic facts have a different significance for the theist and the atheist. According to the atheist, much time is needed to provide the unfolding of unimaginably multiple dynamic forms, allowing the large possibility of random selection, that have led to the development of conscious, reflective creatures who can appreciate it. For the theist, *Allah akbar* (God is great)! No matter in however many universes he brings forth conscious interlocutors, it all shows to the theist, in still finite ways, glimpses of boundless infinity. Such thought little affects different persons' religion because religion usually has much more to do with personal experiences of intimate intersubjective relations. Despite all the recent incomparably great developments of time consciousness, including pushing back our historical consciousness of human experience and out to all peoples, it is the more immediate and intimate historical formation of our daily selves and our personally most important traditions that has by far the most dominant influence on us. When educators integrate "comparative religions" into a spot in a curriculum that otherwise is rather poor in presenting responsibly the historical development of mankind, it is most likely to have the effect of encouraging a woozy relativism.

A way of counteracting this is to build an education around one of the long-enduring, rich traditions. Even when this is done, for instance, by Catholics (as we have attempted to do by mining the rich texts of Balthasar on Christian love) attempting to present a balanced and nuanced view of the many millennia of the Hebrew-Jewish-Christian tradition, the time and resources required make it almost inevitable to reduce glimpses at other great traditions more as sources of objections against Catholicism that have urgently to be answered. Already, it is nigh impossible in a contemporary elementary and secondary school curriculum to present with accuracy and fairness the different forms that Christianity takes in the many different tribal, national, and social class milieus. Finally, it is an illusion to think one can present the living soul of a great tradition that one has not lived, the intersubjective world of that tradition having only a remote influence on the presenter.

THE SECRET OF LIVES THAT "HAVE IT TOGETHER"

This reflection with its depressing dimensions—sad reminders about inadequate, even bad, planning, about the explosive expansion of our sense of time, which we can barely grasp at this point, about manipulation and false loves, fantasy obscuring reality, and the realization that most of the important human realities have to be lived by the one seeking to appropriate them critically—suggests that in conclusion we swing to the opposite, the happy possibilities: we shall find encouragement to wisdom in a final consideration of what it is that, despite all those serious limitations, grounds the possibility of our living coherent, fruitful lives. I cannot be of much use in attempting this for traditions that remain largely foreign to me. I promised earlier, under the rubric of looking more closely at "the secret of saintly lives," to pursue at least the tradition of wisdom in which I have personally been formed, hoping that readers from other traditions can bounce off this experience, reflecting on similar dimensions at the foundation of their own lives and those with whom they have lived most influentially. I am here recalling this appellation *saint*, rather than moving on to *the sage*, because, having proposed for the reader's serious attention the fundamentality for human being of love, I am seeking to develop as many of the dimensions of it as I can, which plunges us into an episteme that is as much will as intelligence. The man of love is better called "saint" than "Nobel Prize winner."

How are saints educated? How in different traditions are they led to break through some of the common limits—especially the self-imposed veils—that obscure life for us ordinary mortals? What is it that then stands revealed to them, to guide them surely on their paths and to aid the development of character of iron protecting hearts of great tenderness and compassion, saving the hearts for moments of meaningful sacrifice as opposed to foolishly throwing away one's life?

To the world, the saint can look the fool—remember the great Dostoyevskian theme. But look again: how is it that the saints are so supremely mindful? This mindfulness I believe fundamental to what is meant here by a "saint." The New Testament portrays Jesus Christ as knowing exactly what he was doing as he marched to his certain doom, doing "not my will but the will of the Father." At the core of every saintliness there is an illumining of a greater reality than that of the saint's limits. The incarnate Logos accepted to march step by painful step to the place of supreme sacrifice, bringing unfolding illumination into finite human history.

In *Being and Truth*, I struggled to clarify the basic human need to pursue "holiness." The word *holy* is from the German, *Heil*, from whence the English words *hale* (as in "hale and hearty" and "hale and farewell," which means I wish you, in undertaking a journey, to enjoy health and to fare well in your enterprise, by staying on [the wise] path). The English words *whole* and *health* both come from this root—health, wholeness, sanctity, and integrity are all ways of expressing the need for the human being (once again the vernacular has it right) "to get his act together." The word *sanctity* has the advantage of bringing to the fore the role of the "sanctum," that ultimate reality, be what it may, which founds the meaning of one's life. How, working from the limits of a human point of view, can such "wholeness" ever be achieved? Here is a glimpse at how one tradition lives out this challenge.

AT THE CORE OF THE *EK-SISTENTIAL* STRUCTURE: FAITH, HOPE, AND CHARITY

For our consciousness to move beyond passive reaction under the assault of what most insistently and spontaneously presents itself, to proceed into the "not yet" with a genuine consistency, based in carefully criticized evidence, the person must believe on firm grounds in the partially unveiled aspects of the object of his quest. In the case of a human creation, one must believe that there is some possibility of its being able to be finished by being installed firmly in existence that is illumined by authentic horizons. If the artist or the searcher despaired, fearing his creation or discovery will prove trivial, he would not continue to invest passion and energy in continuing the creation of it. The researcher will abandon his quest once he begins to believe he is finding only a chimera or a triviality.

To be "genuine" means that a faith is well founded, in the sense that as the quest unfolds the sought-for reality reveals itself in ways that allow critical connection to the already having been, inviting expanding rather than arbitrarily contracting horizons of interpretation. In persons suffering from certain psychopathologies, and in persons of bad character, there is no affording the luxury of paying attention to certain hard realities. Denial does not always take the form of repression of things one has known. There is a way of so structuring one's life that the occasions for some things or persons to demand attention and thought are structured from early on. When first introduced in school to the challenges of mathematics and science one can, with a sweep of the arm, decide forever, "This has nothing in it for me," and so save himself much hard work. The same with great art and music. Parents can spend a small fortune on music lessons, but so self-centered is the adolescent, he lets the matter drop, never to pursue the mysteries of great musical visions. And how casually can the fruits of a long religious education be dismissed when one decides to go another road.

Were the person to engage in the sociopathological unrealism of liberal individualism and thus believe himself somehow absolutely autonomous, his faith would be founded in an illusion. Genuine faith transcends a "whistling Dixie" self-confidence; it is not bravado but, rather, is founded in confidence in Others that has proven sound, a confidence that allows realistic assessment of the ways in which this person or that is or is not to be counted on.

To what extent does genuine faith require profound confidence in a "hero" whose large image attracts within ample horizons and, in so attracting, illumines in breadth and depth the way to wisdom? There is nothing more dangerous than creating for oneself, according to one's comfort level, a phony hero, the kind of idol one might call "a Little Tin Jesus," following one's own projected fantasy. Genuine faith must be precisely an *ek-sistential* (literally, a standing out of oneself) reaching out to "the other than me" precisely as other (for only an other can draw me out to that which is radically new to me, transcending my heretofore limits), the reality of which is to be listened to ("obeyed," but re-sponse-ably, hence critically, the condition of its being able genuinely to enrich my world).

If genuine, it will always be the discovery of a reality that I shall never be able fully to com-prehend ("wrap my prehensors around"). As research or friendship opens onto mystery, which is lurking always just below the surface of present knowledge, anything real opens onto the infinite depths of the cosmos. There we encounter the new coming to be: creation continuing and, in the case of persons, freedom. There is a new surging into the soul and surging from it, as the creations of the soul's interior are ex-pressed. So, I discover and acknowledge the other to be a center of freedom that I am not meant to control, but from whom I learn and with whom I am called to cooperate. Genuine faith then is an *ek-sistential* act of going out from the self to become obedient to the other as *auctor* (the author or the one who increases) of its own being, and to the *auctores* that feed the other's being, faith as a stand that is truly receptively listening, hence seeking to love rather than to control.

A well-founded faith is grounded then in reciprocated love: the other not only pulls the *ek-sistent* out beyond himself but returns assurance of enduring enrichment and support. When someone admires a crystalline rock, the reciprocated "love" of the mineral is minimal, but not inconsequential: it consists in the rock's just being what it is, simply there, involuntarily contributing its crystalline structure as a certain kind of light reflects off it, bringing to the admirer a form. The rock does not actively solicit my attention as my hungry cat does. The feline expresses his satisfaction by purring as he begins to eat, but his owner is fancifully projecting if he interprets those happy sounds as an expression of gratitude.

Expectation that there is ever more good awaiting me—the dimension of loving engagement that is called "hope"—is not "a leap of pure faith" but a logical step in the ongoing discovery and reciprocation of another's love, from the foundations of the material structures of the cosmos to the highest manifestations of gratuitous love. Stephen A. Mitchell, in *Hope and Dread In Psychoanalysis,* seems discouragingly realistic about the limits of genuine hope in another human being.[1] Mitchell maintains that we must found our hope on critical examination of our own experience. This is what the philosopher calls "a necessary condition," but not, your author adds, "sufficient." I believe, for reasons I have not well spelled out in this book, we need the model of a hero much fuller in the realization of one's humanity than hope in ourselves can offer.

Striving for sanctity becomes meaningful only when one has been offered and accepts a great love, which implies accepting knowingly, explicitly. That acceptance may come in a flash, a genuine act of being consumed by love, but more often it is a gradual deepening in one's willingness to let the lover open one out beyond the old limits of a narrow self-centered world. In both instances—flash of conversion or long struggle to open to greater sanctity—it is the ongoing effort to be faithful and hence to deepen and widen one's acceptance of the love that is "the striving for sanctity."

Assume for the moment that the object of that love is altogether real

---

1. Stephen A. Mitchell, *Hope and Dread in Psychoanalysis* (New York: Basic Books, 1995).

and serious enough to be worthy of the kind of devotion one gives it: that love will continue to pour genuine Being into the soul of the one striving for sanctity; the love brings progressive union with the truly *sacrum.* In contrast, "obsession" is a misdirected, twisted self-fascination, masquerading as a love, focused on something unworthy of so much attention, something from which the psychiatrist will be right in trying to help the patient free himself.

The scientist in love with his galaxies, or megamolecules, or pathogens can avoid obsession if her love is a genuine admiration of the structures she is investigating. When the beloved is another person who draws you out of yourself through his own loving generosity, it is more difficult, but still not impossible, to become obsessed. (The loving other—if the love is genuine—will warn if signs of obsession begin to manifest themselves. I am suggesting that genuine love always enlightens; this is an essential sign of its being love.) If one is fantastically projecting himself around a selection of attributes of the other, one hopes the other, seeing this, will find a way to break through to the interior life of the obsessed to help him free himself from his self-obsession.

Love offers education, drawing out beyond the previous bounds of the disciple's horizons. Like all graces, any such opportunities can be refused. Think, for example, of the student who rejects the opportunity to be ignited by his professor's enthusiasm for astronomy because the immature one has allowed his laziness or lack of imagination to interfere with the attraction into that great love.

DISCIPLINE AND THE GRACE OF LEARNING TO LOVE

It is a delicate process, the educative opening of a human being to love. I shall circle back for a moment to the very beginnings to underscore the role of discipline and obedience in building a culture of love.

When the infant discovers that the Provider is not simply a pawn of the baby's screaming and smiling powers, the natural tendency is to use his few capabilities to manipulate, playing up and down the scale of his voice until he finds the screech that drives the Provider "up the wall," and though it takes longer, he learns to use the smile productively. As he masters these games he begins to see the extent to which the Other is not just his plaything but a responsive center who seems somehow to mix together obliging reply beyond screech and smile through a vast range of verbal tools of communication, displaying ever new wonders that develop the child's ability to admire. The consequent complexities bring lessons of deliberate denial for the sake of (horrors!) discipline. Communication—the harmonizing of meanings emanating from distinctive but cooperating worlds—requires discipline, built on habits of power: virtue.

The little child certainly does not understand why Mommy won't let him touch the hi-fi, and he gets joy out of putting her to the test repeatedly. Mommy herself must then show discipline, never yielding, however beguiling her opponent; she must look stern when she really wants to laugh at this unequal test of wills. For this interaction to be soundly formative, her reasons for demanding and refusing must be matters of love, well-founded reasons, or else the love of discipline will not be born, only frustration at the arbitrary. The waffling hero will soon seem hollow. Eventually, however, the imposed strictures, and even positive possibilities, can be verbally explained.

It is crucial to human being who and what we obey—if we listen but receive back only confused signals, integrity will not be advanced. A psychiatrist friend once said to me in a difficult context: "There is nothing worse for children than mixed signals!" The discipline must eventually lead to an appreciable result; given the infant's still limited imagination, this had better be sooner rather than later. Since mother is the Great Provider and Coddler, the Built-in Hero (Father often is not consistently there), her charge may have sufficient confidence in her to feel there is some reason for this "hi-fi arbitrariness," even though for the moment he cannot imagine what. It is becoming clear, though, that, both as provider and as disciplinarian, she is not just a function of me! The infant is not only learning that Mommy loves him—hence he can have faith in her—but also learning to obey, and that this obedience is not necessarily in contradiction with the faith and love he has in her (if what he hears confirms the rest).

Throughout life we are called on constantly, in virtually all worlds, to obey. It is important to distinguish three kinds of obedience:

1. Listening out of terror. I'll do what you demand although I hate it. I have to, because the consequences of revolt are too terrible! From this experience one learns the raw facts about brute power, about ineluctable opposition. That produces kowtowing, the "passive-aggressive" personality, and can provoke a beginning of this fan-

tasy: "I can beat this game . . . just watch me!" It is the opposite of a
school for love.

2. I am confronted by an authority, but instead of kowtowing or rebel-
   ling, I actually hear and hearing, see or at least feel that what the
   other is saying and demanding is generally reasonable and to my
   benefit, and perhaps to the benefit of all to heed. In this way I learn
   that this particular discipline is a function of reality and of love. It
   nourishes my hope.

3. I place myself voluntarily under the authority of the head of an
   organization, willingly (and lovingly) accepting his guidance, or I
   discover that in the intersubjective worlds in which I find myself
   there are always already operative authorities. My submissions can
   happen for any number of reasons, which may be good or bad. Perhaps I accept the authority of the school into which I voluntarily
   inscribe. Or maybe I abandon my responsibility to another blindly
   because I crave the power of being part of a gang.

To the extent that in love I discover the goodness and the benevolence
of another and the cause for which he stands, I should be most willing to
hear his advice in matters where he is competent. One obeys his doctor,
and has confidence in his psychiatrist, just as a child confidently obeys
his mother and father in areas where their competence is far superior to
his own. All such sound authorities nourish hope.

DISCERNING TRUE FROM FALSE PROPHETS

The persons one confidently follows, giving over part of one's life to
them, are like gods offering structure to our lives. Their model furnishes
a future from out of the "already having been." Of course, we all grumble
against all our gods. But it is the degree of genuineness of the "god" that
founds the contrast of the "saint's" love in its integrity over against the
fanaticism of the delusional, obsessive, exalted fool under the sway of a
false prophet. To the extent a prophet is false, the follower, having chosen
to model himself on either someone largely mythical or upon a person
who existed or exists with strong personality and challenging program,
the lacunae of which are plugged by the blindness of fanaticism, creates
what Holzner calls (in the context of contrasting the teachings of Saint
Paul with the pagan Greco-Roman religion of the time), "oriental fanati-

cism and "surexcitism." To the extent certain Jews, Christians, and Muslims display fanaticism, one should reexamine the heroes at the source to judge critically whether the sources show such potential for fanaticism or whether pathological adepts have twisted the vision of the founding heroes. This is a far more serious business than, for instance, hockey fanaticism—the effort of the poor bloke to plug the emptiness of a flat life with made-up heroism on a very narrow base. A good example of how genuine heroes do not of themselves breed fanaticism: there is no hysteria in the music of Bach or Mozart, but with the mighty *Eroica*, inspired by a (false and soon corrected) view of Napoléon, fanaticism in music makes its first (and rather noble!) appearance. Wagner was not far behind.

All of this is to introduce the most crucial of all questions confronting the human being, more important than mere physical survival: *how can one be sure that she has come into genuine contact with a real "god"? How do we recognize "true prophets" of that "god"?* Beyond the very personal loves in the family, source of powerful "hero worship" and through them inevitable influence from the god (if indeed "God is love"), contact for larger-scale matters with the ultimate god—the Zeus of our lives—generally occurs through the god's preferred, historically significant "prophetic instruments." These "prophetic instruments" are human beings who are put forward in very different ways by various kinds of traditions, having been chosen by the Source to reveal itself. For instance, the physics professor has been ordained by the institutional heads (the Ph.D. examiners and then "the bishop," in academe called "the Provost") to pass on authoritatively the faith of physics to trusting undergraduates. The closest one comes in this realm to the divine is in admiration of the "Authors of the Great Breakthroughs"; there is something of "the god" in Copernicus, Galileo, Tyco Brahe, all the way to Einstein, Heisenberg, and perhaps soon the authorities of "string theory." Only other more senior prophets are in a position to criticize authentically the earlier prophets: researchers able to access the deity as intimately and originally as possible. (In this tradition the Source of all intelligibility lies in the cosmic phenomena, mediated through expensive instruments, expressed in a highly developed, indeed arcane, language—mathematics—the whole enterprise governed by the research institutions that provide the data upon which the theories rest [and which even have their own rituals, including nomination to the College of Cardinals . . . pardon the slip, I meant to say the Nobel Prize].) Discriminating between true and false prophets is at the heart of the quest for truth, in all departments of life.

The criteria of judgments are revealed by the nature of the phenomena with which the particular tradition is preoccupied.

I divine grumbling among the readers: "You are stretching a metaphor a bit far in terming, for instance, the authorities within a domain of science prophets." Allow me to clarify. The institutional authorities literally do control exclusive means for receiving the Word from phenomena only those initiated into the "clergy" and given access to those (in physics extremely sophisticated) means can enjoy. They control the vast hierarchical "seminaries" to which the disciple must be called and through which he receives a long and rigorous preparation. Along the way he will gradually be asked to approach the essential research apparatuses. He will stand in awe before the face of the phenomena shown to him "live" for the first time. Now at last he has his chance to join the rank of the prophets if, and only if, he not only succeeds in becoming in his interior life the place of a breakthrough—a kind of revelation—but also manages in publishing it to capture an audience. The old saying "A prophet is without honor in his own country" may here be changed to read, "A prophet may fail to be heard by his own contemporaries, but he is likely to be canonized decades, sometimes even a century, later, as the serious truth of his revelation is at last grasped by the Brotherhood."

There are many prophets who, like the physicists, proclaim only natural truth, in the sense of entirely discoverable by "unaided" human reason, provided the instruments and the culture are developed. Perhaps the exalted title "prophet" should be reserved for the fundamental discoverers, those who expand and often re-create the horizons of interpretation of vast intersubjective worlds. These are surely to be distinguished from mere experts in the field, because the prophets open for all vast new visions of Being. Planck, Heisenberg, and Einstein were prophets; the Assistant Professor of Physics is their Imam in the local temple of science. Yes, I call them prophets here to call attention to the mystery of their great leaps of meaning-creating constructions that endure through centuries of critical reexamination.

It is when the prophets of the "merely natural" yield to the temptation to propose their principles and their theories as absolute and definitive guides to all of human existence that they can mislead millions and damage hundreds of millions. Karl Marx is my favorite example of a false prophet of the merely natural, a prophet who insistently claimed to be "scientific." His fatwas were promulgated as fundamental insights into the natural socio-political-economic structures, that is, as "scientific." It is bad science to present very tenuous vast hypotheses about unstable socio-political-economic structures subject to rapid change as though they were unalterable principles.

Then there are those prophets—perhaps even more dangerous than "the prophets of science"—who insist that the truth they proclaim comes not through unaided reason but as a gift of some form of personal revelation offered them not by just any god but by the Almighty God himself, in the most exalted sense. This light may be intended for all or, in the spirit of "Gnosticism," reserved to an inner elite. When one thinks back on the likes of Marx, Lenin, Stalin, Mao, Hitler, and Goebbels, one is not so sure who is most dangerous, "scientific" prophets or "prophets of God." When, like Osama Bin Laden, the prophet mates the divine revelation to the techniques of terrorism, then, you can be sure, you get the best of both worlds!

One born into a tradition of revelation, be it natural (such as Buddhism—Gautamma not pretending to be a messenger of God but only the Enlightened One who has entered deep within the soul)—or supernatural (Judaism, Christianity, and Islam claiming inputs into history that are alleged to be pure gifts from that which is beyond human inventiveness), can follow along throughout life increasingly molded by the tradition without ever critically appropriating it. It is almost natural ("fallen human nature"!) never to question very profoundly the genuineness of the source of "ultimate light" that has thoroughly formed one and hence to go through life with an intellectually poorly founded faith. (Keep in mind that the fanatic Marxist enthusiast and the straight-staring SS man betray aspects of an uncritical faith, too. So does the closed-minded brilliant physicist.)

As I shall explain in a moment, there is hope for pious persons who struggle to follow genuinely a tradition of which they have a fairly childlike understanding: I believe that through intimate personal contact with genuine saints of a tradition, a person can be brought out of himself into a deeper, more authentic love relationship. In this way he can grow in a less exclusively intellectualized wisdom that manifests itself through a certain cultivated perceptivity. There is a danger in this: that he will lack the sophisticated tools needed to refute false doctrines either "out in the world" or heresies that have infected his beloved tradition. If the saint's follower is not equipped to do much more than largely ignore those critical issues, he runs the risk of contaminating the genuine vision incarnated by his hero. The critical alternative merits being put bluntly:

as one reaches maturity, he can begin to think about the evidence for the genuineness of the founding claims, engaging in what Saint Augustine, perhaps the greatest critical searcher after truth since Plato, termed *fides quaerens intellectum*, "faith searching for insight."

A Jew, Christian, or Muslim who obeys without critical reflection may give himself over to sacred texts, may listen docilely to the Imam, the Magisterium of the Church, the rebbis wise in Talmud, and become enlightened and enriched. But how does he know who is really speaking at the core—who are these "local priests" of the genuine prophets, who is this telling me what Jesus really meant, whence the soundness of the elaborations that take place over time around the core truths? Though the uncritical person's lore will be little open to the challenges of the other great traditions, he may be susceptible to inroads of the popular traditions of the time (Jesus deformed by Carl Jung), and derailed through philosophically half-understood discoveries being made through the sciences of his epoch. Worst of all, there may not be enough genuine dialogue to free him from what his own imagination is spinning around the ancient events and the foundational claims. What is to save him from becoming a false prophet to himself?

From the start I have acknowledged that this introductory anthropology is no place for a critique, from the outside, of significant traditions that have not formed the author's own faith. But it is important for every human today seeking wisdom—even the author of this book—to engage in such critique in due course, for we share the world with such faiths, and they are powerful, from particle physics, cosmology, and evolutionary doctrines to Islam. There is much that is vital to learn from the experiences of others formed by those faiths, there are superb insights to be gained from the others' experiences, and there is much about which one ought to remain leery in what some of their representatives preach and do. Human beings advance in the truth through recognition not only of brilliant breakthroughs and fruitful practices but from errors—their own and those of others.

In *Tradition and Authenticity in the Search for Ecumenic Wisdom*, I promised to explore a critical appropriative process and while doing it learn in a serious way from a great tradition foreign to my own experience: I aspired to face the challenges and hazards of encounter with an other's great tradition. To contrast most relevantly with my own Catholic tradition, Islam was to be the victim of my attention. This choice was made twenty years before 9/11. I continue to probe the limits of the possibility of such dialogical appropriation, made more urgent but not easier by "the events." After twenty years of desultory study of Islam I have become ever more aware of how tenuous are my efforts to enter empathically into the worlds of persons with whom I disagree about some of the most basic truth claims, and whose living milieus I know only superficially, more through books than in flesh and blood. In earlier works I drew on some aspects of the Catholic experience of how this questioning of one's tradition can occur, and how that tradition characteristically does invite it. In *The Catholic Tradition* I showed how that tradition, properly understood (and contrary to empiricist disinformation), invites the most ample use of reason.

In discussing here by way of closing some of the very human aspects of the constellation of what the Christian tradition terms the "supernatural virtues"—faith, hope, and love—and adding a few words now on the "religious counsel" of obedience for the light it may throw on how truth is to be embraced, I am hoping that my readers will understand better the positive historical effect of this tradition's unique teaching of love, presenting a hero, a human being, who is claimed to be love itself. May the reader distinguish those positive elements from every misuse of prophetic traditions for the sake of political power, a real and imminent danger in all the great traditions, including those that emphasize their scientific quality. I hope to be offering here in this farewell something that can be integrated into the wisdom of all persons, whatever their religion, secular or revelational.

THE CENTRAL HUMAN PROBLEM: FALSE GODS

The Walter Kaufmanns of this world have made an act of faith that there is no reality transcending the bounded cosmos, hence nothing that could communicate its intentions "from beyond" for this world: claims of gods revealing their plans for mankind are simply human projections. But suppose for a moment that there is a God and he does want us to reach personal fulfillment, whatever that is in his plan. Then, for any person who believes that, it would be reasonable to strive to hear this truth and to live according to its lights, and as far as possible exactly as God intended, were the divine Source to have made anything at all clear. Put thus simply, such a principle sounds unexceptionable, but obviously only if genuine revelation exists. One way to approach the question of whether revelation has happened would be not only to examine with care what is claimed about how it happened but also to weigh in light of the wisdom one has been able to acquire the attractiveness of the ideal that the supposed Source of the meaning of it all allows to shine forth upon concrete reality as we experience it. There are many problems with this. Not the least is the fact that the moment one reflects on what God is alleged to have demanded, then (in the case of the great "Abrahamic" religions of revelation at least) some serious reasons become apparent that any human being might not want to hear his demands. Remember, the pivotal issue of human freedom is our fear of losing control. That is what the story of the Fall is all about.

The tradition has the merit of facing that very real issue squarely: human nature, in Abrahamists' revelation, is "fallen" precisely because our most ancient ancestors were already not keen on ceding control. As I glance around me I do not see much enthusiasm in everyday life for any giving up of control that can be avoided. Do we not consider "giving over control" where it can be avoided simply weakness, maybe even masochism, in any event irresponsibility? Think of those who seem willingly to turn over much of their lives to "the Party," to "the Guru," to "the authoritarian Church," the confused seemingly eager to hand over responsibility to a tyrannical source. From adolescence on, weak individuals cede control of part of their lives to gain the sense of security that comes from being part of "the gang."

What the Abrahamic God is purported to have revealed to us is in fact shocking to the project of our autonomy. Centrally this: that he is in fact truly God, and given his infinity (as befits a god who really is God) there can be only one: "I shall have no strange gods before me." He describes himself in early Hebrew texts as "a jealous God." "No strange gods" spells disappearance to the legitimacy of even the most pressing of competing gods, I mean "the god at the center": G L O R I O U S ME, this "EGO-Center of Awareness and Initiative"—which, being a knowing and willing individual, endowed with a genuine (but supposed to be re-sponse-able) autonomy, spontaneously wants to be a god too, ruling a comfortable little personal universe that he struggles to keep in hand: "My house is my castle" . . . or "My community [party, gang] is my refuge."

The central problem of human being—to relate to the remainder of reality the autonomy of a creature endowed with a genuine freedom to give of himself, capable of (and the Abrahamists believe intended for) love—brings the challenge that love in all its forms demands self-sacrifice, immolation of the self. Not the self as authentic *autos*, but the egoistic self pretending to be what it is not: the Ultimate, hence the absolute reality. Such giving up of the absurd temptations of the inauthentic self becomes conceivable only once it is understood that what we sacrifice is not our freedom but an illusion that replaces genuine finite freedom: the temptation to believe that I myself all alone am the ultimate source of final meaning. That final meaning is then understood as "just what it means to me." To my students at the university there was one unforgivable sin: for one person TO DARE tell another that what he was doing was right or wrong. The older reader can scarcely imagine how deeply and wisely this sense of autonomy has been accepted.

Paganism, in portraying the constant, bitter strife between the gods, was much closer to the truth than secular humanistic atheistic individualism. Atheist humanism leads to human, all too human, power struggles with no restraint coming from beyond what is commanded (understand: temporarily controlled) by human power; there is no *Zeus Olympikos* to mediate between the gods and to found binding principle. As Nietzsche showed so stunningly, libertarian individualism teeters always on the brink of nihilism. That is why he tried so hard to convince himself that the Superman *(Übermensch)* is genuinely and mysteriously creative as he pulls himself up by his bootstraps.

The Abrahamist belief is that God brought about the evolution of man to some purpose, not just to be dissolved in the cosmic "heat sink" after passing through massive destructions wrought by human power games. Consider the stark contrast of fated cosmic destruction—a principle of physics—with the amazing command of Christ: "Be ye perfect as my heavenly Father is perfect"! To echo Saint Paul: that is either crazy or divine.

Both the Son of God and the *Übermensch* strive for perfection, but the children of Abraham believe that the Source has broken into history to show us to what to devote our energies: *to the common good of all mankind*. Striving for perfection, then, is the same as seeking to be in complete and perfect conformity to reality, a reality that embraces all of mankind. If reality is the fruit of a loving act of creation, if we are informed about the transcendental role of love, then devoting our authentic selves to the overarching (and very difficult—keep the Cross in mind!) project of love leads to fulfillment. God's revelation, upon entering into human history, that the death of the individual human being is not the closure of horizons, is not what life is about; rather, that there awaits us "life everlasting" through the immortality of the soul and the resurrection of the body, then human life must be viewed in entirely new optics.

In that light, why should anyone hold back—why accept imperfection, hence mediocrity, hence destruction? Why believe there is any lasting fulfillment in accumulating estates and mighty motorcars? The folly of meaningless accumulation of material trinkets stands revealed. Upon grave reflection, nothing else but fulfilling love really makes any sense. Fatalism, mediocrity, power struggles, mindless materialism—evil in all its forms leads to . . . nothing.

The great theistic faiths make clear the path, as they allege God to show it. The Christian revelation transmits "the good news" ("Gospel") of the redemption, our being freed from captivity to our own self-centered passions, "the great light" promised by the Hebrew prophets illumining the way; the course of every little fragile human bark is made clear, to paraphrase the prophet Isaiah: "The seas are made smooth." And Jesus: "I am the Way, the Truth and the Life." "Take up your cross and follow me. . . . He who loses his life will gain it. . . . My yoke is light."

POSTSCRIPT

This work tries to articulate key structures and phenomena that constitute the nature of human being, understood in both its historical and its individuated senses. The structure of this book presents these various constitutive elements. These elements are to be understood dynamically, that is, as operating simultaneously and distinctly.

Furthermore, this work also follows a long-standing tradition of philosophical anthropologies. It is not to be read as a series of analytic arguments; rather, it is a work of phenomenology.

Finally, it should be remarked that given that human being continues to evolve and given that new worlds are constantly being created in the dynamic structure I have laid out, this work is not the final word on human being. More work constantly needs to be done to appropriate the rich and constantly emerging and changing senses of what it is to be human. My hope is that this work can contribute to expanding and deepening the discussion.

INDEX

Adoration: defined, 160; preparation for, 162–63; at proper moment; 162–63; and virtues of character, 163

Agape: distinguished from eros, 152, 158–60; and glory, 158, 159; as divine love, 159–61; and institutions, 161–62

Aliquid, 117–18, 119, 120

Analogia entis. See Analogy of being

Analogy of being, 43, 46, 116–24, 125, 128, 130, 150. *See also* Ens

Appreciation, 66, 158, 163, 164–65

Appropriation: of meaning, xv; of worlds, 21, 69; of givens, 31; and love, 67, 156; critical, 68; imagination in, 69; of intellectual capabilities, 103; of being, 112; of human being, 150, 183; by other, 156; of realities, 168; of tradition, 177

Aquinas, Thomas, 57, 117, 124, 157

Aristotle, 124, 162

Art: as music, 58, 78, 99–100, 102; in everyday performance, 95–96; as poetry, 96–97; as painting, 97–98; as drama and cinema, 100–101; as architecture, 101–2

Attitude: in authenticity, 3, 23, 75, 113, 119; of seriousness, 59; as spiritual, 63–64; as passion, 65; of adoration, 160, 162; and virtues of character, 163; of mindfulness, 163

Authenticity: and traditions, 2, 17, 68; as attitude, 3, 23, 75, 113, 119; as drive toward wisdom, 3; and expanding horizons, 4, 9, 22, 25, 27–28, 34, 68; and temporality, 5, 166; and education, 9, 12, 23, 34; and freedom, 9, 21, 135; as responsiveness, 11–12, 23, 25; and weirdness, 12; small and large, 16, 24; in Heidegger, 22; in psychology, 22, 24–25; and goodness,

28; and historicity, 51; and truth, 75, 92–93, 119; as responsibility, 21, 34, 135. *See also* Horizons

Authoritarianism, 143, 144, 147

Autonomy, 137, 141, 143, 145, 146, 180, 181

Autos. See Self

Balance, 15–16, 51, 98, 143, 148, 166

Balthasar, Hans Urs von: and love, 137, 157, 159, 161; and adoration, 160, 163; and hope, 165; mentioned, 154, 162

Beauty: natural, 66, 164; in art, 96–99; as transcendental, 120; as gift, 158–59

Being: and *Dasein*, xiv; illumines reality, 25; and authenticity, 68, 135; as God, 112, 120, 122, 128; as ultimate meaning, 114; as unity of being, 114, 120, 122; as Infinite Source, 118, 120, 126, 128; and being, 121, 121*n1*; Analogy of, 125; as religious dimension, 130, 135; and atheism, 130; and evolution, 136; and evil, 139; avoidance of, 144; as glory, 159; and love, 172; and prophets, 176

Being and Time (Heidegger), xiv, 11, 22

Being and Truth (Langan), 3, 63, 86, 112, 151, 169

Big Bang, 41, 125, 126, 139, 166

Big-souledness, 56–57

Body: in time and space, 6; connected to cosmos, 25, 28, 36, 46, 49; as locus of personal world, 29, 40; governed by soul, 52; habits and skills of, 63–64; as ground of perception, 83–84, 92; of Christ, 106; resurrection of, 182

Breakthrough: in religious traditions, 4; as leap of imagination, 4, 61, 148, 176; artistic, 11; in evolution, 54; as

185